The South:
A Concise History

Volume I

The South:
A Concise History

Jeanette Keith

Upper Saddle River, New Jersey 07458

Library of Congress Cataloging-in-Publication Data

KEITH, JEANETTE.
    The South: a concise history / Jeanette Keith.
      p. cm.
    Includes bibliographical references and index.
    ISBN 0-13-022056-6 (vol. 1) — ISBN 0-13-094198-0 (vol. 2)
    1. Southern States—History. 2. Southern States—Social conditions. I. Title.
F209 .K44 2002
975—dc21
                                                          2001034599

Editorial Director: *Charlyce Jones Owen*
Acquisitions Editor: *Emsal Hasan*
AVP, Director of Production and Manufacturing: *Barbara Kittle*
Editorial Production/Supervision and Interior Design: *Judith Winthrop*
Cover Design: *Kiwi Design*
Cover Image: The Levee; New Orleans, 1884. Library of Congress
Prepress and Manufacturing Buyer: *Tricia Kenny*
Supervisor of Production Services: *Guy Ruggiero*
Cartographers: *Carto-Graphics, Mirella Signoretto*
Copy editor: *Jamie Fuller*

This book was set in 10.5/13 New Baskerville by The Composing Room
of Michigan, Inc. and was printed and bound by Courier-Stoughton
The cover was printed by Phoenix Color Corporation.

© 2002 by Pearson Education
Upper Saddle River, New Jersey 07458

Printed in the United States of America
10 9 8 7 6 5 4 3 2 1

ISBN 0-13-022056-6

PEARSON EDUCATION LTD., *London*
PEARSON EDUCATION AUSTRALIA PTY. Limited, *Sydney*
PEARSON EDUCATION SINGAPORE, Pte. Ltd.
PEARSON EDUCATION NORTH ASIA LTD., *Hong Kong*
PEARSON EDUCATION CANADA, LTD., *Toronto*
PEARSON EDUCACIÓN DE MEXICO, S.A. DE C.V.
PEARSON EDUCATION—–JAPAN, *Tokyo*
PEARSON EDUCATION MALAYSIA, Pte. Ltd.
PEARSON EDUCATION, Upper Saddle River, *New Jersey*

Contents

v

2

The Old South, 1790–1860   53

3

Defending "Our Way of Life": Southern Politics to 1860 *99*

Preface

Although I am a native Southerner, born and raised in rural Tennessee, I teach southern history at Bloomsburg University of Pennsylvania, a small state college in the North. My students think southern history is dramatic, full of exotic characters and exciting events. They are fascinated by the Old South and the Civil War, moved by the Civil Rights Movement, and curious about southern culture and folkways. Their interest is partly practical: many of them will be moving south in search of work after graduation.

For my southern history class, I wanted to assign a series of primary texts, essays, scholarly articles, and fiction pieces, but I knew that my students would need a textbook for background. Unable to find the sort of concise narrative history I wanted, I wrote this book.

The South: A Concise History is one extended story, or history, of the nation's most distinctive region from colonial settlement to the present. In composing this story, I have tried to incorporate new scholarship about race, class, and gender. This is another way of saying that the characters in this story are not just members of the political elite, but also include dirt farmers, Indians, plantation mistresses, slaves, factory workers, civil rights leaders, and all the motley collection of personages that make southern history one of the best stories around.

I have concentrated more on what happened than on detailed explanations of why, in the belief that the route into history comes through narrative: knowledge of the basic outline of events is a necessary precursor to analysis. In that spirit, I urge students of southern history to use this book as an avenue into further exploration of southern history and culture.

The field of southern history is fiercely political and deeply contested. I am sure that southern historians of all political stripes will find things here that offend them. I am also positive that my fellow historians will wish I had done more with this or supplied more information on that. The book is intentionally short. Far from wanting the last word, I hope that readers of this book will be intrigued by the stories they find here and look for more history and analysis, starting with the suggestions for further reading and viewing appended to each chapter.

For their help with and judicious criticism of this project, I wish to thank Tony Allen, Michael Hickey, Susan Stemont, Scott Nelson, Cindy Hahamovitch, Mark Quintanilla, Jeff Davis, Tim Tyson, Mel McKiven, Anastatia Sims, David Carlton, members of the Southern Humanities Council (who heard about the project in a presentation in 1999) and the readers who critiqued the manuscript for Prentice Hall: Eric H. Walther, University of Houston; Tommy R. Thompson, University of Nebraska at Omaha; Richard L. Hume, Washington State University; Norman G. Raiford, Greenville Technical College; Christopher Waldrep, East Illinois University; Robert Thurston, Miami University. All sins of commission and omission in this work are my own.

Most of all, I wish to thank my students at Bloomsburg University of Pennsylvania, where I have taught American history for the past twelve years. Over the years, their comments and questions have enlightened me as to what students can be expected to know, and not to know, about the history of the South. They have also been very forthright about what they would like to know more about, and what they would not. If this book proves readable and entertaining as well as useful, much credit is due to them.

The South:
A Concise History

Introduction

Why Study the South?

In the summer of the first year of the new millennium, the state of South Carolina removed from its statehouse the Confederate flag, a symbol of a nation that had been dead for 135 years. Raised above the capitol in 1962 in commemoration of the centennial of the Civil War, the flag of the defeated rebellion had other meanings as well. For some South Carolinians, the flag symbolized "southern heritage," a complex of emotions and ideas including loyalty to home and honor to ancestors, particularly those who fought for southern independence against the federal government in the 1860s. For others, the flag symbolized slavery, and they considered it a shameful reminder of past racial injustice and present-day racism.

When the National Association for the Advancement of Colored People (NAACP) called on tourists to boycott South Carolina until the flag was removed, the battle lines were drawn. Southern heritage advocates, overwhelmingly white people, insisted that the flag had nothing to do with racism, while the NAACP and its supporters, both black and white, retorted that the flag signified both slavery and white supremacy. Meanwhile, the

1

tourism boycott hurt businesses in the state, and businessmen of all races began pressuring the state government to take the flag down.

Finally, the state's governor worked out a compromise: the flag would be removed from the capitol spire but placed above a Confederate memorial on the grounds nearby. In July, cadets from the Citadel, a state-funded military school located in Charleston, ceremoniously removed the flag and, accompanied by an honor guard dressed in gray uniforms, carried it to its new location. At the event, crowds representing both sides waved flags and picket signs and shouted insults at each other. Unsatisfied, the president of the NAACP called for the continuation of the boycott and bitterly criticized the black South Carolina legislators who had voted for the compromise.

Two other southern states, Georgia and Mississippi, had replicas of the Confederate flag built into their state flags. Students of the issue expected the controversy to continue for years to come.

· · ·

Why study the South? In this time of global markets and international business, when Americans from Maine to California share the same popular culture with people all over the planet, shouldn't we concentrate on the big national picture? Aren't all Americans pretty much alike anyway, regardless of which region they live in?

As the saga of the continuing controversy over the Confederate flag indicates, the answer is—not exactly. While southerners of all races today are more like other Americans than they are different, the differences can still be striking. Where else in this country do people get so mad over history? But of course, no other region in the United States has a history like the South's.

At the core of that history is the Civil War, a major turning point not only in regional but in national history. The war grew out of decades of sectional conflict revolving around the issue of slavery. Prevalent in all the states when the nation was founded, slavery was abolished in the northern states early in the century, thus becoming the South's "peculiar institution." By the 1850s slavery seemed the essential cornerstone of southern life to most of the region's political leaders. They viewed the creation of the Republican Party as a threat, since the Republicans built their politics around promises to prevent the spread of slavery into newly acquired western territories. Many southern leaders believed that the Republicans, once in power, would not be content with stopping the spread of slavery but would move to abolish the institution in the South. The election of Republican Abraham Lincoln in 1860 provoked the crisis: convinced that their peculiar institution was no longer safe in the federal union, the Deep South states seceded to form the Confederate States of America. When Lincoln called for troops to put down the rebellion, most of the upper tier of the South joined the Confederacy. The ensuing war lasted for four years (1861–65) and still heads the list of the nation's most deadly conflicts, having claimed the lives of 600,000 American men.

The war established the United States as a nation, not just a conglomerate of affiliated states. It settled the question of states' rights: the federal government is sovereign over the states. Beginning as a war of national unification, the Civil War ended as a war of liberation, setting free millions of Americans of African descent. Although the Union did not fight the war to free the slaves—ending slavery did not become federal policy until two years into the conflict and was then prompted by military necessity—generations of Americans have chosen to gloss over that fact, creating a mythology of the nation as crusader for freedom. Socially, politically, and economically, the United States as we know it today was born through the destruction of the Old South.

But within the region old times were not forgotten. The nation's designated losers, the only Americans (until Vietnam) to ever lose a war, white southerners built a cult of loss and remembrance that reverberates in political conflicts today. Their unwillingness to let go of the Old South also reflected the dearth of economic choices available in the region after the Civil War.

During the late nineteenth and early twentieth centuries, the South was the nation's poorest region, with the vast majority of the population, regardless of race, working in low-wage jobs or in agriculture. The region's states anchored the bottom of every statistical list measuring progress, having the nation's worst schools, poorest health, lowest incomes, and so on. It was a full century after the Civil War before the southern economy began to draw even with the rest of the nation.

During this time of poverty and defeat, white southerners created a system of legal structures that cut blacks out of the political system then denied them equal access to public facilities and state-funded services. The "Jim Crow" system, as it was called, segregated blacks from whites in all public places. Middle-aged southern whites and blacks today can still remember segregated schools and water fountains labeled "White" or "Colored." When black southerners began to struggle for their rights, sometimes with the somewhat reluctant help of the federal government, many white southerners resisted defiantly; it was during that period, in the 1960s, that the Confederate flag appeared again over the South Carolina capitol.

Today the South is as officially racially integrated as any other part of the nation. Legal segregation having ended almost forty years ago, black professionals have created a small market in the memorabilia of Jim Crow, buying up the "Whites Only" and "Colored Only" signs as antiques. After decades of leaving the region for better jobs and living conditions in the North, African-Americans began in the 1970s to move back to the South, a trend that continues. Black politicians serve as mayors of major southern cities, sheriffs of southern counties, and legislators throughout the region.

But southern memories are long. The South's greatest writer, Nobel Prize-winning novelist William Faulkner, once had a character say that the past was not dead: "Hell, it isn't even past." As the flag controversy shows, southerners sometimes act as if Faulkner was right. In the South, history matters, and bad history—history that tells lies about the past— can have serious contemporary political consequences. For people living in the region, a sense of history can be an essential social, cultural, and political skill. Those contemplating moving south would do well to at least familiarize themselves with the outlines of southern history, to avoid costly social and business faux pas.

However, studying the South can be useful for other reasons, according to historians. One group of historians says that we should study the region because the South is historically separate, or "distinctive," from the rest of the nation. Therefore, studying southern history allows us to make comparisons that help us understand national or world history. Other historians argue just the opposite: that the American South is "America squared," in the words of historian Steven Stowe. This is another way of saying that you cannot understand America without understanding the South: southern history *is* American history. Dominant themes in national history can be seen most clearly in the history of the South.

Southern Heritage Politics

"We, the founders of the Southern party, acting in the spirit of our Southern colonial and Confederate fore-fathers, believing American civilization derives its greatest strength from its historic Christian faith and its fidelity to limited constitutional government. . . ." Thus begins the "Asheville Declaration" of a new political party, founded in 1999.

The Southern Party's Declaration (which can be found on its web site, http://www.southernparty.org/) provides a useful summary of distilled "southern heritage" rhetoric. The Southern Party insists that the Constitution created a government with limited powers, delegated to it by the states. States reserved the right to withdraw from the compact if needed to protect their liberties. But when the Southern states withdrew from the Union in 1861, they were "illegally invaded and conquered," before being subjugated, "the effects of which are still being felt today in the form of predatory taxation, an imperial presidency, and a tyrannical judiciary." Currently, the declaration says, the culture of the South is under threat from political correctness, as purveyed in schools, churches, and media, all designed to destroy southern culture.

In other publications, leaders of the Southern Party deny any intention to reestablish white supremacy, and protest the use of the Confederate flag and other Old South symbols by hate groups.

This tiny political party has big plans. The Southern Party's goal is to increase local and state autonomy, ultimately leading to southern independence. It states that the process may take a long time but holds out as examples successes scored by nationalist movements in Quebec and, especially, Scotland, which recently convened its first independent parliament in almost 300 years.

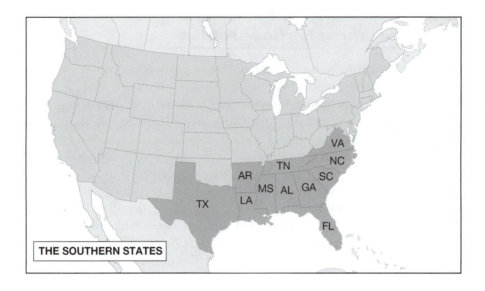

THE SOUTHERN STATES

But history is not just for professional historians. History buffs—those who study history because they love it—seem especially attracted to the history of the South, perhaps because it contains some of the most dramatic stories around. Those who study history because they are fascinated by human character find southern history to be full of examples of people exhibiting the worst, and the best, qualities found in human nature. Whatever else it may be, southern history is never boring, and it is studied in colleges from Atlanta to Tokyo.

Where Is the South?

It depends on whom you ask: linguists, historians, sociologists, and geographers tend to have different answers. Linguists point out that various forms of the southern accent can be found from Maryland to central Florida, west through Texas, and north into southern Indiana and Illinois, which were originally settled by southerners. Sociologists suggest that the South can be

defined as that place where people think they are
southerners; by this definition, places like northern Virginia
and southern Florida are not in the South. Geographers
might define the South by growing season and rainfall,
thereby eliminating northern Kentucky and Virginia by
temperature and western Texas for lack of rain. Historians
have generally used two other factors to define the South:
slavery and the Civil War. Historians argue that since slavery
as a labor system is the most important difference between
North and South, the South can be defined as composed of
those states that still had slaves in 1860. By that definition,
the South includes Delaware, Maryland, Kentucky, and
Missouri. Other historians argue that the South can best be
defined by the experience of the Civil War: the southern
states are the ones that seceded, went to war, and were
defeated. This book uses the last of these definitions. For
our purposes, the South is composed of the states of the
former Confederacy: Virginia, North and South Carolina,
Florida, Georgia, Alabama, Mississippi, Louisiana, Texas,
Arkansas, and Tennessee. However, students will find
occasional references to events in the border states as well.

Separating History from Legend

For almost as long as there has been a United States, Americans
have told stories about the distinctive qualities of the South. Much of what
Americans think they know about the region falls under the category of
myths and legends, both positive and negative.

Southern historians sometimes refer to the legend of the prewar
Old South as the "moonlight and magnolias myth." Created by songwriters
and novelists, enshrined in movies like *Gone with the Wind,* the mythologi-
cal romantic Old South of gallant white men, spirited belles, and happy
slaves is still attractive to a large portion of the American public. People
with no ancestral connection to the South dress up as Confederates to reenact Civil War battles, take tours of antebellum mansions, and watch *North*

and South every time the miniseries plays on television. Very few people, however, choose to reenact the role of plantation slave.

Nonsoutherners helped create the myth. Stephen Foster, the man who wrote the moonlight-and-magnolias music—those songs about Susannah, the Old Kentucky Home, Camptown Races, and all that doo-dah—was born in Pittsburgh and worked out of New York City. *Gone with the Wind*, the film that fixed the Old South myth in the public mind, was of course a Hollywood creation, although based on a novel written by a Georgian. White southerners have also been enthusiastic molders of the legend, creating their own myth of the Old South that both justifies and memorializes the Southern men who fought for independence in the Civil War. Many white southerners express pride in the South's distinctive past and loyalty to southern ways, including traditional notions of hospitality, courtesy, courage, and honor.

On the other hand, many Americans despise the myth of the romantic South. For them, the region is America's heart of darkness. This attitude dates to the 1830s, when antislavery writers, attempting to convince a northern audience that slavery was evil, depicted white southerners overwhelmingly as morally depraved, sexually predatory, and ferociously violent, not to mention ignorant, backward, and lazy. For many Americans, this stereotype has been too useful to let die. Even today it allows people in other regions of the country to cherish their own moral superiority and to congratulate themselves on the progress shown by their own institutions, without ever putting those assumptions to a reality check.

Historians find some truth, and a lot of nonsense, in both mythologies. Yet we must be aware that myths, however historically inaccurate, condition the way that people look at southern history and at the South today, and take that into account when studying regional history.

Regional Stereotypes

Sociologist John Shelton Reed has been studying the South for decades, with interesting and often amusing results. He began by studying self-identification, asking people if they thought they were southern. Among his findings from the 1970s was the following: the more education and money a white southerner had, the more important was southern identity. While less educated and sophisticated whites identified most with their own community, more educated and traveled southerners surveyed identified with "the South." What did being southern mean? In 1987 Reed polled self-identified white southern students at the University of North Carolina, gave them a list of terms, and asked them which applied to white southerners, which to white northerners, and which to Americans in general. Southern traits picked by the students included tradition-loving, very religious, courteous, and loyal to family ties; they labeled white northerners industrious, materialistic, progressive, aggressive, arrogant, loud, and rude.

Themes

Although there are many ways to look at the history of the South, in this book we will trace several interrelated themes. Look for the following topics to come up, with variations, in each chapter:

Race, Class, and Gender

For many Americans, the major theme of southern history is race. Those who know little about the region are still likely to remember that the Old South's society and economy depended on racially based slavery. Others remember the Jim Crow South. To some Americans, southern history is about white supremacy in the region that was home to the overwhelming majority of the nation's African-American population until well into the twentieth century.

Recently, however, historians have begun to look at the issue of race in southern history in a new light. Guided by the insistence of biologists that race has no scientific meaning, historians and social scientists have come to see race as socially constructed. That is, human beings chose to see some differences, and to ignore others, to create categories of difference

Courtesy of Bruce Plante, *Chattanooga Times.*

This cartoon appeared during the Confederate flag controversy. What stereotypes does it reflect?

that often serve the ends of the people in power. In the United States, most of the work of socially constructing race was done in the South, beginning in the colonial period: it was there that constructs of blackness and whiteness still influential upon American life first emerged. Today historians study the role of race in the South to see how the concept evolved, changed, and was used by various groups in the region's history.

Throughout most of southern history, white racial solidarity required that all white men be considered equal and equally responsible for keeping black men subordinate. All white men gained status by keeping blacks down. That was the way the southern system worked—in theory. However, white southerners understood quite well that all white men were not truly equal. The southern white upper class considered itself an aristocracy and expected deference from those with less money, status, and power. Other whites often resented the power of the elite and expressed that resentment through politics. African-Americans, well aware of class differences among whites, looked down on very poor whites, whom they labeled "trash," and even within slavery developed their own system of rank. With emancipation, class differences sometimes led to conflicts within the black community. Among southerners of all races, class divisions led to bitter cultural and political struggles, some of which continue to shape southern politics to this day.

The traditional power of white men derived from their gender as well as their color. When southerners said that the South was a white *man's* country, they were not kidding. In the Old South, being a man meant being a master. White men demonstrated masculinity through their control of their households, including their slaves. Black men understood that in the South, gender intersected with race: to be denied equal rights with white men was to be denied manhood, and to assert equality was to assert masculinity. Southern gender roles for women were also shaped by race. White men justified slavery and segregation on the basis of gender, claiming that they did what they did to blacks to protect "white womanhood." On the other hand, one of the perks of white masculinity was sexual access to black women, with or without their consent. The history of southern gender roles has meant that struggles for racial justice always had gender implications, while attempts by women of both races to attain equality have been complicated by racial issues.

Religion

Today the South is as much distinguished by religion as by race. Yet the region sometimes called the "Bible Belt" was not always so. Colonial New England was settled in part by religious zealots, but the white leaders of the southern colonies came to America to make money. How the South got religion, and what black and white southerners did with their religious beliefs, is a major theme of southern history. The region is dominated by evangelical Protestants, Christians who believe that being "saved" is the most important event in a person's life. Southern blacks and whites share religious fervor, although they still mostly worship in separate congregations. To secular Americans, the force of southern religion is almost incomprehensible, and those who move into the region are astonished to be asked, "What church do you go to?" right after questions about name and occupation. Yet in southern history, religion has played a role in everything from slavery to the Civil Rights Movement to present-day politics.

Politics and Government: The Defense of Liberty

In 1784 Thomas Jefferson, the American revolutionary from Virginia, wrote to a French acquaintance that his fellow southerners were "zealous for their own liberties, but trampling on those of others." This contradiction is central to southern history: the slave society of the Old South produced many of the nation's most ardent proponents of freedom. Over the last 400 years, white southerners have defended liberty, as they understood it. Sometimes they believed that the greatest threat to their liberties was in the very organizations designed to defend them: governments, whether local or national. Since antebellum days, some white southerners have felt either that other Americans were hostile toward the South's institutions (especially slavery and segregation) or that the rest of the nation treated them as second-class citizens. On the local level, white southerners have been resistant to government regulation of private property, with impact on matters ranging from gun laws to zoning. Ironically, white southerners have often combined suspicion toward the government with willingness to grab as much government largess as possible. Southern politicians have long been masters of pork-barrel politics, ensuring that their districts get ample shares of federal appropriations. Distrust of government, defense of liberty, and pork-barrel politics provide three interlocking themes of southern political history.

To understand the South, we must begin with the history of the region at a time when, as historian Wesley Frank Craven said, it was not yet "the South." The roots of southern history lie in the clash of cultures and people produced by the European colonization of the Americas.

Suggestions for Further Reading

PETER APPLEBOME, *Dixie Rising: How the South is Shaping American Values, Politics, and Culture* (1997)

JOHN BOLES, *The South Through Time* (1995)

ROY BLOUNT, ED., *Roy Blount's Book of Southern Humor* (1994)

W. J. CASH, *The Mind of the South* (1941)

WILLIAM J. COOPER AND THOMAS E. TERRILL, *The American South* (1991)

CARL N. DEGLER, *Place over Time: The Continuity of South Distinctiveness* (1977)

LARRY J. GRIFFIN AND DON H. DOYLE, EDS., *The South as an American Problem* (1995)

TONY HORWITZ, *Confederates in the Attic: Dispatches from the Unfinished Civil War* (1998)

JACK TEMPLE KIRBY, *Media-Made Dixie* (1978)

JOHN SHELTON REED, *One South: An Ethnic Approach to Regional Culture* (1982)

————, *1001 Things Everyone Should Know About the South* (1996)

WILLIAM R. TAYLOR, *Cavalier and Yankee* (1961)

CHARLES REAGAN WILSON AND WILLIAM FERRIS, EDS., *Encyclopedia of Southern Culture* (1989)

C. VANN WOODWARD, *The Burden of Southern History*, 3d ed. (1993)

1

Did Liberty Grow from Slavery?

When the United States was young, European cartoonists used to draw the nation as "Brother Jonathan," a lanky country boy with a big floppy hat and a whip, signifying his status as a slaveholder. Five of the nation's first seven presidents (Washington, Jefferson, Madison, Monroe, and Jackson) were southern slaveholders. Europeans found it hard to understand: how could a people who fought a revolution for freedom justify having slaves? The answer lies in the history of the colonial South, a society whose legacy to later Americans included a profound allegiance to liberty and an equally profound commitment to the institution of slavery.

Origins

When Columbus claimed the Bahamas for Spain in 1492, he set off a race between Western European nations to explore and exploit the territory they called the New World. Among the wonders they found were the native inhabitants of the Western Hemisphere, the peoples they mistakenly called Indians. In North America alone there were hundreds of different native groups, ranging from small hunter-gatherer bands to highly organized empires with cities rivaling anything in Europe.

In the area that would become the southeastern United States, loosely confederated tribes under the leadership of paramount chiefs supported themselves through agriculture (corn cultivation having been imported from Mexico) and by hunting. Anthropologists have labeled this culture "Mississippian," and locate its center in a series of towns along the Mississippi River. Although the tribes were culturally similar, however, it would be a mistake to think of the Mississippian culture as politically unified and peaceful. To the contrary: tribes fought each other constantly for territory, especially the coveted rich farmlands along rivers. They practiced diplomacy and politics in their intertribal struggles. When southeastern Indian groups encountered Europeans, their first reaction (after wonderment and shock) was to try to fit these strange newcomers into their existing political and diplomatic systems.

Divided politically, culturally and linguistically, southeastern Indians shared with all other natives of the continent a fatal susceptibility to the new diseases brought in by the Europeans. Descended from peoples who migrated into the New World from western Asia, possibly as long as 60,000 years ago, the Indians had not evolved immunities to the many ills of Europe and Africa. Diseases that Europeans considered childhood nuisances, like measles and mumps, were deadly for the Indians, while the poxes and plagues that killed many Europeans wiped out whole villages of Indians. In the hundred years after Indians first encountered Europeans in 1492, the population of the New World declined, as wave after wave of epidemics swept across the land. Historians, archeologists, and anthropologists disagree about how many natives of the Western Hemisphere died, but the estimates range up to 75–90 percent. The death rate was probably highest in urban centers in Mexico, and probably less among the smaller, more isolated settlements in what would become the American South. Nonetheless, epidemics weakened the Indian tribes at a time when they faced invasion and conquest.

In the early 1500s Spanish explorers, moving out from their nation's early settlements in the Caribbean, began to investigate the Southeast. Some Spanish adventurers kidnapped southeastern Indians from the coasts of present-day Florida and South Carolina and carried them off to serve as slaves in the Caribbean colonies. Others had stranger goals. In 1513, Ponce de Leon explored the west coast of Florida in search of a fabled fountain of youth. But the Spanish expeditions (*entradas*) mostly looked for gold. After Spanish adventurers led by Hernando Cortes conquered the fabulously rich Aztec Empire, looting its wealth and subjugating its population, the possibility of another such coup was never far from the dreams of would-be *conquistadores.*

For four years, from 1539 to 1543, an expedition led by Hernando De Soto wandered from Florida up to the Tennessee River, down again into Georgia and Alabama, and across the Mississippi. De Soto's forces were surely the first whites ever seen by the Indians of the southeastern interior, and the first blacks as well: DeSoto's expedition included slaves from Africa. It cannot have been a pleasant introduction. The Spanish moved into villages and demanded food and service. They slept with Indian women, whether willing or not, leaving behind a crop of babies. (This attempt at sexual subjugation occasionally backfired: several of De Soto's party, including some of the Africans, deserted the expedition rather than leave their new Indian wives.) They kidnapped Indians for use as porters and guides. When resisted, they used the superior military technology of Europe—steel swords, crossbows, guns, horses, and war dogs—to slaughter Indians. This onslaught destabilized the entire Mississippian culture, leading to fragmentation and the emergence of new tribes, often composed in part of refugees from tribes decimated by the Spanish.

Despite their years of effort and warfare, however, the Spanish search for wealth failed: the hills and river valleys of Florida, Georgia, and Alabama did not produce the kind of riches found in Mexico. For that reason, the Spanish paid less attention to the southeast than to their new possessions in Mexico, Central, and South America. Spanish settlements along the Atlantic and Gulf coasts tended to be mission outposts staffed by Catholic priests and monks, and military garrisons. It was not until the 1560s that the Spanish, concerned about French attempts to claim Florida, built a lasting outpost at St. Augustine, thus founding the first European town in the present-day United States.

A similar pattern prevailed to the west, in what is now Texas. In 1528 *conquistadore* Cabeza de Vaca, shipwrecked on the Gulf Coast (probably at present-day Galveston) began an epic six-year journey back to Spanish settlements in Mexico, thus providing Spain with a claim to the territory

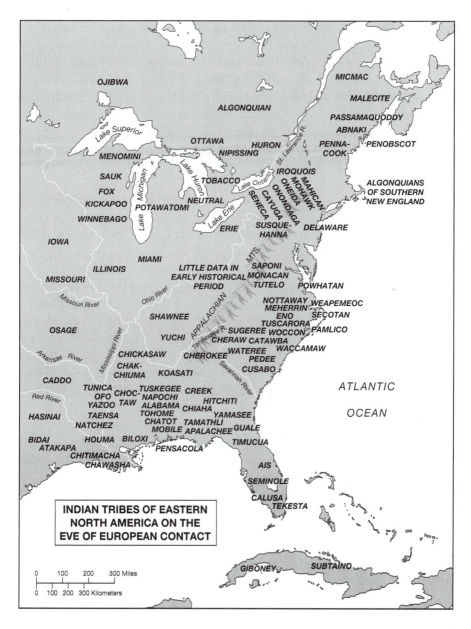

Indian tribes of Eastern North America on the eve of
European contact.

17

he passed through. In 1540 Francisco Coronado embarked on a two-year search for the "Seven Cities of Cibola," mythical cities of gold rumored to be hidden somewhere in the North American interior. In his wandering, Coronado passed through northern Texas. Despite these explorations, however, Spanish hold on the area remained quite limited. It was not until the 1700s that the Spanish established mission towns at San Antonio, Goliad, and Nacogdoches. Even then, relatively few Spanish settlers came to these isolated New World outposts. Most of the subjects of the Spanish empire's northern borders were Indians or *mestizos,* the children of Spanish and Indian parents.

However, the Spanish explorers introduced European imports to the entire region. These included trade goods (iron, mirrors and textiles being especially valued); new species of plants and animals (pigs, escaping to southern forests, became the ancestors of the famed "razorbacks") and most significantly, diseases. Everywhere the Europeans went, the Indian population sickened and died. Historians estimate that in 1492 between 5 and 10 million Indians lived in the territory that became the United States. By 1800, there were only about 600,000 left.

The Columbian Exchange

Published in 1972, Alfred W. Crosby's book *The Columbian Exchange: Biological and Cultural Consequences of 1492* has become a classic study of what began to happen to world ecology in 1492. According to Crosby, "The two worlds, which God had cast asunder, were reunited, and the two worlds, which were so very different, began on that day to become alike. That trend toward biological homogeneity is one of the most important aspects of the history of life on this planet." Europeans introduced a large number of domesticated animals to the Americas, including cattle, hogs, and horses, and the grains, such as wheat, rye, and barley, that were the staples of European diets. But the plants of the Western Hemisphere, those first cultivated by Indians, transformed the world diet: corn (maize), beans, potatoes, tomatoes, sweet potatoes, manioc, squashes,

> pumpkin, chili peppers, cocoa, pineapple, papaya, avocado.
> Among the nonfood plants originating in the New World
> are tobacco and rubber.

By the early 1600s, Spain faced new competition for territories in the New World, fueled by new religious rivalries. In the 1500s, Catholic Europe experienced a period of religious upheaval as reformers first attempted to change the Church, then split off into new Christian denominations, collectively called Protestant in memory of their origins in protest. Spain remained Catholic, as did France, although a significant minority in the latter country became Protestants. But in Britain, Catholic unity was replaced by multiple ways of being Protestant, ranging from the nation's official faith, the Church of England, to the Presbyterians, the Puritans, and the Quakers. Despite their differences in doctrine, British Protestants agreed that the nation's mission in the world included opposing Catholicism; the Catholic nations felt the same way about the Protestants. Therefore, European conquest of the New World took on a new urgency, as nations moved to block the expansion of rival faiths.

As a reult of previous voyages of exploration financed by kings of England, England claimed territories on the Atlantic coast of North America between the French to the north and the Spanish to the south. In 1585, under the reign of Queen Elizabeth I—the "Virgin Queen," for whom the colony of Virginia would be named—Sir Walter Raleigh sponsored the establishment of a colony on Roanoke Island on the Outer Banks of the Carolina coast. This colony proved unsuccessful. In 1590, a relief expedition to Roanoke found that all the settlers had disappeared. In 1607 the English tried again, north of Roanoke in the Chesapeake Bay, at a place they named for their king, James I.

Jamestown

The first English colony on the American mainland was founded as a business proposition. To raise money for the adventure to Virginia, wealthy merchants and gentlemen of London formed a joint-stock company, the Virginia Company of London, and sold stocks. The investors talked about converting the Indians and glorifying King James, but as colonist Captain John Smith said, "We did admire how it was possible such wise men could so torment themselves and us with such strange absurdities and impossibilities; making Religion their colour, when all their aime was nothing but present profit."

The investors in the Virginia Company hoped to do in the Chesapeake what the Spanish had done in Mexico: get rich. In 1607 they sent gold refiners, jewelers, and many "gentlemen adventurers" to Virginia. In the 1600s "gentleman" referred to a member of the English upper class, or gentry. Young men of the gentry could ride, fight, and command, but they knew little about survival in the wilderness. Smith, himself a farmer's son and mercenary soldier, grumbled that common soldiers would have been of more value than so many would-be officers, and that a man who knew how to handle "a pickaxe and spade, is better than five Knights."

Personnel, climate, disease, and sheer bad luck combined to make the Virginia Company's venture in the Chesapeake a disaster. The colonists spent much of their time hunting for gold and quarreling with each other. As the president of the Virginia Company himself said, "A more damned crew hell never vomited." Since the colonists did not take time to plant crops, they starved. They had located their settlement along the James River, from which they got their water, and into which they dumped their sewage. The combination of salty tidewater and waste gave the colonists dysentery, and many died of dehydration. They were unable to coerce the neighboring Indians into working for them. Faced with starvation and abuse from their gentleman masters, some of the colonists "deserted" and took refuge with the Indians. By January 1608, only 38 of the original 120 colonists were alive, and they owed their survival mostly to Captain Smith. The middle-aged mercenary soldier became the colony's governor, imposed martial law on the surviving colonists, forced the gentlemen to work, and negotiated with the neighboring Indian tribe for enough food to keep the colony going until reinforcements arrived from England.

The Names of America

When Columbus arrived in the Bahamas in 1492, he thought he had found the East Indies, the islands off the coast of China. Therefore he called the inhabitants "Indians." Some people today, finding this nomenclature both inaccurate and politically incorrect, prefer to use the term "Native American." However, the name "America" itself refers to an Italian mapmaker, Amerigo Vespucci, and has no historical connection to the people who were here in 1492. "Native American" seems to this author therefore to be no great improvement over "Indian." Wherever possible, I have tried to refer to the peoples who preceded Europeans in the South by the names they used for themselves: Susquahannock, Doeg, Yuchi, Shawnee, Cherokee, Choctaw, Creek, Powhatan.

The Indians of the Chesapeake

In 1607, the natives of the Chesapeake region had created a settled way of life that supplied them with a standard of living enviable to the English settlers. Indian women farmed corn and other vegetables, while men hunted and fished. Although the Indians in the region shared this way of life, they had their own political divisions. In the Chesapeake region alone there were about forty different small tribes, most of which did not get along well with each other.

In 1607 the dominant tribe in the region, the Powhatan, was headed by a chief who had begun to draw together neighboring tribes in a confederation against their enemies in the hills to the west. Given that the Spanish had been landing on the coast for decades—and occasionally snatching Indians for use as slaves—the chief of the Powhatan (known to the English simply as Powhatan) cannot have been too surprised at the arrival of Europeans on his territory. He seems to have seen the English as potential allies in his own empire-building plans. He sent food to the colonists and allowed his daughter, Pocohontas, to visit them frequently. When Smith went out to explore the surrounding territory, the Powhatan captured him and took him to their village. There the chief staged a symbolic ceremony in which Pocohontas rescued Smith from threatened execution. Historians are unsure as to what, exactly, Powhatan meant by this; perhaps he was dramatizing his own power and Smith's weakness, or trying to win Smith's alliance by ceremonially adopting him. Powhatan's attempt to communicate failed, and relations between the English settlers and the Powhatan confederation deteriorated rapidly. In 1609 war broke out between the English and the Indians. This conflict continued, with full-scale wars in 1622, 1625, and 1644.

Despite spirited attempts to defend their territory, the Powhatan were wiped out as a military force long before the end of the century. Neither Powhatan's tribesmen nor any other of the Chesapeake Indians could fight disease. Epidemics and warfare destroyed entire tribes in the Chesapeake. Surviving Indians made their way as refugees to other tribes, worked for the English as laborers, or were enslaved. In 1607 there were about 20,000 Indians in Virginia. By 1669 only about 2,000 were left.

Colonization of the Chesapeake

Each Thanksgiving Americans celebrate the first English settlement in Massachusetts, that of the Pilgrims at Plymouth. No national holiday commemorates Jamestown, a settlement that began badly and became worse, reaching its nadir in the winter of 1609–10. Captain Smith had been injured and was evacuated to England. The colonists ran low on food, and those who tried to hunt were attacked by Powhatan's warriors. Governor George Percy recorded that the Virginians ate their horses first, then "were glad to make shift with vermin as dogs, cats, rats and mice." The starving colonists finally resorted to digging up corpses and eating them, "And amongst the rest, this was most lamentable, that one of our colony murdered his wife, ripped the child out of her womb and threw it into the river, and after chopped the mother in pieces and salted her for his food, the same not being discovered before he had eaten part thereof." By the spring of 1610, despite reinforcements, only ninety people were left in the colony: about one hundred had died of disease and hunger, thirty-three had been killed by Indians, and thirty-seven had deserted. The settlers decided to abandon the colony, and had actually taken ship to leave when they met a relief ship coming up the James River. Under orders, the settlers returned to Jamestown.

From 1610 to 1622, the Virginia Company tried in various ways to take control of its investment and make it profitable, but without success. The death rate continued to be very high and the company continued to lose money. In 1624 the King of England revoked the charter of the Virginia Company and took over the colony.

Meanwhile, the colonists had discovered the crop that would make them rich: tobacco. The natives of the Western Hemisphere had long used the plant in religious ceremonies. Sir Walter Raleigh and other English explorers brought tobacco home from the New World and made smoking it a fashionable fad, despite the disapproval of King James, who wrote a pamphlet condemning smoking as unhealthy and disgusting. The first Virginia settlers found tobacco growing in Virginia, but the variety was not acceptable to English tastes. In 1612 John Rolfe introduced into Virginia a better variety of Trinidadian tobacco, and in 1614 he shipped the first barrels home. For the colonists, tobacco was an ideal crop. The more Europeans bought and smoked, the more they wanted. In vain both the Company and officials of the Crown protested and forbade the colonists to grow the noxious weed. The Virginians had found their economic niche, and they refused to give it up. Virginia became internationally famous for tobacco.

In 1634 George Calvert, Lord Baltimore, founded a new colony, Maryland, north across the Chesapeake from Virginia. Calvert, an English Catholic, hoped to provide a safe refuge for his people, who faced persecution and public hostility in England. Although Maryland's early settlers included a number of Catholics, the colony was quickly swamped by Protestant settlers, most of them planning to get rich quick by growing tobacco. By the 1640s tobacco culture dominated life in the Chesapeake region.

Tobacco, Labor, and Lives

It is hard to overestimate the impact of tobacco. The crop required land, so planters moved out of Jamestown to take up isolated farms along the rivers, pioneering a pattern of dispersed settlement that would be typical of the rural South well into the twentieth century. On isolated southern farms and plantations, the owner, or "master," became effectively a law unto himself; he could do as he pleased without worrying about interference. Tobacco is a labor-intensive crop, requiring many "hands," or workers. Planters soon realized that the more workers they had, the more tobacco they could grow, and the more money they made. Needing workers, planters got them from all available sources, starting with the mother country, where a changing economy had left many men without jobs or prospects. In search of opportunity in Virginia, thousands of Englishmen signed indentures, or contracts, that bound them to work for a certain number of years (usually four to seven) for the man who bought their contract. The master also got the servant's headright, a land grant promised to all immigrants to Virginia. Thus by importing more labor, the master also got more land.

Between 1645 and 1670, historians estimate that between 40,000 and 50,000 British settlers came to the Chesapeake region, and that approximately 75 percent came as indentured servants. Although indentured servants were not slaves, that distinction often became blurred in Virginia. Planters bought and sold contracts, and even gambled for them, transferring the servants from one master to another at will. In 1625 an English sea captain refused to carry indentured servants to Virginia because, he said, "servants were sold . . . up and down like horses."

In truth, the planters of Virginia treated the servants worse than horses. A horse would have been an investment, while servants were but rental property. Many people who came to Virginia got sick during the first year, a process that Virginians called "seasoning," and the death rate remained high thereafter. Knowing that servants were likely to die before their contracts expired, masters drove them hard, determined to extract all the labor value they had paid for, and physically abused them as they pleased. Historians estimate that during the 1600s about 40 percent of the servants brought to Virginia died before their contracts ran out; those who did survive received minimal "freedom dues" (corn and tools) to help them survive as freed men.

Not all servants came to Virginia voluntarily. "Spirits," kidnappers who "spirited away" British men and women to service in the colonies, plied their trade in port cities like London and Bristol. In the 1640s and 1650s the English government shipped over Irish and Scottish soldiers who had been taken as prisoners of war. British law at that time had harsh penalties for even the most minor crimes. Stealing a sheep or hunting rabbits on a nobleman's land were hanging offenses. Some magistrates humanely preferred to send felons to Virginia rather than to the gallows. On the other hand, prominent men who owned profitable plantations in the Caribbean were accused of deliberately accusing innocent men of crimes so they could transport them as servants.

For the first fifty years or so of settlement, Virginia planters preferred indentured servants to the other labor available, enslaved Africans. Even in the 1670s, indentured servants outnumbered slaves three to one. Indentured servants were cheaper. Paying a higher price for the lifetime labor of a slave made no sense if the slave, like other newcomers to Virginia, died within a few years. Concerns about the legal status of slave property may also have led planters to prefer servants. The rationale for slavery was religion, not race: Christians could hold non- Christians as slaves until they converted. A slave who could gain freedom by baptism made a risky investment. Some planters seem to have resolved the question by assuming that slaves and servants were legally the same. These masters set their slaves free after seven years of service. Until Virginians began to clarify the differences between slaves and servants, planters chose servants over slaves.

Historians think that most of the slaves in Virginia in the early 1600s were "saltwater Negroes," people of color from slave societies in the Caribbean and the African coast, where European colonization had been under way for well over a century. They would have been familiar with European culture, and probably spoke at least one European language (possibly Spanish or Portuguese.) Many had Spanish names. These men and women of color worked with white servants, slept and ate with servants, had sex with servants. If set free, as several were, they married white servants, bought property, and became landowners and masters in their own right. Others served for life and saw their children follow them in slavery.

Early Virginia was a man's world in which white women were a scarce commodity. The high death rate at Jamestown derived in part from the absence, not only of women, but of any kind of settled household existence. Moreover, lacking women, the colony certainly had no prospects of growing by natural increase. Accordingly, the first Virginia Assembly (meeting under the sponsorship of the Company) stated that "in a new plantation it is not knowen whether man or woman be more necesary." To encourage the migration of women to Virginia, the governor and the assembly sent for a shipload of "woemen, maids young and uncorrupt to make wifes to the inhabitants" (Brown, 80, 81).

Despite colonial leaders' best efforts, English women did not migrate to Virginia in large numbers during the 1600s. Most of the white women who did came as indentured servants. Sponsors of the colony tried to attract white women to Virginia by promising that they would not have to do field labor, thereby raising them in status above African or Indian slaves. However, records indicate that English women, whether servants, wives, or daughters, worked tobacco when needed. They also cooked and cleaned for households that might include dozens of male servants, as well as the master's family. Female servants were subject to harsh physical discipline. Moreover, Virginia laws required servants who got pregnant to work additional years. The laws had to be modified when the assembly realized that some masters were deliberately impregnating their women to keep them in service. Historian Kathleen Brown's research into women in colonial Virginia verifies the truth of a contemporary ballad that described the hard life of a woman servant in Virginia and urged English women to stay home, "For if you do here come, you all will be weary, weary, weary, weary, O."

Virginia did offer one major incentive to immigration for English women: the possibility of improving their social status through marriage. For most English men and women in the 1600s, marriage was more about economics than romantic love. As seventeenth-century Englishmen saw it, women existed to work and to bear children for men. In such a world, single women had few options and usually worked as unpaid servants in their relatives' homes. To escape this fate, some women journeyed to Virginia, where there were three men for every woman. If a woman was blessed with an immune system that allowed her to survive Virginia's various diseases, she could marry her way into wealth and social position. Given the high death rate in Virginia, the average marriage lasted about seven years. Some strong and healthy women married and were widowed four or five times, and wound up as "founding mothers" of several prominent colonial families. Even servant women could usually count on marriage, usually to a landowner. Former servants would then become mistresses in their own right. Operating in a seller's market, canny women could negotiate marriage settlements and widow's portions that gave them far more power and property than normal back home in England.

The Virginia colonists were not the "gentlemen" and "ladies" of the later plantation myth. From the low ranks of English society, Virginia settlers had little chance to acquire polish on the frontier. Even the richest Virginians lived in primitive, simple wooden farmhouses and farmed on lands hacked out of the forests. Devoting most of their time to tobacco, Virginians depended for food on kitchen gardens and herds of hogs and cattle, imported into the colony and allowed to fend for themselves on the open range. For recreation, Virginians of both sexes drank, gambled, danced, fought, and fornicated. Virginia's court records indicate that colonial women specialized in creative and exuberant cursing, slander, and gossip. Colonial courts tried to control women's rowdy behavior, handing out punishments for women who cursed or defamed their neighbors, beat people up, or had sex outside of marriage, but some women were defiant. One woman, assigned to stand in front of the church wearing a sheet to show her repentance for having fornicated, was punished again when she spitefully tore holes in her sheet.

Virginia was built by violence and coercion. To survive, let alone succeed, Virginia planters used force to take land from the Indians, then grew their export crop, tobacco, with coerced labor. In the first century of settlement, most of the labor force was still white and indentured rather than black and enslaved, but the pattern was in place. This new society, like that of the mother country, had a class system; but unlike England, early Virginia offered a great deal of social mobility. In England, where class status was assigned at birth, impoverished nobles outranked rich commoners. In Virginia, where almost everyone was a commoner, rank could be achieved. Since English women were scarce, possessing one as wife became a sign of high status, generally reserved for planters and denied whenever possible to servants or slaves. Life in Virginia was often brutal, but it offered great financial and social rewards to the survivors.

Government, Power, and Rebellion

In 1618 the Virginia Company, desperately trying to salvage its investment in Jamestown, had given the colonists some limited self-government through an elected assembly. This assembly, which became known as the House of Burgesses, was the first American legislature. When Virginia became a royal colony in 1624, the king appointed a governor who then chose a council of the elite to advise him on policy. However, the House of Burgesses continued to meet without the governor's sanction. Ultimately, royal governors found that they could not govern the colony without the advice and consent of the planters who made up the burgesses. With royal approval, Virginia developed a three-tier government: the royal governor, the council (which advised the governor and acted as the colony's supreme court), and the House of Burgesses. This pattern would become typical of most of the southern colonies by the 1770s.

Virginia also set the pattern for local government. In other English colonies, such as those in New England, colonists lived close together in towns and governed themselves through the town meeting. Since Virginians lived on widely dispersed plantations and farms, the Virginia assembly divided the colony into counties. Each county had a "commander" and an elected "court" of magistrates, or justices of the peace. The county court provided what little administration rural counties needed and also acted as a judicial body, hearing small-claims cases. To keep the peace, each county had a sheriff and eventually a county court clerk to keep legal records. Southern counties use modifications of the same structure of government today.

Although Virginia's government featured elected assemblies, it would be a mistake to see Virginia as a democracy. Indentured servants, slaves, and women could not vote. Although small farmers could vote, in practice they deferred to the colonial elite, of whom the colony received a fresh infusion in the 1640s and 1650s. In the 1640s the English Civil War pitted the forces of the king against those of the English Parliament. When Parliament won and established a government under the leadership of General Oliver Cromwell, some defeated royalist "Cavaliers" took refuge in Virginia. Governor William Berkeley quickly incorporated them into the ruling elite but also made sure that Virginia maintained good relations with Cromwell's government until the monarchy was restored in 1660. Berkeley, who ruled Virginia from 1645 off and on for more than thirty years, molded the wealthiest Virginia planters into a tight-knit ruling party of less than 400 men, with most power vested in the planters closest to the governor. Many of these men held multiple colonial offices: one man might be simultaneously the tax collector, constable, and judge for his district. Berkeley and his clique used their control of the colonial political system to enrich themselves, then displayed their wealth by building grand estates.

In 1674 Nathaniel Bacon, a twenty-seven-year-old English gentleman, fled to Virginia after legal and personal problems made his future in England problematic. Related to several prominent Virginia families, including that of Governor Berkeley's wife, Bacon quickly insinuated himself into the governor's inner circle. However, in 1676 Bacon became the leader of a faction of planters determined to rid Virginia of its "Indian problem" and wound up leading a rebellion against Governor Berkeley.

Planters along the frontier had long complained that Berkeley's government was too friendly to the Indians. In 1675 members of the Doeg, irritated by the encroachment of white settlers, took a planter's hogs and killed a colonist. In retaliation, Virginians killed some Doegs and some Susquehannock who had not been involved in the original incident. In revenge, the Susquehannock mounted attacks on frontier settlements. Berkeley made peace with the Susquehannock, then proposed that Virginians safeguard their frontier by building a series of forts.

Berkeley's proposal made frontier planters furious. Berkeley's forts would be paid for by a tax increase, and planters felt that the taxes they paid on their servants, slaves, and tobacco exports were already too high. Moreover, most colonists wanted to expand Virginia's territory to the west. By the 1660s, increasing numbers of indentured servants were surviving their terms of service and wanted land. Freed servants and ambitious planters alike considered the colony's remaining Indians to be nuisances who deserved to be wiped out. In April 1676, planters in Charles City County began to arm in preparation for attacks on the Indians, and they asked Bacon to take command. Although Berkeley refused to approve Bacon's war against the Indians, the young man and his army attacked and enslaved Indians wherever they found them, whether friendly or hostile. Relations between Berkeley and Bacon deteriorated until, in the summer of 1676, war broke out between the supporters of the two men. Bacon led an army against Jamestown and burned it.

The rebellion was brought to an end by disease, Virginia's great equalizer. Bacon caught swamp fever and died of dysentery. Berkeley took revenge by hanging many of Bacon's supporters. In 1677 a royal commission arrived to sort out the politics of Virginia. The commissioners condemned the Virginians who "seem[ed] to wish and aime at an utter extirpation [extinction] of the Indians." The commission also faulted Berkeley's methods as governor, and he was removed from office and sent to England.

Bacon's Rebellion has been the subject of much debate by historians. Was the rebellion a preview of the Revolution? Was Bacon a prototype of American patriots fighting for liberty? Historians who believe so have stressed that Bacon's army included many frontiersmen, servants and even slaves, and that Bacon portrayed himself as a champion of "the people." Other historians note that Bacon himself was no friend of the common man. He scorned the Virginia elite as men of inferior family background and poor education.

More recently, historians have labeled Bacon's Rebellion a turning point in the development of American race relations. Bacon rebelled against the governor because Berkeley would not let him massacre and en-slave all the Indians in Virginia, including the friendly ones. At the end of the rebellion, not many more than 1,000 Indian men were left alive in Virginia. Colonists took the last of Indian lands and enslaved those Indians they could capture, thus effectively ending the colony's "Indian problem."

Some historians contend that the impact of the rebellion was even greater upon that small percentage of the Virginia population that was African. In order to diffuse class conflict in Virginia, these historians argue, the colonial elite set out to divide their labor force along racial lines.

The Southern Social Contract

Bacon's Rebellion highlighted a problem of concern to Virginia planters: what to do about the freed servants? By the 1670s the worst of the colony's dying times were over. Although the death rate continued to be higher than in England or in Massachusetts, planters could no longer count on almost half of their servants dying before they finished their term of service. When the servants went free, most could not afford land or wives and thus had no stake in maintaining the peace and prosperity of Virginia.

Masters noted with fear that Bacon's armies included many servants and slaves, who looted the houses of Berkeley's wealthy supporters, burned account books where the debts of poor men were recorded, and drank toasts to each other with the masters' wine. Among the last of the rebels to surrender was a group of eighty Africans and twenty white servants. The prospect of a rebel army of Africans and servants deeply worried Virginia's upper class.

Bacon's Rebellion seems to have been the catalyst for a major shift in Virginia's economy and its political system. Beginning in the 1670s, planters began to replace departing servants with slaves. By this time, improved economic conditions in England had reduced the number of men willing to risk indentured servitude in Virginia. As the supply went down, servants cost more. On the other hand, slaves cost less because of the entry of the English into the African slave trade. With the death rate declining, purchasing a slave's labor for life became a better bargain. To make this kind of property safe, the old confusion about the status of slaves now had to be clarified.

In the last decades of the seventeenth century, Virginians began to create a legal code for slavery. This process involved both defining slavery and distinguishing slaves from servants. In 1662 the assembly placed slavery on a racial foundation and tied it to gender by passing a law stating that the children of enslaved African women would be slaves even if the father was a free Englishman. Children of a free woman, whether white, Indian, or African, would be free. In 1667 the assembly removed the religious restrictions on slavery, stating that Africans who converted to Christianity could still be held as slaves. In 1682 the burgesses declared that all "non-Christian" servants imported into the colony would be slaves for life; this act applied to Africans and to Indians taken captive. With these laws, Virginians laid the legal foundation for the slave South.

Other laws drew new racial lines between British servants and Africans, whether slaves or free. Servants and slaves frequently ran away together. In 1661 the assembly required that white servants who ran away with slaves would serve "for the time of the said negroes absence" (Morgan, 311). In 1680 the assembly ordered that "any negroe or other slave [who] shall presume to lift up his hand in oppostion against any christian" should receive thirty lashes in punishment. This meant that servants could strike slaves and slaves could not legally retaliate. In 1705 the assembly enacted a measure allowing masters to punish slaves by "dismemberment" (usually cutting off fingers or toes); the same law made it illegal to "whip a christian white servant naked, without an order from a justice of the peace." Slaves had been allowed to own property, but the 1705 law ordered that all property belonging to slaves be seized by local authorites, sold, and the money made used for the relief "of the poor of the said parish."

Through further enactments the colonial assembly constructed a new definition of masculinity that united white men while excluding blacks. Free white men were expected to serve in the militia, the citizen's army that guarded the colony from attack. As the population of African slaves increased, so did the potential for a slave insurrection. In the early 1700s Virginia assemblies required that freed servants be given guns as part of their freedom dues. With this action, the assembly assured that all white men, regardless of class, would join together to protect white property. In the militia, planter and servant served as comrades in arms, further strengthening racial unity. Although free blacks were allowed to have guns, they were denied the right to serve in the militia. Solidifying the status of white men, the Crown insisted that all freed white servants be awarded fifty acres of land. From the late 1600s on, white southern men would measure their liberty by their access to land, guns—and women.

In the last decades of the seventeenth century, Virginians passed laws designed to control the sexuality of white women and to reserve them for white men only. In 1662 the assembly enacted punishments for inter-racial fornication. As enforced, this law targeted white women who had children by black men. In 1691 the assembly prohibited interracial sex inside or outside marriage. They stated that their purpose was "prevention of that abominable mixture and spurious issue which hereafter may encrease in this dominion, as well by negroes, mulattoes, and Indians intermarrying with English, or other white women, as by their unlawful accompanying with one another". Free white women who had children by black men faced stiff fines. The biracial children of white women were bound out to service until age thirty. The law called for banishment for any white person, male or female, who married across the color line. On the other hand, white masters could, and did, have sex with the black women they owned without punishment. The children of such unions became the slaves of their fathers.

Virginia's way of life became a pattern for later English colonies in the South. Like Virginia, such colonies would produce "staple crops," agricultural commodities that could be stored and packed for shipment overseas to international markets. Like Virginia, the other southern colonies would develop economies and societies dependent on racially based slave labor. Historian Edmund Morgan has pointed out that Virginia also pioneered the southern social contract, the unwritten understanding that raised the status of all whites in exchange for their support for the slave system.

The Colonial Slave Trade and the South

By the time Virginia was settled in 1607, Europeans had been shipping slaves out of West African ports for about 150 years. When the Europeans began to trade with West Africans in the 1450s, they tapped into an existing market in slaves. Africans enslaved captives taken in war, and heads of families sometimes cleared debts by selling children into slavery.

Slavery within African villages seems to have been different from slavery as it developed in the New World. In West Africa, women did the farming. Heads of families put enslaved women to work alongside their wives, producing the crops that fed the kinship group. Their children were treated as family members.

However, Africans also traded slaves on the continental market. Until the Europeans arrived off the coast of West Africa, Arab traders controlled most of the continent's long range slave trade, marching long caravans of slaves out of West Africa to markets in the Middle East, where they stood at auction with other captives, including white men and women from Christian areas in Europe. Slavery had no racial basis; that would come later.

The trans-Atlantic slave trade began to grow in the 1500s. To exploit the New World's mineral and agricultural resources, Europeans needed labor. West Africans supplied the necessary bodies, being eager to trade captives for textiles, iron, horses, guns, and luxury goods. Much of the slave trade seems to have been under the direct control of African states, whose leaders used European goods to increase their political power. To supply the trade, African leaders embarked on a series of wars, sending their millions of captives to the international slave markets.

For two hundred years, from the early 1600s through the early 1800s, African peoples made war on their neighbors, took captives, marched them to the Atlantic coast, and sold them to Europeans. On the beaches, the captives were stripped, inspected, branded with a slave mark designating their status, and confined in corrals, sometimes for weeks. Many captives died of despair or suicide. Others were convinced that the Europeans, having confined them like animals, planned to eat them. At that point they faced another ordeal, that of the ocean voyage to the New World called the Middle Passage.

Slave ships stank so badly that people could smell them for miles across the open sea. Slavers lost about 10 to 15 percent of their cargo—and their crew—to disease on every trip. Sharks followed the ships to feast on the bodies of the sick and the dead tossed overboard. Male captives spent their voyage confined below decks, packed in so closely that they could not easily move, and awash in their own vomit and other body wastes. Captains usually brought the slaves up on deck once a day and "danced" them, requiring the captives to jump up and down in their chains to restore circulation. Slavers confined female captives only at night, keeping them on deck in the daytime so that they would be available for the sexual use of the crew.

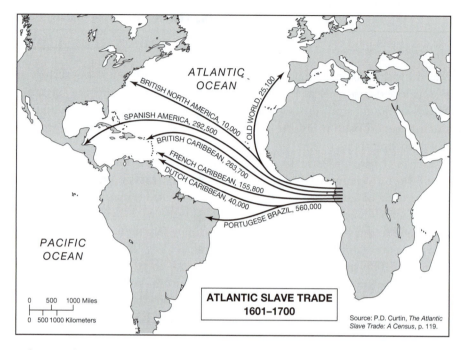

Atlantic slave trade, 1601–1700.

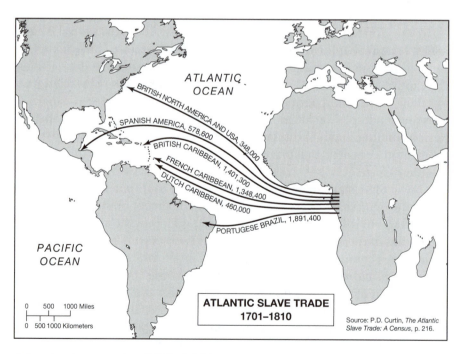

Atlantic slave trade, 1701–1810.

In most West African religions, suicide was the ultimate offense. Yet Europeans recorded that Africans on the slavers jumped into the shark-infested waters, starved themselves, hung themselves in their own chains—all in hopes that death would free them to be reincarnated back home. Others revolted against their captives and fought with their chains against swords and guns, generally to no avail. Those who submitted and survived the Middle Passage arrived in New World ports and were sold, often at public auction.

For many years historians have tried to imagine what the Middle Passage did to the minds and hearts of the people who survived it. Some historians have suggested that the shock of the passage was so great that it effectively stripped Africans of their memories, culture, and tribal identity, making it easier for their new owners to force them into the routines of slave life. More recently, however, others have noted that African tribal cultures survived in the New World, especially in areas with a large African population, like Brazil and the sugar islands in the Caribbean. Even in the English colonies in North America, where the slave population was relatively small, African ways became a major influence upon southern culture.

The Africans shipped to America did not think of themselves as "African," any more than the Virginian colonists thought of themselves as "Europeans." Although blacks and whites certainly perceived each other as different in color, they also recognized many differences between groups of people that had nothing to do with color. Newly arrived slaves identified primarily with their original tribes, thinking of themselves as Hausa, Wolof, Fanti, Ewe, and Ibo, just as newly arrived indentured servants thought of themselves as Scots, Irish, Welsh, and English. Moreover, the "saltwater Negroes" who had been the first slaves in British North America tended to look down on the newcomers from Africa, with whom they had little in common. It would take several generations for new racially based identities to replace old loyalties.

Slavery Today

In his magisterial book *Slavery and Social Death*, historian Orlando Patterson notes that slavery is such an ancient and pervasive system of domination that there is hardly anyone alive who is not descended from slaves. Sadly, slavery continues in the modern world. The American Anti-Slavery Group estimates that 27 million people today are held in some form of bondage. (See the Anti-Slavery Group's home page, www.anti-slavery.org, and that of Anti-Slavery International, www.antislavery.org, for further details.)

The old slave markets of the chattel slave system have mostly been closed, but slavery still exists in Mauritania, Sudan, Saudi Arabia, and the United Arab Emirates, despite legislation and decrees outlawing the practice. Much more common today are systems of forced or bonded labor. In many parts of the world, people unable to pay their debts are forced to work for their creditors. Children are sold as debt slaves and work as domestic servants or in factories to pay off their parents' debts. However, the average American is most likely to encounter slaves in the international sex trade. The brothels of Asia, popular ports of call for some American tourists and military personnel, are staffed by young men and women who are effectively slaves. Most die of AIDS.

Today many who are shocked at the brutality of the slave trade wonder how the English colonists could have behaved so cruelly to other human beings. English masters who had worked English indentured servants to death surely had no sleepless nights over slavery, a system of labor then found throughout the world. All the New World empires—the Spanish, French, and Portuguese—had slavery, although the systems differed according to the customs of the European colonizers' home country. Some historians argue that English culture predisposed the colonists to think of dark-skinned people as bad and therefore deserving of slavery. (In English folklore, the devil is black, while beauty is always "fair.") Others note that pre-1492 Europeans justified slavery on the basis of religion, not race: Moslems thought it correct to keep Christian slaves, while Christians thought the same about Moslems. This religious justification apparently still held some force in the colonial Chesapeake, where legislatures enacted laws stating that Africans' conversion to Christianity would not set them free. When in later years masters needed to defend the institution, they did so by labeling the enslaved brutish, heathen, and savage (like the Indians often enslaved beside them). Therefore, some historians contend that American racism did not precede slavery but was socially constructed to justify racially based slavery.

In the Atlantic slave trade, the numbers of people sold to British North America were but a drop in the bucket. Phillip Curtin, the foremost authority on the trade, estimates that less than half a million slaves were taken to the British North American colonies from the 1600s through the early 1800s. By contrast, the Spanish imported some 1.5 million slaves into their American possessions, while the French and British each brought over 1,600,000 slaves to their island possessions in the Caribbean. Brazil was the largest slave importer, in part because slavery lasted longer there (well into the late 1800s) than in other New World countries. Traders carried at least 3.5 million slaves to Brazil.

The slave system that emerged in the southern English colonies in the eighteenth century was in one way unique in the Western Hemisphere. British North America was the only place in the New World where the slave population grew by natural increase. Slave owners in other areas, anxious to make money quickly, worked their slaves to death cultivating sugar or mining silver. Planters in the eighteenth-century South could make profits without killing their people, and they quickly realized that encouraging slaves to pair off and form families led to the production and survival of children, and therefore a dependable source of labor. Rather than constantly importing labor from Africa, southern planters raised their own.

New Settlements, New People

As citizens of a very young country, Americans tend to telescope events in the nation's colonial past, jumping from Jamestown to the Declaration of Independence as if there were not over 160 years between. During those decades, Indian tribes disappeared, while new ones were formed. Native Americans who learned to deal with the Europeans prospered while becoming increasingly dependent on trade goods. The British colonies in

Maryland and Virginia were joined by others, north and south, and the French reached out from their colonies in Canada to found new settlements along the Mississippi. European immigrants poured into the region, and thousands of unwilling migrants made the trip to the New World in the hulls of African slavers.

The Carolinas and Georgia

South Carolina was founded in the 1660s as a proprietary colony, given by King Charles II of England to a group of noblemen to whom he owed political debts. The proprietors planned to lure settlers to Carolina with generous grants of land but expected to govern the colonists with an extremely old-fashioned system vesting most authority in the proprietors and their deputies and friends. But when planters from Barbados, Bermuda, and the Bahamas poured into the new colony, the proprietors found that they could not govern from England, and the settlers developed their own forms of self-government, including a civil constitution that allowed an amount of religious toleration unusual for the period.

In the seventeenth century South Carolina's wealth came from the Indian trade in deerskins and slaves. Colonial leaders played tribes like the Creek, Choctaw, and Chickasaw against each other and bought the prisoners of Indian wars for slaves. Meanwhile, the Carolinians and the Virginians negotiated for trade with the Cherokees in the mountains to the west, drawing that tribe into the sphere of English influence.

Planters who came to the Carolinas from the Caribbean were accustomed to exploiting slave labor and do not seem to have ever seriously considered any alternative workforce. Once they found their staple crop in rice, they imported slaves from rice-growing areas of Africa, such as Senegal and Sierra Leone, to work the plantations. To control their workforce, the planters implemented slave codes based on those developed in the West Indies. Frequently masters lived in Charleston most of the year, visiting their plantations only occasionally. While Charleston operated as an outpost of the Caribbean sugar islands, visitors commented that South Carolina plantations looked like African villages.

African slaves made up the majority of the population of South Carolina as early as 1708, and by the 1730s outnumbered white colonists in some areas by as many as eight to one. Most African-Americans today probably have at least one ancestor who came to America through the slave market and quarantine center on Sullivan's Island in Charleston Bay. In South Carolina the customs of many African tribes fused into a new African-American culture. By 1740, South Carolina's 40,000 slaves had developed their own language, Gullah, a mixture of several African tongues and English. (Gullah is still spoken today on several coastal islands.) Whites in South Carolina, highly conscious of their minority status, worried about slave rebellions. To control the slave population, Carolinians assigned the militia to ride regular mounted patrols along "beats" in the countryside.

White Carolinians feared the slave population with good reason. In 1739 a group of Angolan slaves began an insurrection, the Stono Rebellion, that resulted in the deaths of about twenty-five whites and about thirty-five rebel slaves. Colonial authorities quickly crushed the rebellion and spent months hunting down and punishing escaped rebels. After Stono, the South Carolina assembly enacted slave codes that greatly restricted even the minimal liberties that had been allowed previously. Yet Carolinians continued to live in fear, plagued by frequent rumors of rebellion. As Virginian Thomas Jefferson noted, those who depended on slavery had taken the wolf by the ears: it was no longer safe to hold on or to let go.

North Carolina began as an outpost of settlers from Virginia and South Carolina. A very old southern joke says that North Carolina was "a vale of humility between two mountains of conceit." In Virginia and in South Carolina, a plantation elite quickly grew to dominate colonial politics and society. Although there were plantations in North Carolina, the joke points out that North Carolina society contained many more common folk than plantation aristocrats. North Carolinians made their living as small farmers and in the production of "naval stores," including turpentine and tar. They angered visiting Virginians with their refusal to defer to the Virginians' aristocratic pretensions; the Virginians retaliated by describing backcountry North Carolinians as barbarous, dirty, lazy, ignorant, and (most irritating of all) under no compulsion to obey their "betters." Besides, as a visiting missionary complained in the 1760s, their women wore their clothes too tight and their hair slicked up Indian style with bear grease. (What the Carolina women thought about the minister escaped the historical record.)

Georgia, founded in 1733 as the last of the English North American colonies, had an idealistic origin unusual in the South. The founder of Georgia, Colonel James Oglethorpe, hoped that his colony would become a place where poor English debtors could find a new start. The first capital, Savannah, was also a southern rarity: a planned settlement, complete with gridded streets and open, parklike squares. The proprietors of Georgia thought slavery incompatible with their aims and forbade it, but without success; by the 1740s planters from the Carolinas began to move into Georgia with their slaves.

The Backcountry

Political conflicts between tidewater and backcountry became standard in the southern colonies well before the Revolution. In the 1760s bands of thieves roamed the South Carolina backcountry. Protesting that the colonial government did not care enough about them to bother to enforce the laws, the frontiersmen formed the "Regulators" to hunt down the robbers. Backcountry North Carolinians complained that their area of the state lacked adequate representation in the colonial assembly and that even local governments were controlled by officials from the eastern part of the state. In 1767 they formed their own Regulators and shut down the county courts. The Regulator rebellion continued until 1771, when militia from the eastern counties under the command of the royal governor broke up an army of 2,000 disgruntled frontiersmen at the Alamance River. The Regulator rebellions demonstrated that unity among whites was fragile and could be shattered along class lines. In both Carolinas, western farmers charged that tidewater planters cared more for their slaves than for free whites.

The Scotch-Irish

During the 1700s a new variety of British settler began to appear in American ports, passing through on the way to the western frontier. These people have been labeled "Scotch-Irish," a name that still persists after 300 years, despite its historical inaccuracy. Some of the new settlers were indeed Ulster Scots, descendants of Scots Presbyterians sent by the British over to Northern Ireland to fight the Catholic Irish and generally hold the fort for the British crown. Others were from the north of Britain, or the

Scottish lowlands. Contrary to present-day southern-heritage rhetoric, very few were Scottish highlanders. (Indeed, as lowland Scots, they were the highlanders' traditional enemies. There were highlander settlements in the Carolinas, but those people never thought of themselves as Scotch-Irish.) Perhaps vaguely Celtic in ancestry, most spoke not Gaelic but dialects of English.

In the 1700s, approximately 300,000 Scotch-Irish immigrants came to America. In Britain, they had been frontier people, cattle and sheep herders, prone to raid their enemies across whatever border they happened to live on. In the New World, they took up lands once again on the border, following the Great Philadelphia Wagon Road through the backcountry from Pennsylvania down to Georgia. In the South, they formed the majority of many frontier settlements. Having once fought the Irish, they now fought Indians.

They were a tough population to manage, whether in Northern Ireland or in western North Carolina. Proud, independent, and violent, they also differed in religion from the English who settled along the southern coast. Most of the southern white lowlanders were members of the Church of England (known today in America as Episcopalians). The Scotch-Irish were Presbyterians, Calvinists whose version of God tended to be as vengeful as themselves. In Pennsylvania, Benjamin Franklin called the new immigrants "white savages." Back home, English people referred to the Presbyterian "scum" of North Britain by a special nickname: "rednecks."

The Latin South

In the early 1600s the French began to establish colonies in the far north, in what is presently Quebec. Early French colonies revolved around the Catholic mission and the fur trade, a highly profitable enterprise, and one that took French woods runners (*coureurs des bois*) deep into the continental interior. More systematic explorations followed in the late 1600s. In 1682, the French explorer René-Robert Cavelier sieur de La Salle floated down the Mississippi and claimed its valley for King Louis XIV, naming the entire region, from the Appalachians to the Rockies, and north to Canada, "Louisiana" in his honor. Further explorations of the Gulf Coast led to the establishment of a French outpost at Biloxi, founded by the Sieur d'Iberville in 1699. A settlement at Mobile followed in 1711 and one at Natchitoches in 1715. In 1718, Jean Baptiste Le Moyne, Sieur de Bienville (d'Iberville's brother) founded New Orleans.

New Orleans drew commerce and people from the southern Mississippi valley and the Caribbean, and sailors from all over the world. Although the settlers of Louisiana grew rice, indigo, and tobacco, the colony lived primarily by trade. The French, like the Spanish, did not sponsor wholesale migrations of their people to the New World. Nor did they encourage religious dissidents to emigrate, as the British did. As a result, the European population of Louisiana remained small. In terms of the French empire as a whole, New Orleans was an expensive, rather unprofitable outpost, important mostly for its geographic location at the mouth of the Mississippi. In 1762, the French crown signed over New Orleans to Spain. The French hoped that the Spanish could keep Louisiana out of the hands of the British; the Spanish wanted the colony as a buffer between their Mexican possession and the British colonies on the east coast. The Spanish held Louisiana officially until 1800, when it fell again under nominal French control before passing by treaty to the United States in 1803. Thus Louisiana, and especially New Orleans, added Spanish flavor to an already diverse mixtures of cultures and peoples.

Cajuns and Creoles

In Spanish and French New World colonies, people born in the New World of European parents were called "Creoles." In Louisiana, Creole came to refer not only to American-born French and Spanish people, but also to the varied peoples of color of New Orleans. Partly because of the Latin slaveholder's tendency to emancipate his children by slave women, New Orleans developed early on a sizable population of free people of color. Many of the *gens de colour* became property owners; some inherited plantations and slaves.

The Acadians, or "Cajuns," were French settlers in Canada, evicted from their homes as the result of a French-British war in the mid-1700s. They came to Louisiana as refugees, and took up residence in the bayou country north of New Orleans.

Maturing of Anglo-American Colonial Society

In 1750 the tidewater settlements in Virginia were 140 years old; those in South Carolina, almost 100 years old. In the tidewater, planters built great houses of brick that signaled their intention to make America their home and to rear their children as ladies and gentlemen, complete with educations fitted to their status. The sons of Virginia's elite went to the College of William and Mary, established in 1693. As gentlemen, planters'

George Washington's home at Mount Vernon, like many Virginia plantation houses, faced the river, a more reliable source of transportation than colonial roads. Mount Vernon illustrates well the ways in which Virginia planters used architecture to signify their dominance and their status as leaders of colonial society. Published in 1800. Library of Congress.

sons were expected to be familiar with the liberal arts—that is, the arts suited to liberty. They read history, political theory, and law.

The master's wife and his daughter displayed the family's status through their accomplishments. Eliza Lucas's father gave her a plantation in South Carolina to manage when she was sixteen. Successful in that endeavor, Miss Lucas turned to horticultural experiments, working out ways to cultivate and process the plant that produces indigo dye, and then encouraging her neighbors to grow and market this new crop. She eventually married Charles Pinckney, whom she adored. When his death left her a young widow with young children, she managed several plantations and supervised her sons' English education through streams of letters to friends overseas. Eliza Lucas Pinckney's offspring grew up to become Founding Fathers of the American republic. Although Eliza Lucas Pinckney was extraordinary, other women of the colonial elite shared her ability to move from business management to decorative arts to domestic concerns while maintaining the calm, refined demeanor appropriate to an upper-class lady.

Although the slave population included newcomers from Africa, the descendants of slaves imported in the seventeenth century now spoke English, and some had become Christians. Tribal distinctions still mattered, both to slaves and to their masters, who often preferred to purchase people from one select ethnic group. However, slavery was beginning to act as a melting pot as men and women from different tribes married and had children. Slaves, like masters, were building a unity based on race.

Indentured servants still came to the colonies, served their terms, and took up their freedom dues, often moving west to the frontier that stretched north and south along the foothills of the Appalachian Mountains. For servants or immigrants, survival and upward social mobility depended on access to new land, and they continually pushed against the Indians on the frontier. Meanwhile, Indian tribes became increasingly dependent on English trade goods.

As colonial society matured, a new political culture emerged. Over the years, the southern colonies (like those in the north) developed systems of self-governance that usually included some form of elected legislative body. Even the most snobbish would-be aristocrat could not gain power without appealing to "the people"—that is, the white small farmers who formed the region's voting majority. Virginia, in particular, had a lively political scene, featuring campaign rallies that included all the food and drink the voters could consume, paid for by the would-be officeholder. (Some cynical politicians referred to this as "swilling" the voters.) Voting became a symbol of white manhood, enacted in public before crowds, so that everyone would know what stand a man had taken.

It was through these political systems that leaders like George Washington, Thomas Jefferson, James Madison, James Monroe, and others emerged to lead the American Revolution. Like the colonial leaders of the previous century, they were wealthy slaveholders; unlike Berkeley and Bacon, they based their claim to power not on birth but on their ability to speak for "the people."

The life and career of George Washington illustrate how this new colonial elite could make such a claim. Although his family was wealthy and powerful, young Washington himself did not inherit much money. As a young man he learned to survey land, an outdoor occupation that required travel into the backcountry. His class status earned him a position as captain in the Virginia militia, but he learned to command by fighting alongside ordinary farmers in the French and Indian War. As an adult, Washington acquired an estate, Mount Vernon, when his beloved older half-brother died; his marriage to a widow, Martha Custis, brought him wealth. Washington worked hard to live up to his fortunate position. He was a careful and methodical master, paying much attention to the well-being of his land and his slaves. Afflicted with a violent temper, he learned to control it. Although his wealth, education, and demeanor distinguished him as a gentleman, like his neighbors he was a farmer whose prosperity depended on the caprices of nature and the turns of English markets; like them, he was constantly in debt to English middlemen. Despite great differences in class status, Washington and Virginia's ordinary farmers shared common interests.

Washington, a reserved and dignified man, hated "swilling the voters," but like other southern white politicians, he had to court the common man to attain power. Through years of public service, Washington built a reputation that Thomas Jefferson would later summarize: "He was, in every sense of the words, a wise, a good and a great man."

Revolutions

To the British government, the American colonies were only one part of a worldwide empire, and not the most profitable part, either: Barbados and Jamaica made more money for Britain than Virginia and all the other colonies combined. Striving to increase their empire, the British went to war with France in 1754. American colonists fought in this "Seven Years War," which they called the "French and Indian War." The war ended with a British triumph. By treaty, the French gave to the British their territories north, west, and south of the thirteen colonies (present-day Canada, the Midwest, the trans-Appalachian South, and Florida.) New Orleans had already passed from French to Spanish control, but the Spanish ceded their claims to Florida to the English. The American colonists were jubilant, believing that the lands west of the Appalachians would be theirs to exploit.

Their high hopes turned into anger when the British government announced in 1763 that the trans-Appalachian lands would be reserved for the Indian tribes who lived there. In the South, wealthy planters who had invested money in speculative claims to western lands felt betrayed, while poor farmers who understood that upward mobility for their children depended on access to new land joined in condemning the British decision. The colonists' anger grew when the British, attempting to pay for their recent war, tried to raise revenues by taxing the colonies. Since the 1600s the colonists had accepted that the British had the right to tax exports from the colonies in order to regulate imperial trade. The new taxes proposed by the British (a sugar tax in 1764, a stamp tax in 1765, and later the famous tax on tea) were taxes on internal commerce. The colonists protested that only they, through their elected assemblies, could enact such taxes. Colonial leaders called for boycotts of the taxed goods. The British insisted on their right to tax the colonies, and in the 1770s sent troops into Massachusetts to quiet colonial protests. Fighting broke out in 1775 between the Massachusetts militia and British troops attempting to find a hidden arsenal of weapons and ammunition.

Although the Revolution began in the northern colonies, southerners, especially Virginians, quickly emerged as leaders. The colonists' new assembly, the Continental Congress, placed George Washington of Virginia in command of the rebel army. It is not an exaggeration to say that many men joined the Revolution, and later supported the American republic, because they trusted Washington. When the Congress decided to declare independence in 1776, a delegate from Virginia, Thomas Jefferson, composed the Declaration. Congress had a very practical reason for encouraging Virginians to take command: Virginia was the most populous and wealthy of the colonies, and the rebellion could not succeed without her support.

The causes of the American Revolution remain debatable. While historians take seriously the colonial elites' fears that British policy aimed at destroying their liberties, they also point out that colonial leaders' radicalism had other sources as well: economics and pressure from below. In most of the colonial South, the "founding fathers"-to-be were deep in debt to the British merchants who acted as middlemen for the marketing of the region's staple crops. It is probably an exaggeration to suggest (as early-twentieth-century historians did) that the Revolution was mostly a way to get out from under these debts, but it did have that effect. Even more significantly, new historical research suggests that the colonial upper class, at least in Virginia, was pushed into revolution by their small-farmer neighbors, who hoped that the Revolution would bring them more political power.

Talking Liberty, Talking Slavery

White southerners who supported the Revolution brought to the cause a special understanding of liberty that derived from both their experience as colonists and their familiarity with slavery. Over the years, colonial assemblies had jealously guarded their right to make tax laws, since the power to tax was the power to control or destroy the very property that helped to distinguish a free man from a slave. To tax a free man without his consent (expressed through his elected representatives) took away his liberty. Virginia assemblyman Patrick Henry expressed this view in a speech against the new British taxes, concluding, "Give me liberty, or give me death." White southern patriots accused the British of attempting to turn free Americans into slaves. White southern Loyalists, or "Tories," also used the language of liberty and slavery, accusing the rebel leaders of rank hypocrisy for talking about freedom while holding slaves.

In 1775 the royal governor of Virginia, Lord Dunmore, promised freedom to all slaves who would join the king's forces. Some historians credit Dunmore's proclamation with solidifying Virginia patriots' commitment to the Revolution. As one southerner wrote, "Hell itself could not have vomited anything more black than this design of emancipating our slaves." Dunmore's proclamation certainly convinced the majority of African-Americans that the British were their best chance for freedom. Though some of the colonies' small free black population supported the patriot cause, most of the slaves did not.

Emboldened by Dunmore's promise of liberty, thousands of slaves escaped to the British army, where they served in the Black Regiment of Guards and Pioneers. The passage of British troops through any slave-holding area in the South precipitated mass escapes. The British transported hundreds of former slaves from the South to New York, and then at the end of the war evacuated 2,000 of them to Nova Scotia, where they formed the largest settlement of free blacks in North America.

The War in the South

When the French began to support American independence, the Revolution turned into a worldwide conflict, involving the British against the French and Spanish. For the British, putting down the rebellion became something of a sideshow. Annually during the summer British armies were dispatched to the colonies; annually Washington and his men fought (and usually lost) and retreated past the reach of the British to fight again the next year. Up until 1778 most of the fighting was done in the northern colonies, but in that year the British shifted their operations south, hoping to use southern ports as bases for their naval battles with the French for control of the Caribbean sugar islands. The British believed that many of the southern colonists were secret Tories, who would rally to the Crown if given the opportunity.

The British southern campaign focused at first on the Carolinas. In 1778 the British captured Savannah, and in 1780 they took Charleston, before crushing the American defense under the command of General Gates at Camden, South Carolina. With British troops to back them up, Tories attacked their rebel neighbors, bringing the war home to the southern countryside. British Colonel Banastre Tarleton earned a reputation for brutality when he refused to allow defeated rebels to surrender, ordering his troops to kill them instead. This "no quarter" policy backfired, as many previously neutral Georgians and Carolinians were pushed into joining rebel guerrilla bands such as the one led by Francis Marion, "The Swamp Fox." The neighbors' war in the Carolinas became increasingly vicious, with atrocities committed by colonists on both sides.

In October 1780, the British commander, Lord Cornwallis, attempted to advance into North Carolina, but when a band of "over-mountain boys" from the Appalachian frontier destroyed a loyalist army in battle at King's Mountain, Cornwallis fell back to South Carolina.

Meanwhile, the rebels organized an army under the command of General Nathaniel Greene, sent by Washington to take command in the South. In 1781 Greene succeeded in luring Cornwallis into chasing the rebel forces through the countryside. This war of mobility exhausted the British forces, leaving them vulnerable to attack. In January, a portion of Greene's army destroyed Tarleton's forces at the battle of Cowpens, and in March the armies fought an indecisive battle at Guilford Courthouse. Cornwallis withdrew, leaving the Deep South under rebel control, and made his way to the coast, eventually arriving in Yorktown, Virginia, in the summer of 1781.

There the British commander found a combined French and American army waiting for him, and a French fleet blocked any escape via the Chesapeake. Cornwallis surrendered to General Washington and the French commanders in October 1781, bringing the war for American independence to an end. In 1783 representatives of the new United States of America met with the British, French, and Spanish to sign an official peace treaty. By this treaty the Americans obtained title to lands reaching west to the Spanish possessions along the Mississippi, south to the thirty-first parallel (roughly the northern border with Florida, which was returned to the Spanish), and north to the border with Canada. For the southern colonists, the road to the West now opened, and in the 1780s and 1790s they poured across the mountains to take up new lands.

The South in the New Nation

As the United States developed its new system of government, southerners could be found on all sides of every political controversy. The first national government, created in 1781 by the Continental Congress, was a loose alliance of states under the Articles of Confederation. Although the different states cooperated for defense and foreign policy, each state operated like an independent country in its own territory. As the articles explained, "each State retains its sovereignty, freedom and independence." Having just fought a revolution against a king, many Americans feared that any kind of strong government might become a danger to the liberties of the people. Therefore, many Americans preferred to place most power in the hands of state governments, which were close to the people and could be watched carefully for signs of potential tyranny. This was the point of view of southern leaders such as Thomas Jefferson.

However, other political leaders across the country began in the 1780s to call for a stronger central government that would be able to regulate international commerce, keep the new settlements in the West aligned with the nation, and create a stable financial system. A Massachusetts farmers' tax revolt in 1786 dramatized the need for reform. In 1787 delegates from twelve of the states met at Philadelphia to revise the Articles of Confederation. Under the leadership of the Virginia delegation, which included Edmund Randolph, George Mason, and James Madison, the convention decided to scrap the articles and start fresh with a new constitution, a written framework for a republican national government.

As the delegates hammered out their new constitution, it quickly became clear that slavery already divided North and South. Slavery had been legal in all the thirteen colonies. In the postrevolutionary period, most northern states had enacted legislation gradually emancipating their slaves. In the new government, seats in the House of Representatives would be apportioned by population: the more people, the more representation. Other nonvoters, such as women, children, and landless men, were counted for apportioning representatives, but the northern states objected to counting slaves. The delegates worked out a compromise that allowed the southern states to count all their free citizens, including indentured servants, and three-fifths of their slaves. Thus was slavery written into the Constitution. The delegates also forbade Congress to outlaw the importation of slaves until 1808, and required that fugitive slaves who ran away across state lines be returned to their masters.

Having written their constitution, the Federalists (as they were now called) had to get it ratified by the states. Some of the strongest opposition to the new government came from old southern revolutionaries like

Patrick Henry, who thought that the new government would trample on the liberties of the people. Thomas Jefferson, at that time serving as ambassador to France, expressed similar concerns but did support ratification. Others worried, with just cause, that this new government would destroy state sovereignty and concentrate power at the federal level. However, George Washington had acted as president of the Constitutional Convention, and his support for the new plan went a long way to convincing southern white voters. To win further support, Madison promised that the first Congress elected under the new system would enact a Bill of Rights. Ratified in 1791, the Bill of Rights protected citizens from the national government, guaranteeing freedom of speech, assembly, press, and religion. The Second Amendment protected the state militias by upholding the right of the people to keep and bear arms, and the Tenth Amendment reserved to the people or the states all rights not specifically given to the federal government.

The new nation had been created, and was to be governed, largely by southerners. A Virginian, Thomas Jefferson, wrote the Declaration of Independence; his fellow Virginian, James Madison, was instrumental in formulating the Constitution and the Bill of Rights. The Virginian George Washington commanded the Revolutionary Army. From Washington to Andrew Jackson, every president except John Adams and his son John Quincy Adams came from a southern state. By the time that Jackson left office in 1837, the sectional differences between North and South, already visible at the Constitutional Convention, had begun to deepen.

Suggestions for Further Reading

JAMES AXTELL, *The Indians' New South: Cultural Change in the Colonial Southeast* (1997)

IRA BERLIN, *Many Thousands Gone: The First Two Centuries of Slavery in North America* (1998)

KATHLEEN M. BROWN, *Good Wives, Nasty Wenches and Anxious Patriarchs: Gender, Race and Power in Colonial Virginia* (1996)

COLIN G. CALLOWAY, *New Worlds for All: Indians, Europeans and the Remaking of Early America* (1997)

CATHERINE CLINTON AND MICHELLE GILLESPIE, EDS., *The Devil's Lane: Sex and Race in the Early South* (1997)

PETER COCLANIS, *The Shadow of a Dream: Economic Life and Death in the South Carolina Low Country: 1670–1820* (1988)

ALFRED W. CROSBY, JR., *The Columbian Exchange: Biological and Cultural Consequences of 1492* (1972)

PHILIP D. CURTIN, *The Atlantic Slave Trade: A Census* (1969)

——, *The Rise and Fall of the Plantation Complex: Essays in Atlantic History* (1990)

DAVID BRION DAVIS, *The Problem of Slavery in Western Culture* (1966)

DAVID HACKETT FISCHER, *Albion's Seed: Four British Folkways in America* (1989)

MICHAEL ANGELO GOMEZ, *Exchanging Our Country Marks: The Transformation of African Identities in the Colonial and Antebellum South* (1998)

WOODY HOLTON, *Forced Founders: Indians, Debtors, Slaves, and the Making of the American Revolution in Virginia* (1999)

RHYS ISAACS, *The Transformation of Virginia, 1740–1790* (1982)

WINTHROP JORDAN, *White over Black: American Attitudes toward the Negro, 1550–1812* (1968)

ALLAN KULIKOFF, *Tobacco and Slaves: The Development of Southern Cultures in the Chesapeake, 1680–1800* (1986)

EDMUND S. MORGAN, *American Slavery, American Freedom: The Ordeal of Colonial Virginia* (1975)

PHILIP D. MORGAN, *Slave Counterpoint: Black Culture in the Eighteenth-Century Chesapeake and Lowcountry* (1998)

GARY B. NASH, *Red, White and Black: The People of Early America*, 4th ed. (2000)

ORLANDO PATTERSON, *Slavery and Social Death: A Comparative Study* (1982)

MECHAL SOBEL, *The World They Made Together: Black and White Values in Eighteenth-Century Virginia* (1987)

JOHN THORNTON, *Africa and Africans in the Making of the Atlantic World, 1400–1680* (1992)

ERIC WILLIAMS, *Capitalism and Slavery* (1944)

PETER H. WOOD, *Black Majority: Negroes in Colonial South Carolina from 1670 through the Stono Rebellion* (1974)

GORDON S. WOOD, *The Radicalism of the American Revolution* (1992)

2

The Old South, 1790–1860

Once there was a world of gracious living, gallant men, and lovely ladies, and loyal slaves . . . Or was there? No past time and place is more vivid in the fantasies of Americans than the Old South. On the basis of films, books, and television shows, most Americans believe that they know what the Old South must have been like. Images of a feudal world populated by beautiful women in crinolines, gallant soldiers in gray, and slaves brutally forced to work in cotton fields uneasily coexist in the public's memory, along with an understanding that the Old South, having been formed by slavery, disappeared with slavery at the end of the Civil War.

The history of the Old South contradicts the moonlight-and-magnolias myth. Although slavery formed the region's economy and society, the institution was not as widespread as the mythology would have us believe. In 1860, three-fourths of white southerners did not own slaves. Those who did may have wanted to see themselves as landed aristocrats living lives of leisure and grace surrounded by faithful slave retainers, but the economics of slavery contradicted that wistful dream at every turn. To survive and prosper, planters had to be businessmen. The region's wealthiest people used the oldest labor system, slavery, to produce cotton, America's most valuable export and an essential component of the rising industrial system in Europe and in the northern United States.

Studying the history of the Old South provokes questions. What was the world that slavery made really like? Did slavery really form the South? How could it, since most white southerners did not own slaves? Most of all, why did white southerners fight a war to preserve slavery?

Becoming Southern: The Emergence of the Old South, 1790s–1830s

By the end of the eighteenth century, white Virginians had already begun to complain that the soil, so rich a century before, was losing its fertility after repeated crops of tobacco. Planters, deciding that tobacco no longer brought enough profits to compensate for the damage it did to their land, began to switch from tobacco to wheat and other food crops that required less labor and therefore fewer slaves. Thoughtful white Virginians foresaw a gradual and distant end to the institution: when slaves cost more to feed than they earned as labor, planters would set them free. Meanwhile, to preserve and increase the value of the slaves they held, planters supported state laws that prohibited the importation of additional slaves from Africa or the West Indies. Nonetheless, thousands of Africans were brought to the Deep South before 1808, when the federal government finally ended the importation of slaves.

Washington, Jefferson, and Slavery

The existence of slavery in a republic founded on principles of liberty concerned the Founding Fathers. In the northeast, the revolutionary generation passed laws freeing the slaves. In the South, many expressed vague hopes that the institution would gradually fade away.

None of the Founding Fathers had a more tortured

connection with slavery than did Thomas Jefferson. The author of the Declaration of Independence believed in human liberty. Yet Jefferson also believed that Africans were probably inferior to whites. As a practical politician, he also knew that his constituents adamantly opposed any suggestions that blacks and whites could live in community as equals.

Jefferson's personal life complicated the issue. Jefferson liked to live well, buying good foods and wines and lavishing attention on his estate, Monticello. Slave labor paid for his luxuries.

For generations, the descendants of slaves at Monticello have insisted that Jefferson kept a slave mistress, Sally Hemmings, by whom he fathered numerous children. Recent DNA testing indicates that these family legends are probably true. The Hemmings children were allowed to walk away from Monticello to freedom, but the rest of Jefferson's slaves were sold after his death to help clear his debts.

A much more straightforward man than Jefferson, George Washington freed his slaves in his will.

In 1792 Catherine Littleton Greene, widow of Revolutionary War general Nathaniel Greene, entertained at her Georgia estates a visitor from New England, Eli Whitney, a young tutor then looking for a job in the South. While at the Greene estate Whitney heard Mrs. Greene and other visitors discussing the commercial possibilities of cotton. In the sea islands off the coasts of Georgia and South Carolina, planters cultivated a variety of cotton with fibers loosely wrapped around the seeds, making it relatively easy to remove the seeds, spin the fiber into thread, and then weave the thread into very fine, silk-like cloth. Sea island cotton required such a long growing season that it was not suitable for cultivation in the inland South. Upland cotton, grown for home use as far north as Virginia, had seeds that were tightly matted into the fiber. Though housewives laboriously pulled the seeds out, combed the cotton, and used it for quilt battings and clothing, the difficulty of removing the seeds made the crop unsuited for commercial cultivation. Mrs. Greene and her neighbors explained this problem to Whitney, who then proceeded to invent a machine, or "engine," to remove the seeds. The cotton gin was so simple that others quickly copied it. The new machine transformed southern agriculture and with it, the economy of the United States and the world.

Cotton was the essential raw material that made possible the Industrial Revolution. In the 1740s, English inventors began to create machines to do the spinning and weaving that had traditionally consumed many hours of women's lives. When Whitney invented the cotton gin, English manufacturers manifested an immediate interest. Before the end of the century, planters in Georgia and South Carolina were shipping out bales of cotton to English mills to be spun and woven into cheap, durable, washable cloth for the world. By 1840, English manufacturing districts depended on shipments of southern cotton in much the same way that Detroit now depends on Middle Eastern oil. By 1860, more than 60 percent of the world's cotton supply came from the South, and the fiber crop made up more than half of the nation's exports.

In Massachusetts, inventors pirated English textile machinery and opened up the first American textile mills in 1815, setting off the first industrial revolution in the United States. As industrialization spread through New England, New York, and Pennsylvania, a new way of life began to develop. The northeast's economy was increasingly characterized by industry and wage labor. Although northeastern textile mills depended on southern cotton, northeastern and southern economic interests began to diverge. Not all of the areas of the North industrialized. Even in the northeastern states agriculture remained important, and it dominated the economies of the newly settled midwestern states like Ohio, Indiana, and Illinois. Small farmers there had much in common with small farmers in the South. However, as the decades of the early nineteenth century passed, midwestern farmers were increasingly linked to the economic interests of the northeastern industrial centers, for which they produced food.

For most people, the Industrial Revolution eventually provided a higher standard of living than had ever existed previously in human history. However, the revolution took its casualties. The workers in English textile factories, many of them children, labored under horrendous conditions; the estimated life expectancy of a child worker in a Manchester, England, mill was about nineteen years.

Less obvious casualties could be found in southern cotton fields. The invention of the cotton gin revitalized the institution of slavery. Like tobacco, cotton was labor-intensive. Planters quickly adapted the systems of labor pioneered in tobacco cultivation to use in the new fields of cotton. As a result, the number of slaves did not decline but grew. In 1790 there had been 697,897 slaves in the United States; by 1860 there were 3,953,760. As northern states abolished slavery and federal legislation prohibited its transplantation into the Middle West, the institution thrived in the former southern colonies and traveled west.

Westward Migration

At the time when Eli Whitney was talking to Mrs. Greene about the problems of cotton, white southerners had already begun to migrate across the Appalachian Mountains to settle lands in the West. A man who owned land was master of his own estate, regardless of size or wealth. The children of indentured servants understood well that a landless white man had no place in southern society. The term that slaves used for such people captured their marginality: "white trash."

Understanding his countrymen's land hunger, President Thomas Jefferson acquired more territory west of the Mississippi by buying the Louisiana territory from France in 1803. Even before the purchase, white American settlers had begun to move into the Louisiana territory, taking up lands north along the Mississippi River. The purchase also brought into American control New Orleans, the vital port at the mouth of the Mississippi, through which passed the produce of the new trans-Appalachian South, and the Middle West as well.

Louisiana

With the Louisiana Purchase, the French-speaking colonists of Louisiana became American citizens. These new southerners were culturally quite different from the settlers of British descent. They were Catholic, not Protestant. The Creoles of Louisiana generally disdained the Americans as barbarians, acceptable as business associates but unwelcome socially. Because the French and Spanish kept tighter rein upon their colonies than had the British, the Louisianans had little experience with local self-government. However, Louisiana shared with the other new southern states a dependence on slave labor.

The plantation system developed late in Louisiana, not really taking hold until the late 1700s, when planters turned from the cultivation of rice, indigo, and tobacco to sugar. Like tobacco or cotton, sugar was a labor-intensive crop, particularly at harvest time, but it was very profitable. For workers, Creole masters and white American newcomers purchased slaves from Africa, often drawing from different tribes than had been purchased by planters in Virginia and the Carolinas. Planters also imported slaves from the islands of the Caribbean. These slaves brought with them the religion created there, *voudon,* a synthesis of African and Catholic elements that Americans referred to as "voodoo."

On the Road

For white southerners of all classes, owning land meant independence. They bought land from the federal government or from land speculators who had purchased large tracts in years past to hold until the time for development arrived. Some received grants of public land for service in the Revolution. Small farmers often migrated in family groups, settling new lands in company with relatives by blood or marriage. Planters sent their sons west with a supply of slaves, marched under guard to the Mississippi Territory, or sold slaves to traders who transported them to eager buyers in the new territories. Frederick Law Olmstead, a New Yorker who traveled extensively in the antebellum South, recorded this impression of the migration west in the 1850s:

One of these trains was made up of three large wagons, loaded with furniture, babies, and invalids, two or three light wagons, and a gang of twenty able field hands. They travel ten or fifteen miles a day. . . . The masters are plainly dressed . . . keeping their eyes about them, noticing the soil, sometimes making a remark on the crops by the roadside, but, generally, dogged, surly and silent. The women are silent, too, frequently walking, to

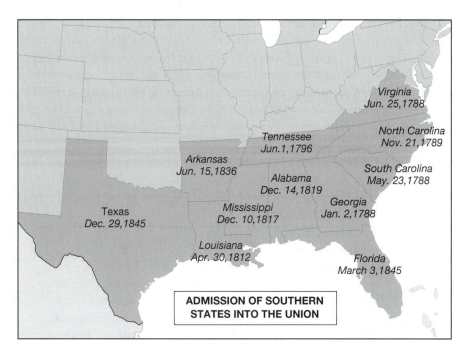

Admission of states into the Union.

relieve the teams, and weary, haggard, mud be-draggled, forlorn, and disconsolate, yet hopeful and careful. The negroes, mud-incrusted, wrapped in old blankets or gunny-bags, suffering from cold, plod on, aimless, hopeless, thoughtless, more indifferent than the oxen to all around them.
(Olmstead, *The Cotton Kingdom*)

Indian Removal

Westward migration brought southerners in conflict with the remaining Indian tribes in the region. Of these tribes, the most numerous and powerful was the Cherokee Nation, whose lands stretched along the southern Appalachians from north of present-day Chattanooga, Tennessee, into present-day northern Georgia and Alabama. By the early 1800s the Cherokee had been in contact with whites for about 200 years and had adopted so many English ways that they earned the reputation as the "most civilized tribe." Cherokees lived in houses, grew the same crops as their white neighbors, belonged to Christian churches, and intermarried frequently with whites. They chose tribal leaders through elections and owned slaves. In treaties, the federal government had guaranteed the Cherokee Nation control over their own land.

Cherokee Women

For Cherokee women, becoming "civilized" was not always a blessing. Traditionally, the nation had been matrilineal, tracing descent through the mother's line. Under white law, the child belonged to the father's family, not the mother's. Traditionally, women controlled access to land. Under white law, married women had no property, since anything they brought with them to marriage became their husband's. To protect tribal control of land, the Cherokees had to enact laws exempting their women from this provision. Traditionally, Cherokee women had a role in tribal councils. As the nation became more assimiliated, they created elected representative governments and (like whites) denied women access to the vote.

In the 1820s white settlers began to move onto Cherokee land in north Georgia. Some coveted the tribe's cleared and cultivated farmlands. The discovery of gold deposits drew others. To fight white encroachment, in 1828 the Cherokees declared themselves sovereign over their own territory. When the state of Georgia denied this claim, the Cherokee Nation sued Georgia and in 1832 won an assurance from Chief Justice John Marshall that the land was theirs to govern. Marshall said that treaties between the Indian nations and the federal government had guaranteed Indian independence.

Unfortunately for the Cherokee, the rest of the federal government did not share Marshall's respect for treaties made with Indians. President Andrew Jackson was a Tennessean whose military career began in war against the Creeks. He expressed the views of most Americans when he suggested that if the eastern tribes wanted to survive as nations, they should go along with a government plan to remove them to the "Indian Territory," present-day Oklahoma. There, Jackson said, they could maintain their traditional ways. In addition, their passage west would free up their lands for white settlers.

Under the 1830 Indian Removal Act, the federal government made an offer to the Cherokees and the other eastern tribes: sell your lands in the east and receive new lands in the Indian Territory. The president of the Cherokee Nation, John Ross, took the issue to his people, holding an election in which the overwhelming majority of Cherokees rejected the offer. However, a small contingent, apparently convinced that the offer was the best thing for their people, signed the Treaty of New Echota, giving up the tribe's lands in Georgia for $5 million and land in the Indian Territory. Although Ross denounced the treaty, Congress ratified it. In 1838 the federal government sent the army into Cherokee territory to oust the people from their homes and set them on the road to Oklahoma. Without adequate preparation or food, the Cherokees died by the thousands along the "Trail of Tears" from north Georgia through Tennessee and across the Mississippi to Indian Territory. White settlers took over their houses, their farms, and their prized peach orchards. A small remnant of the tribe escaped from the army to take refuge high in the Great Smoky Mountains. Sheltered there by white friends, they became the ancestors of the Eastern Band of Cherokee, still in residence today in Cherokee, North Carolina.

If the Cherokees, a numerous, powerful people, could not stand against the federal government's Indian removal plan, the smaller and weaker tribes had no chance at all. By the end of the 1840s Indian removal was complete: the tribes had been transported across the Mississippi. Indian removal did not evict all Indians from the South. Those who lived among the white community, and particularly those women who had married white men, were not touched. However, the Indian nations no longer impeded white appropriation of their land.

The Old South in Full Flower, 1830–1860

By 1860 a distinctive society had emerged throughout the southern states. South Carolina was not like Mississippi, nor was Virginia like Arkansas: each place had its own geographic, climatic, economic, and political variations. Neither was the Old South unified politically or socially. The social divisions among whites that emerged before the Revolution continued to play a role in the region's politics in the early nineteenth century, as planters and small farmers clashed over issues of state and local politics. The regional white elite had its own divisions. Virginians and Carolinians looked down their noses at the newly rich "cotton snobs" of Mississippi and condemned "Southern Yankees" who worked their slaves too hard in pursuit of profit. Yet despite all that, a southern "way of life" developed, based upon the region's economy and its race relations. First, the vast majority of southerners made their living by agriculture. Second, the perceived necessity of controlling a subject race brought all whites, regardless of class, together in alliance to maintain white supremacy. Finally, many white southerners held in common values that derived in part from religion and in part from an ancient code of masculine honor.

A White Man's Country

When southerners said that their region was "a white man's country," they were making reference to gender as well as to race. Rich or poor, southern white men shared a style of masculinity that derived from their dominant position in the region's racial and gender hierarchy. They were masters, responsible for the governance and guidance of the dependents in their household. As head of the household, a white man controlled the family's property, holding sole title to land and slaves and making all important economic, social, and political decisions for the family. Society expected wives, children, and slaves to show deference to the master.

Historians have labeled these family and gender roles "patriarchical" or "paternalistic." Such patterns of family life did not originate in the South. They were typical of most of Europe and the United States prior to the Industrial Revolution. However, by the 1830s economic developments in the northeast had begun to lead to changes in gender roles and family life there. Industrialization took men out of the home and away from constant daily involvement with their dependents. As a result, middle-class women in northern industrial centers gained more power in the home, taking over most daily decisions about household management and, above all, the dominant role in raising children. By the 1840s, northern newspapers and magazines had begun to praise a new style of middle-class family life in which men concentrated on winning wealth and power in the public world while deferring to women's domestic expertise and moral superiority within the home. Not all northern men and women bought into this new lifestyle, but those who did criticized southern family life as old-fashioned and barbaric. For their part, white southerners thought that gender roles in the North defied nature, producing masculine women and effeminate men.

Honor

The foundation for southern white masculinity rested on the concept of "honor." Honor is not the same thing as self-respect, dignity, or self-esteem, all modern concepts that refer to the individual's feeling about himself. Honor derives from the opinions of others. Through his behavior, a man earned honor from his neighbors; conversely, he could lose his honor by being shamed before other men. To have honor, a man had to show himself courageous, truthful, and protective of his dependents. Of these virtues, the most important was courage. A man demonstrated courage by being willing to take physical risks and, above all, by being willing to fight. Honor also required truthfulness: southern white men prided themselves that their word was their bond. Finally, honor required that a man be protective of his dependents, particularly women. If another man insulted a woman of his family, a southern white man was honor-bound to try to avenge the insult.

Southern white men of all classes manifested an understanding of honor, although they acted out the concepts in ways appropriate to their status and age. For example, no young man could with honor insult a man too old or infirm to avenge himself. In addition, gentlemen held themselves too honorable to fight poor white trash, who were beneath contempt;

a man might use a horsewhip on such people, but one did not lower one-self to their level by fighting them man to man. Other men might refuse to fight because of religious principles and still maintain community respect as long as they did not appear to be afraid. Honor helps explain why the Old South was such a violent place, leading the nation in murders per capita. Southern juries often refused to convict a man who killed another in an affair of honor.

Honor was an ancient concept, once understood throughout Europe and the United States. In the early 1800s, men throughout the country still upheld their honor through violence. Alexander Hamilton, the nation's first Secretary of Treasury, died in a duel in 1804. As a young man, Abraham Lincoln came close to fighting a duel over politics. West-erners and frontiersmen, like southerners, clung to old concepts of mas-culinity, but members of the growing northeastern middle class con-demned dueling as barbaric and primitive.

Southern white men of all classes participated in unifying ritu-als of manhood. Regardless of rank, men were expected to be able to ride, shoot, and fight. Men displayed these skills at races, shooting matches, and hunts. These competitions brought gentleman and dirt farmer together, creating a masculine community that cut across class lines. Being a man also meant living up to the duties of citizenship, which included commu-nity defense and self-government. In most states, only white men served in the militia, the volunteer citizens' army. On militia days, white men of all ranks met to drill under the leadership of elected officers and afterward drank and caroused together on the county's mustering grounds. Politics was another predominantly male arena. At political rallies, men drank whiskey, ate barbecue, and cheered candidates who could stand before a crowd and defend a political position, using words to fight as ordinary men used their fists or guns.

White women lacked similar communal occasions. Confined by work and custom to the farm, rich and poor women might encounter each other at church, but even there contact was probably minimal. Historians have contrasted the experience of women in the antebellum South with that of women in the urban North. In the 1830s, women in the North be-gan to develop a concept of womanhood based on the common experi-ences of motherhood and homemaking. Working together in charitable and reform organizations, northern urban and small-town women formed networks of female friends that reinforced a feeling of solidarity—sisterhood—based on gender. Most southern white women lacked such outlets. In the overwhelmingly masculine world of the Old South, white women's primary identity came from their relationships with men, and their primary relationships were with the men and women in their households

Life on the Plantation

Historians, like other Americans, have been fascinated by the planters, who left behind records of their lives in letters, diaries, and memoirs. In fact, by 1860 the planter class formed a tiny minority of the southern population. Three-fourths of the southern white population owned no slaves. Of those who did, about 70 percent owned fewer than ten slaves. Those who owned at least 50 slaves numbered about 10,000 families out of a white population of about 8 million. Only about 3,000 families owned more than 100 slaves.

Although relatively few white southerners lived on plantations, the plantation still deserves the attention it has received. Plantation owners were the richest men in the South, and wealth brought with it political influence and power. The plantations dominated the southern economy: they were the big businesses in a landscape of small farms. Finally, and most important, plantations were the environment in which most black southerners lived.

The Plantation as a Business

A plantation was a large farm on which staple crops like tobacco, cotton, rice, or sugar were cultivated. To be successful, the planter had to think constantly about two different, but connected, things: what did the crop itself need, in terms of growing season, cultivation, fertilizer, and water, and how could he best manage his slave labor force?

The requirements for growing southern staple crops varied. Cultivating rice and sugar necessitated that a planter invest a major amount of capital up front. Rice lands had to be irrigated and systems of water control installed. To cultivate sugarcane for market, a planter had to buy a mill and

Table 2-I
Slave Population and Distribution, 1790 and 1860
Percentages Represent Proportion of Slave to Total Population
of Nation, Region, or State

	1790	1860
United States	697,897 (17.8%)	3,953,760 (12.6%)
North	40,370 (2.1%)	64 (0.0%)
Border states		
Delaware	8,887 (15.0%)	1,798 (1.6%)
Maryland	103,036 (32.2%)	87,189 (12.7%)
Kentucky	11,830 (16.2%)	225,483 (19.5%)
Missouri	———	113,931 (9.7%)
Southern states		
Virginia	293,427 (39.2%)	490,865 (30.7%)
North Carolina	100,572 (25.5%)	331,059 (33.4%)
Tennessee	3,417 (9.5%)	275,719 (24.8%)
South Carolina	107,094 (43.0%)	402,406 (57.2%)
Georgia	29,264 (35.5%)	462,198 (43.7%)
Florida	———	61,745 (44.0%)
Arkansas	———	111,115 (25.5%)
Alabama	———	435,080 (45.1%)
Louisiana	16,544* (51.6%)	331,726 (46.9%)
Mississipp	———	436,631 (55.2%)
Texas	———	182,566 (30.2%)

*As of 1785; Louisiana was not part of the Union in 1790, so this number is not included in national total.

Source: Adapted from Peter Kolchin, *American Slavery, 1619–1877* (1993), 242.

to carefully supervise the process by which cane juice became sugar: a small mistake could destroy an entire year's profit. (It should be noted that the federal government helped assure sugar's profitability by placing high tariffs—import taxes—on sugar produced outside the United States.) Both rice and sugar required a subtropical climate and were therefore largely confined to South Carolina (rice) and Louisiana (sugar). Small farmers rarely had the capital or the labor to grow rice or sugar. They could, and did, successfully grow tobacco and cotton, but with family labor they could cultivate only limited amounts of these crops and still have time to grow food and raise livestock. In tobacco and cotton, the planter had the advantage of size: with more labor, he could plant, cultivate, and harvest more land, and make more money.

The requirements of staple crops and slave labor shaped settlement patterns in the Old South. Although all southern states had plantations, these giant farms tended to be concentrated in low-lying areas, usually near rivers. Small farms dotted the plantation districts, but most small farmers settled in the hills, where land was cheaper and more easily cultivated by family labor. In the hill districts, the population was mostly white and free; in the plantation districts, mostly black and enslaved.

The Plantation Family

Plantation masters and mistresses frequently referred to all the people in their households, slave or free, as "the family." Away from the plantation on business, the master might ask his wife for news of the family, black and white, or instruct his wife to say "howdy to the servants." Return letters from the mistress often included news and salutations from slaves. Slaves who could write sometimes sent respectful but affectionate letters to masters. Yet the same letters and diaries that describe affectionate relationships between white owners and black slaves also describe the use of physical violence and threats to discipline slaves. Slaves left in the historical record their own recollections of masters whose treatment of their human property varied from savage brutality to cruel indifference. One former slave, recorded in the twentieth century, stated that if he were ever threatened with slavery again, "I would take my gun and end it all."

A Note on Sources

Historians get most of their information about the past from the records people leave behind them when they die. Such records may include private material such as letters,

THE COTTON PRESS.

RATION DAY.

SOWING.

THE CALL TO LABOR.

HOEING

A.R.Waud

PLANTATION GRAVEYARD.

SATURDAY EVENINGS DANCE.

SCENES ON A COTTON PLANTATION.

Scenes from a cotton plantation. At left, a bugler
sounds a wake-up call for the plantation workers. at
top, men and women plant cotton; at bottom, they
are shown hoeing it. This illustration first appeared in

68

diaries, and account books, as well as more public sources like newspapers, books, and published documents. Historians call information from the time period being studied "primary sources."

In studying the antebellum South, primary sources include the letters and diaries of plantation families, public materials like *DeBow's Review,* speeches made by southern politicians, and so on. The process works like this: a plantation mistress writes in her diary; the diary, hidden during her life, is put up somewhere in the house after her death; generations later her family donates the diary to a public document archive, usually at a university or historical society. Then historians read the private thoughts of a woman long dead and write books about it.

The fact that primary sources are usually written or printed means that historians write mostly about the literate. This had a major impact on the writing of the history of slavery.

For many generations after slavery ended, historians drew information about the institution from the words of slaveowners. Not until the 1960s did historians begin to search for primary sources from slaves. Once they did, they found narratives composed by fugitive slaves and published by the antislavery movement before the Civil War, and memories of slavery recorded during the 1930s as part of a federally funded local history project run through the Works Progress Administration (WPA). With these sources, historians pieced together a picture of slavery much less benign than that remembered by whites.

Ironically, few people have yet bothered to do the same for the South's non-slaveholding small farmers. Today, historians know more about slaves and their masters than about the Old South's white majority.

(*Figure continued*) 1867 in *Harper's Weekly,* but the methods of growing cotton shown here would have been typical in the slave South since the early 1800s. Library of Congress.

Plantations were businesses, designed to make a profit. But plantations were also homes in which "the family," black and white, lived in close proximity to each other. Although slavery was based upon economics, the people enmeshed in the system did not see each other only in economic terms. Rather, masters and slaves encountered each other as human beings in a relationship rife with emotions. Some slaveowners found that they could not in good conscience abuse the people under their control, and they allowed their slaves a level of liberty just one step below freedom. Other slaveholders' innate sadism blossomed with the knowledge that they could do anything they pleased to their human property. Most slaveholders and slaves fell somewhere in the middle. Masters would have preferred docile, obedient, hardworking slaves; slaves would have preferred to be free. Since neither masters nor slaves could get exactly what they wanted, both muddled through a perpetual dance of intimidation and accommodation. Slavery in the South was a very human institution.

For plantation masters, a tension existed between their role as head of the family and their role as businessman. As businessman, a master's job was to maximize profits, but as father figure, he was supposed to take care of "his people," black or white. Some masters tended to favor one role over the other. In the 1830s, Louisiana planter Bennett Barrow recorded in his diary his obsession with getting as much work as possible out of his people. When slaves did not pick as much cotton per day as he wanted, he whipped his entire crew, hard workers and malingerers alike. At the other extreme were planters whose fondness for slaves reminded one English visitor of ladies' affection for their lapdogs. Most planters would have condemned either extreme; good managers did not allow their emotions to rule their business.

Masters discussed the best methods of labor management in agricultural magazines like the *Southern Agriculturalist,* the *American Farmer,* and *DeBow's Review.* Writers in these periodicals praised orderly, regimented plantations where masters had little contact with slaves: "All conversation with a negro is forbid, except about his work. This is important; he should be kept as far from his master as possible, but with no accompanying *harshness*; he ought to be made to feel that you are his superior, but that you respect his feelings and wants." To get the most out of the investment in slaves, writers urged masters to provide adequate food, comfortable shelter and clothing, and a system of incentives for good behavior that included rewards and opportunities for recreation. Working slaves too hard was counterproductive, as was harsh punishment. Masters advised beginners to establish a routine for work and enforce it daily. Similarly, beginners were urged to think about punishments and devise levels appropriate to the "crime," including but not limited to whipping. Experienced masters believed that the certainty of punishment was more important than the severity as a deterrent to bad behavior.

Above all else, writers urged that slave management be undertaken in a spirit of calm rationality and self-control. The frequency with which masters were urged to think first, not simply react to something a slave had done, indicates how hard it was to do so. Southern records are full of stories of masters, and mistresses, who lost their tempers and took their anger out on slaves.

Masters who owned very large plantations or who had more than one to supervise preferred to delegate the day-to-day management of slaves to overseers. The overseer had a difficult and delicate role to play. Usually the son of a small farmer, the overseer was beneath the plantation owner in status but supposedly far above the slaves. Yet he lived and worked with the slaves while reporting only intermittently, and often by letter, to the master. Masters often made impossible demands on overseers: extract maximum labor from the slaves, but keep them happy at the same time. Masters often fired overseers for brutality. Conversely, masters fired overseers if they failed to make an adequate and profitable crop. Finally, masters fired overseers if they got too friendly with the slaves; some masters complained that overseers who took slave mistresses totally disrupted life in the slave quarters and caused bitter jealousy among slave men. The tenure of an overseer at any plantation was likely to be short.

In addition to slave management, masters had to pay attention to international economics and politics. Most southern cotton was exported to Great Britain, so that country's economic up-turns and slumps directly affected southern plantations. A war in Europe could stimulate demand for southern products or cause the demand to decline. Closer to home, planters worried about the impact of federal banking policies and tariffs on international exports, both of which could create a hostile climate for southern agrarian interests.

Planters prepared their sons for their future responsibilities through careful education. Many masters hired tutors for their children or sent their sons to boarding schools. The sons of the very elite usually attended college, sometimes traveling north to Ivy League schools. (Although Robert E. Lee's son attended Harvard, the school of choice for southerners was Princeton.) To keep up with economic and political issues, planters often subscribed to major regional newspapers and periodicals and sometimes took the New York papers as well.

If successful plantation management required that masters be alert, businesslike, and disciplined, the demands of southern culture mandated that masters not appear to be working too hard. Southern whites admired a man who could command his workers, and his family, with such light-handed ease that his control was almost invisible.

The Plantation Mistress

Antebellum southern whites sometimes illustrated the differences between southern and northern values by pointing to their women. Southern white men stereotyped northern women as plain, hardworking, intellectual, and cold. They argued that slavery freed plantation mistresses from the grubby details of household management and allowed them to cultivate the feminine graces: sweetness, beauty, gentleness, and ease. In southern rhetoric, women were fair flowers, whose lives and honor white men were sworn to protect.

In reality, the plantation mistress often disguised hard work and care behind a veneer of gentility and hospitality. A plantation mistress's job was to feed, clothe, and nurse her household, including the slaves, while remaining feminine, submissive, and sweet to the man who was her husband and her master. To do the job well required both management skills and a talent for command, plus the ability to hide these skills from public view: plantation mistresses had to be bosses without appearing bossy. Learning how to balance the conflicting demands for southern womanhood began in childhood.

As small children, daughters of the plantation elite were often tomboys. Growing up in a rural environment, they learned to fight, shoot, and ride just like their brothers. As the daughters neared puberty, mothers began to teach them more feminine skills, including sewing, cooking, and household management. Even though a young white woman of the planter class might marry into wealth and never use these skills, mothers thought it was important that they know them, if for no other reason than to be able to supervise servants properly.

By the 1830s, wealthy planters had begun to send their adolescent daughters to academies, institutions that combined aspects of present-day high schools and colleges. Plantation daughters traveled from remote frontiers to convent schools like the famous Ursuline Academy of New Orleans. In other locales, parents joined together to found schools for their daughters. In most schools, young women polished their skills in reading and writing. Ladies corresponded constantly; bad grammar, faulty composition, and incorrect spelling reflected poorly on a woman's upbringing. Good penmanship counted too. Women also studied the Bible, the classics of English literature such as Milton and Shakespeare, and (at the better schools) foreign languages, history, science, arithmetic, and philosophy. The goal of such an education was to create a young woman who could accompany her husband into any station of life to which he might be called, whether that be a frontier plantation or the American embassy in Paris.

Once married, plantation mistresses commenced bearing children, some giving birth annually from marriage to menopause. While middle-class northerners had begun to value smaller families, white southerners of all classes praised the prolific mother. Individually, however, both wives and husbands complained about the cost—financial, physical, and emotional—of such large families. Childbirth itself was painful at best, dangerous at worst: many southern women's diaries contain mournful accounts of the death of a dear friend, sister, or mother from "child-bed fever," an infection caused by unsanitary conditions during delivery, or from simple exhaustion and hemorrhage after a long, difficult labor. Historian Catherine Clinton's researches into plantation women's lives indicated that many women died young; one white woman memorialized a friend as follows: "In her youth, she had been a beautiful, petite woman but she had never been strong. The strain of giving birth to fourteen children in twenty-two years and of rearing them had been too much for her delicate body."

Few plantation mistresses presided over white-columned mansions furnished with style and taste. Most plantation "big houses" were nothing more than overgrown farmhouses, surrounded by outbuildings including the kitchen (placed outside to reduce heat and the danger of fire), storeroom, smokehouse, chicken coop, barn, and slave cabins. The plantation mistress's workplace included not only the house but also the farmyard. It was her job to supply food, clothing, and medical care for the household, black and white. A good plantation mistress oversaw the home production of almost everything consumed by the white family and the slaves: vegetables and fruit, eggs and milk, pork, beef, and chicken. In addition to the daily routine of caring for poultry and dairy cows, mistresses put out huge gardens and dried, pickled, or stored vegetables for winter. Once a winter, plantation families butchered hogs, smoking hams and salting other cuts of pork for future use. Food was usually kept under lock in storehouses. Mistresses carried the keys and doled out food supplies on a weekly basis to slave women: so much meat, so much cornmeal. In the early 1800s, mistresses and slave women worked together to spin, weave, cut, and sew clothes for the entire plantation. By the 1830s cheap machine-made cloth was available, and mistresses bought bolts of it for slave clothing and bedding. In 1837 a North Carolina woman wrote to her sister, "I have about two months sewing to do. I never was so tired of sewing in my life. My fingers are worn out."

Finally, the plantation mistress acted as estate doctor. Old southern cookbooks often contain formulas for medicines alongside cake recipes. Mistresses' diaries describe all-night vigils at the bedside of a sick slave and the great grief felt upon losing a patient: "When I saw that Death had the mastery, I laid my hands over her eyes, and in tears and fervor prayed that God would cause us to meet in happiness in another world."

White Sexuality and Slavery

In southern culture, women were expected to bear life's griefs without outward complaint; ladies told their secrets only to their diaries. Even there, most did not confide their anguish about one of the most common features of slavery, sexual relationships between married masters and their slave women.

As a rule, masters treated their slave children no differently from other slaves, particularly if those children had been produced by casual matings rather than by long-term relationships. At most, fathers might employ mulatto children as family servants rather than field hands. A very few masters freed their slave children, educated them, and gave them property; this pattern was much more common in Louisiana than in the Anglo South.

Southern white men argued that using black women as sexual outlets allowed white men to preserve the chastity and purity of white women. By this logic, sex was a dirty job delegated to black women so that white women could be free of it. This construction may tell us more about white male attitudes toward sex than it does about the attitudes of women of either race. Records do indicate that many white women were not happy to delegate to slaves the chore of having sex with their husbands. Some white women refused to share their husbands with slave mistresses. They requested divorces from husbands who chose "obstinately persisting continuously to live in a negro house with his negro woman," or husbands who "had more regard for a female domestic" than for their white wives. Others went wailing home to their parents, demanding that fathers intervene to make husbands give up their black lovers. Some women bided their time until their husbands died, then took jealous vengeance on the husband's mistress and his black family. Other wives placidly turned blind eyes to their husbands' behavior. One prominent South Carolina woman wrote in her diary, "Like the patriarchs of old, our men live all in one house with their wives and their concubines; and the mulattoes one sees in every family partly resemble the white children. Any lady is ready to tell you who is the father of all the mulatto children in everybody's household but her own. These, she seems to think, drop from the clouds. . . ."

Despite social restrictions and the horror of white men, who often refused to believe that any white woman could want a black man, southern white women of all classes sometimes did risk interracial sex. Because sex between white women and black men was the ultimate violation of southern social rules, most such liaisons were carefully hidden and enter the historical record only occasionally. Sometimes a letter might include news that a plantation daughter had seduced a slave and that the daughter had suddenly disappeared from the community. Sometimes white men sued for divorce, charging that their wives had taken black lovers. As in the colonial South, poor white women sometimes lived as common-law wives with black men, or maintained secret relationships with black men. Sometimes a white woman caught in the act with a black lover tried to save herself by crying rape, maintaining her reputation at the cost of her partner's life.

The Enslaved

Most African-Americans are descended from men and women enslaved to work the fields of southern plantations. For planters, slaves were property, valued for the amount of work they could do. By the 1850s a "prime field hand," a young black man in peak physical condition, sold for about $1,500, the equivalent of the price of a small house, and planters estimated the value of slave babies at $200 each. However, slaves did not think of themselves as commodities but as human beings with a world of their own outside the view of white people. Masters controlled slaves' labor and tried to control their lives; through stealth, flattery, and defiance, slaves won back some small amount of treasured autonomy.

The slave work experience varied. Some slaves were house servants, while others worked on small farms, and others did highly skilled labor in southern towns and cities. Others were enslaved on tobacco and rice plantations, where the work routine was not the same as that on cotton plantations. In tobacco and rice cultivation, slaves worked by task, without so much direct supervision by owners or overseers. Nonetheless, the cotton plantation experience was the norm for the majority of the slave population.

Visitors to well-run southern cotton plantations described highly organized operations. Overseers or slave "drivers" (foremen) blew horns or rang bells each morning before dawn. Slaves ate breakfast, then assembled in front of their houses for the day's assignment. Both male and female slaves worked in gangs assigned collectively to a job, such as picking cotton, under the supervision of a driver or overseer. Individual slaves might be assigned other chores, such as minding livestock or working in kitchen gardens. Slaves worked until dinner at noon and rested for the hottest part of the day before resuming their labor, which lasted as long as it was light enough to see (almost 10 P.M. at midsummer in the Deep South.) After supper, usually prepared by slave women for their families in the cabins, a slave's time was his or her own until the horn blew again the following morning. For cotton plantation slaves, this was the general routine, Monday through Saturday morning; most slaves got Sunday off.

As the above description may indicate, masters tried to run their plantations in an efficient manner, imposing order and discipline on their labor force. The effect reminded some visitors of army camps. However, all forms of agriculture depend on the seasons and the weather. If slaves worked twelve-hour days six days a week during harvest season, they did lighter work during the winter months and during bad weather. Planters insisted that their slaves worked no harder than free white farmers or northern factory workers, and that they received compensation for their labor in food, shelter, and clothing equivalent in value to wages for the average northern factory worker. Modern economic historians have disputed these claims. By their calculations, slavery made southern agriculture so profitable in part because the cost of slave labor was less, over the lifetime of a slave, than paying a free worker would have been. The comparison is only academic, since southern planters would not have used free white labor even if they could have hired it at (literally) slave wages. Free labor could ruin an entire year's profits by leaving at a critical juncture, say, just before harvest. Even more than cheap labor, planters needed control.

On some plantations, slaves worked under constant white supervision from the planter or his hired overseer. On others, planters delegated authority to foremen, or drivers, who were themselves slaves. Planters encouraged drivers to keep their fellow slaves on task by rewarding them with money or privileges for work well done. Occasionally a slave driver did so well that planters dispensed with white overseers and put the slave in charge of the entire plantation. Such men succeeded in moving up the small amount allowed them by slave society, but at the cost of alienating their fellow slaves, who often complained that drivers were more brutal than white overseers.

About 25 percent of the southern slave population belonged to masters who owned fewer than 10 slaves. Many of this group of slaves worked on small farms, toiling beside members of the master's family, and had living conditions similar to those of their master (not always a good thing, on a hardscrabble southern farm). Planters reported with some amusement that slaves insisted they preferred to be owned by a rich man rather than a poor one. Historians have determined from slave narratives that slaves who worked alongside their masters were much less likely to be beaten or whipped. Nonetheless, slaves seemed to have preferred larger plantations, however brutal, because the size of the operation gave them more privacy and more room to maneuver. Most of the small number (2.4

percent) of slaves whose masters owned more than 200 people rarely had to deal with the man face to face. However, for most slaves the plantation experience fell between these two extremes. About 49 percent of the slave population belonged to men who owned between 10 and 49 slaves, while 22.5 percent belonged to owners of 50 to 199 slaves.

A small minority of slaves worked as house servants. Northern visitors, unaccustomed to the presence of any people of color at social occasions, found the intimacy exhibited between white families and their black servants highly disconcerting. When a plantation belle traveled, her black maid accompanied her, often sitting beside her in the train, sharing snacks and giggling. A white man's "body servant," or valet, knew more about him than his wife did, and he accorded his old nurse, or "mammy," almost as much respect as he gave to his mother, and sometimes more affection. White northerners did not allow such familiarity from even their white servants. They also looked askance at black maids who appeared in last year's Paris fashions, handed down from their white owners. Being a house servant did have some advantages. Since house servants appeared in public, their owners preferred that they be well dressed. They ate the leftovers from the white table, so they had better food. They were less likely to be sold: a planter would dispose of any number of field hands before selling a good cook. Finally, they were of all slaves the most likely to learn to read and write. Although after the 1830s many southern states passed laws forbidding whites to teach slaves, many masters and mistresses defied the laws, feeling that even slaves should be able to read the Bible. Other slaves learned their letters almost accidentally by attending white children at their lessons. Because of their close proximity to whites, house servants found out news and could pass it on to field hands. On the other hand, being a house servant had liabilities. Because masters often wanted house servants to act as their spies in the slave quarters and to keep them informed of any developing trouble, other slaves did not trust them. A house servant's life could be quite lonely. Worst of all, a house servant, unlike a field hand, had literally no time and place of her own. She was on call twenty-four hours a day and rarely free of white supervision.

Southern whites carried out a thriving trade in slave rentals, particularly in urban areas. Conservatives cautioned that allowing skilled slave workers to contract with white employers, bargain for their own wages, and split the proceeds with their owners gave slaves too much freedom. Nonetheless, owners often allowed skilled workers to control their own work and even to rent rooms for themselves in town and live outside their owner's supervision. Through the rental trade, slaves sometimes managed to buy their own freedom and that of family members.

Housing, Clothing, Diet

Living conditions for slaves varied widely depending on the prosperity and the attitude of the master. Some masters took pride in supplying their slaves with food, shelter, and clothing at least as good as that of poor whites. Others were more interested in maximizing profits and took care that slaves got no more than the minimum necessary to keep them healthy and fit to work.

Slaves lived in "quarters" close to the plantation owner's house. Although some slaves lived communally in barracks, masters usually preferred to place each individual family in its own cabin. Some cabins were well constructed, resembling brick duplexes, while others were one-room dirt-floored shacks that barely kept out the weather. A slave cabin generally contained a fireplace for heat and cooking and possibly some small items of furniture such as a table, chairs, and bedstead. Many slave families slept on the floor, on corn-shuck mattresses if they were lucky, on bare planks if not. As minimal as slave housing was, many white farmers' families had no better.

The same could not be said of slave clothing. Visitors to the South were often shocked at the near nakedness of slaves. As noted above, plantation mistresses and their slave assistants sewed clothing for the entire plantation, buying bolts of cheap cloth and processing it into shirts and pants for men, simple shift dresses for women. (Plantations often gave sewing supplies and cloth to slave women so that they could make their own garments.) Slaves also received wool coats or jackets, and usually a store-bought pair of shoes, "Negro brogans." On many plantations, a slave got only two new sets of garments per year. Given the wear and tear of agricultural labor on cheap cloth, many slaves went around in rags and froze in the winter. Masters used clothing as one more way of maintaining control over the slaves, issuing slaves bright-colored cloth as a reward for good behavior or as a Christmas bonus. Having access to nice clothing was one of the perks of house servants and one of the rewards given to slave drivers or to exceptionally able workers.

Plantation records indicate that slaves received from their masters rations sufficient for a filling, if monotonous and sometimes nutritionally deficient, diet. Each slave family received a set amount of meat (usually fatty pork) and cornmeal per person for the week. On some plantations, slaves also received rations of sweet and Irish potatoes, vegetables in season, and molasses. Masters encouraged slaves to grow part of their food on their own small garden plots and to raise poultry. They often allowed slaves to sell their produce in nearby towns, feeling as did one South Carolina overseer: "Surely if industrious for themselves they will be so for their masters, and no Negro with a well stocked poultry house, a small crop advancing, a canoe partly finished or a few tubs unsold, all of which he calculates soon to enjoy, will ever run away." Being able to grow their own food probably saved slave families from hunger and certainly from dietary deficiency diseases. In addition, men supplemented the somewhat meager allowance of meat by fishing, hunting, and trapping.

The Southern Diet and Modern Health Concerns

The cuisine created by slaves and poor whites in the antebellum South is known today as "soul food" or "country cooking." It featured vegetables, including white and sweet potatoes, corn, greens, tomatoes, okra, and many varieties of beans, bread made out of cornmeal, and for protein, chicken and pork. Traditional southern cooking rarely used beef, which was hard to preserve in the hot southern climate. Chickens could be slaughtered and eaten quickly, while hog meat could be salted and smoked for long-term storage.

Southern cooks started the day serving up bacon or ham and eggs. They saved the pork grease and used it to season almost everything. While wealthy families had fire-heated ovens, most poor whites and blacks did not. Instead, they fried foods in a skillet over a flame, using bacon grease, lard, or butter for oil. Such delicacies as fried corn, fried okra, and fried apples were delicious but contained much more fat than they would if baked or broiled. The famous southern hoecakes were cakes of cornmeal batter spread over a greased hoe and held in a fire to cook. The result resembles a tortilla.

Although some southern dishes have British roots, food historians have noted a strong African influence in dishes like beans and rice, hoppin' john, and greens. Others have found connections between southern cooking and that of Mexico, which uses similar ingredients.

When done correctly, traditional southern cooking is high in nutrients, but it is also very high in fat. The fat calories in the southern diet provided quick energy for people who were doing farm labor. However, the vast majority of the present-day regional population never sets foot behind a plow, and the traditional diet is probably a contributing factor to the high rates of hypertension and heart disease among African-Americans and white southerners.

Although most historians agree that the slave diet met minimal standards of nutrition, slaves knew that plantation masters ate better. Masters and mistresses complained that unless plantation stores were kept under lock and key, slaves would pilfer sugar, hams, and chickens. For their part, slaves thought it was not a crime to, as one said, "put master's chicken inside master's nigger." Through songs, slaves indicated their understanding of their situation:

> We raise de wheat,
> Dey gib us de corn;
> We bake de bread,
> Dey gib us the cruss;
> We sif the meal,
> Dey gib us the huss;
> We peal de meat,

Dey gib us de skin
And dat's de way
Dey takes us in.

Creating Families in Slavery

Families gave the slaves most of what made their lives worth living: affection, a sense of belonging, and hope for the future. In the South almost all slaves lived in families, usually composed of man, woman, and children but often extended to take in grandparents, aunts and uncles, cousins, and what anthropologists call "fictive kin," people who are not blood relatives but who become adopted members of a family. The slave family helped slaves survive, but it was also used by masters to perpetuate slavery. The most rebellious man or woman could be brought into line by threats to family members.

Slaves had very few chances to make decisions for themselves: masters chose their houses, their work, their clothing and even their food. However, slaves generally had the right to choose their own life partners. Although some planters attempted to choose matches for their slaves, most preferred not to intervene in slaves' choices of mates. Perhaps because the right to choose was so rare and precious, enslaved men and women carried out elaborate rituals of courtship that culminated in a public wedding ceremony before a minister, often himself a slave. Slaves took the same vows of faithfulness as did free men and women, although slave marriages had no standing in law. According to legend, slave ministers sometimes modified the vows. Instead of joining the couple "til death do you part," they said, "til death or the white man do you part."

Slave marriages carried heavy burdens. As Christians, enslaved men and women shared many of the same values held by their white owners, but enslavement made it hard, and sometimes impossible, to live up to those values. A master could at his whim break up a slave's home. Sometimes masters refused to let slaves choose their own mates, assigning partners for breeding purposes or giving a favored slave more than one woman. Black men could not protect their women from beatings administered by masters, nor could a slave stop a master from having sex with his wife. Many chose to marry women on neighboring plantations and visit them only on Sunday. Since slave marriages had no legal standing, divorce was never an issue. If a couple could not get along, they could separate. Despite it all, most slaves did marry, and were successful in staying together and raising children.

Slavery and the Law

Under southern law, slaves were a peculiar "species of property," as southern judges noted. As property, slaves could not make contracts and therefore could not marry, buy property of their own, or establish legal ownership over things they considered theirs, from personal items to children. Slaves could not testify in court or bring suit against nonslaves. Under southern law, the crime of rape did not apply when the victim was an enslaved woman. Technically, the damage done by rape to a slave was not to her—she did not own her body—but to her owner. However, slaves were not property in the same way that animals were. Southern courts recognized the humanity of slaves. Though a master might, with impunity, kill a slave more or less accidentally while punishing him or her, the willful murder of a slave was still murder.

Southern jurists considered legal matters concerning slaves to be in the same category as matters concerning wives and children: domestic.

Like children on most nineteenth-century American farms, slave boys and girls worked from an early age, taking on more and harder labor as they grew older. Unlike whites, however, slave children learned early on that their parents could not protect them from being hurt by white owners or by the owners' children. Commonly, white owners gave black children to their own offspring so that the white child could learn to command and the black one to obey. Whether growing up in such close proximity to whites or not, most black children came to understand while still very young that white people could not be trusted. Part of growing up enslaved was learning to wear a mask over one's thoughts and feelings.

Resistance and Survival

Masters lived in constant fear of slave rebellions. To protect themselves, they created patrols who rode through plantation districts nightly to make sure that no slaves gathered in the darkness to plot revolt or escape. Although slave rebellions in the United States had been infrequent, small in scale, and easily crushed by white authorities, planters knew that could change. They talked uneasily of revolutions in the Caribbean, where slaves had risen against their French masters in 1791 and won their freedom, creating the present-day nation of Haiti. Southern whites' anxieties increased with every rumor of poisoning, arson, and rebellion, peaking when occasional revolts actually emerged. In 1800 planters thwarted a rebellion in Henrico County, Virginia. In 1811 Louisiana slaves rebelled and marched on New Orleans, only to be stopped by U.S. army troops. In 1822, authorities in South Carolina uncovered a plot led by Denmark Vesey, a free black, to set off a full-scale revolt; whites noted uneasily that the conspirators included some of the most trusted house servants in Charleston.

In 1831 the masters' fears came true in Southampton County, Virginia, when a thirty-one-year-old slave preacher named Nat Turner led a rebellion that sent waves of anxiety throughout the South. Taught to read and write by his parents, Turner studied his Bible, prayed, and fasted until he received a vision: "white spirits and black spirits engaged in battle, and the sun was darkened—the thunder rolled in the Heavens, and blood flowed in streams—and I heard a voice saying, 'such is your luck, such you are called to see, and let it come rough or smooth, you must surely bare it.'" Feeling called by God to rescue his people, Turner began to plan his rebellion, gathering around him a small cadre of equally determined men. In the night of August 20, 1831, Turner set off the rebellion by attacking his master while he slept. Turner's men then made their way from plantation to plantation, massacring all the whites they found and gathering rebels for their army, which ultimately numbered sixty men. When Turner's band turned toward the little town of Jerusalem, they were met by armed resistance from whites and scattered in panic. Turner escaped and tried to re-form his tiny army, but aroused whites called in the state militia and effectively locked down the plantations. After hiding out for two months, Turner was captured, tried, and executed. While in jail, he dictated a statement to white lawyer Thomas R. Gray, who described the prisoner in the following terms: "He is a complete fanatic, or plays his part most admirably . . . the calm, deliberate composure with which he spoke of his late deeds and intentions . . . clothed with rags and covered with chains; yet daring to raise his manacled hands to heaven, with a spirit soaring above the attributes of man: I looked on him and my blood curdled in my veins." When Gray asked Turner if his defeat did not shake his faith, Turner answered, "Was not Christ crucified?"

Turner's rebellion curdled the blood of whites all over the South. As slavery went, Turner's lot had been an easy one. He had been allowed to learn to read and write and to travel in relative freedom to preach. His master had been kind and trusting. Yet Turner and his men had attacked sleeping white families in the middle of the night, killing without regard to age or gender. The lesson that most whites learned was that giving slaves small liberties encouraged them to reach for more. Following Turner's rebellion, southern states strengthened already existing laws restricting slaves. (It was at this point that many southern states made teaching slaves to read and write illegal.) In practice, the slave codes were enforced when whites wanted them to be and ignored otherwise, especially by masters who thought such laws a violation of their own liberty to do as they pleased with their property. More seriously, southern states forbade anyone to speak or write against slavery or to say anything that might encourage a rebellion. These laws squelched the small number of antislavery southerners, forcing them to be silent in their own land.

Every slave soon learned that rebellions resulted in vicious reprisals from whites of all classes. After the 1811 Louisiana rebellion, the heads of scores of executed blacks were placed on poles along the Mississippi levees. After Turner's rebellion whites in Southampton County tried and executed many of his followers and murdered even more: at least forty blacks paid with their lives for the fifty-five whites killed. All the attempts at rebellion failed. For most slaves, outright rebellion was a gamble that seemed sure to lose. Trying to survive in captivity, they limited their rebellion to individual acts of defiance and self-assertion.

Resisters and Runaways

In theory, masters had total control over slaves' behavior. In practice, both masters and slaves knew better. Disgruntled slaves had ways of getting back at masters who treated them badly. A slave could be whipped into the fields and forced to work, but no master or overseer could really make a man work well. Masters complained continually about slaves' "laziness," or unwillingness to do more than the minimum required of them. Moreover, masters said, slaves were careless and stupid, overworking and abusing farm animals, leaving farm implements out to rust, leaving gates open so that cattle escaped, and so on. What masters saw as stupidity was more likely a low-level form of resistance, typical of the powerless throughout world history. Northern visitors noted the inefficiency and waste of slave labor and attributed it to the very nature of slavery itself: why should a slave work hard when hard work brought no rewards? Many masters recognized the problem and built into their systems of control rewards as well as punishments.

Slaves also resisted by running away. Most runaways did not go far or stay long. Tired of work or abuse, slaves sometimes hid out in forests and swamps for a week or two. Others took unauthorized furloughs to see family members or spouses on other plantations. Planters often punished such behavior severely but to no avail: some slaves, having had all they could take, would persist in taking bits of freedom a little at a time.

Others made the more dramatic and difficult decision to try to escape from slavery permanently. Although no absolutely proven statistics exist, historians estimate that the total number of people who fled slavery in the years from the founding of the Republic to the Civil War may be as high as 100,000. Slaves in the upper South, and especially in the border slave states like Maryland and Kentucky, could escape by crossing over to the free states just to the north. Some runaways tapped into a loosely organized network called the "underground railroad." Composed in part of free blacks, the underground railroad also drew support from antislavery whites, such as the Quakers of Pennsylvania, who helped smuggle fugitives further north. Slaves in the Deep South sometimes escaped west, to Mexico, where the institution was illegal. Before Indian removal, slaves could sometimes find refuge with southeastern tribes such as the Seminole. No matter which way a runaway went, however, the trip to freedom was dangerous and hard. Few families with children could attempt it, nor could the elderly. Most runaways were young people. They left believing they would never see their families again. Those who made the choice knew they also risked brutal punishment if caught.

From a master's point of view, a runaway slave was property that had stolen itself. Federal law required that runaways be returned to masters, but in the early nineteenth century they rarely were. Fugitive slaves blended into free black communities in northern and border state cities or moved further north into Canada. In the 1830s, former slaves and runaways became leaders of the growing antislavery movement, in demand as lecturers because they could speak from personal experience. Runaways provided clear and personal refutation of the myth of the contented slave. As such, they became a political issue and the targets of a new, stringent Fugitive Slave Act in the 1850s.

The Interstate Slave Trade

The southern labor system depended on the interstate slave trade. During the antebellum period, masters sold thousands of slaves born

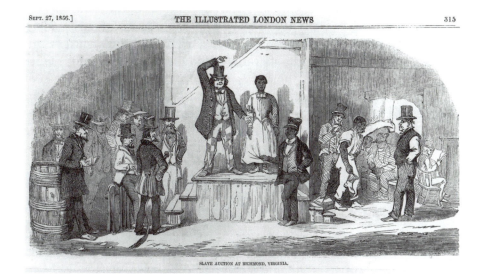

This illustration of a slave auction at Richmond first appeared in the *London News* in 1856. Less sensational than many abolitionist engravings of slave auctions, it nevertheless captures the nature of the event. Note particularly the body language and facial expression of the woman on the auction block. Library of Congress.

in the Chesapeake or the Carolinas to slave traders, who transported them to new lands in the West. At auctions, slaves were often stripped so that prospective buyers could see their physique and check for whip marks. (Scars on a slave's back lowered his market value, being seen by prospective buyers as a sign of bad attitude.) Standing on the auction block, women endured comments from auctioneers about their potential as "breeders."

Paternalistic planters found slave auctions as emotionally disturbing as any northern visitor. When possible, such planters preferred to sell slaves in family groups to people they knew. Other planters had no such scruples and went to slave auctions in the same spirit as they went to livestock auctions. The southern upper class elite looked down on slave traders, considering them boorish, crude, and untrustworthy: everyone knew that slave traders who promised to keep families together or sell them to kind masters broke their word routinely in pursuit of higher profits. Upper-class southerners insisted that slave traders never gained access to the higher levels of white society. However, very successful slave traders of gentlemanly demeanor easily bought their way into the regard of the southern elite. Isaac Franklin of Franklin and Armfield, the South's most successful slave brokers in the 1830s, retired rich to Middle Tennessee, bought a plantation, and married into the Nashville, Tennessee, elite. John Armfield, Franklin's partner, used part of the proceeds of slave trading to create Beersheba Springs, an elite resort in southeastern Tennessee patronized especially by prominent members of the Methodist church.

Free People of Color

Although white southerners tended to divide the people they knew into two groups, white and free versus black and enslaved, in fact there never was a time in southern history when all blacks were enslaved. As we have seen, even colonial Virginia had a small component of free black landowners. The percentage of free blacks in the population was highest in the upper South, where the revolutionary generation had occasionally lived up to its rhetoric by setting chattels free. As a result, 10 percent of the black population in Virginia was free as of 1860. Further north, in the border slave states of Maryland and Delaware, the proportion of free blacks was even higher: 49 percent in Maryland, and 92 percent in Delaware. By contrast, only .2 percent of the blacks in Mississippi were free.

While most slaves lived and worked in rural areas, most free blacks were urban folk. They worked at service professions like cooking and catering, did skilled labor as carpenters or bricklayers, ran restaurants and barber shops, or loaded cargoes on the docks in southern port cities. Runaway slaves sometimes sought refuge with these working-class blacks, and rented slaves found living quarters and community among them.

However, the free black community also had its upper class, most notably in the cities along the Gulf Coast. There, people of color with Caribbean connections acquired property and sometimes owned plantations and slaves. Usually descended from white masters and their slave concubines, these Creole free people of color often had no more than one African grandparent or even great-grandparent. Many of the free people of color in towns like Mobile and New Orleans in 1860 were the grandchildren of colored people who left Haiti in the 1790s, refugees from a slave insurrection and revolution that targeted colored and whites alike. Creoles of color felt little sense of racial solidarity with the enslaved black majority but were not completely accepted by the white community either. As a result, most concentrated on their own community institutions, creating a world of their own.

Plain Folk: The Non-Slaveholding Majority

Fascinated by the plantation world, historians and the public alike have paid less attention to the majority of the southern population who did not own slaves. These people lack even an accurate descriptive label. "Poor whites," a term used by plantation masters, skirts closely to the insulting "poor white trash." Others have preferred the term "yeoman farmers," implying a self-respecting, hardworking class of small landowners. One of the few historians to study antebellum southern farmers called them by a name they might have used themselves: "plain folk."

Freeholders

Whether on plantation or small farm, southern white landowners valued their independence. A man who owned his land free of any mortgage or debt had the economic basis for social independence. Planters, accustomed to commanding their slaves, often found their plain-folk neighbors extremely irritating. Freeholders could not be bossed around but had to be appealed to for support as if they were the equals of men of wealth and power.

Masters on their own lands, white farmers controlled their family's labor and directed that labor to produce sufficient goods for survival. Although poor white farmers raised cotton, tobacco, and livestock for sale to plantations and to town markets, most of their work went toward growing things for home consumption. Small farmers raised corn and vegetables and kept dairy cows and chickens. Since most southern states did not enact "fence laws," requiring farmers to confine livestock, until after the Civil War, hogs and cattle ran free and fed themselves on the region's open range. Farmers in the plantation districts marketed their surplus to nearby plantations, while hill-country farmers drove herds of livestock to markets in towns.

Southern farm life could be harsh and difficult, especially for women. Farmers' wives usually worked the fields beside their husbands and any slaves the family might own, produced large families of children, and (like planters' wives) fed, clothed, and nursed their households. Unlike planters' daughters, the women of the plain folk had few opportunities for education and were frequently completely illiterate. They rarely aspired to the image of gentility and fragility carefully cultivated by the ladies of the planter class.

Although some southern white plain folk lived in plantation districts, most were located in the hills, mountains, swamps, and other marginal lands around them. To survive, white plain folk created elaborate networks of kinship and shared labor. Farm families often joined together for large projects. A man, his sons, and slaves might help a neighbor clear new ground or pick cotton; the neighbor's family would then reciprocate. Some farmers kept records of how many days' work they owed and were owed. Turning work into social events, farm families gathered for corn huskings, barn raisings, and quiltings. The result was tightly knit communities, bound together by need and reciprocity, and usually, as years passed, by marriages and kinship ties.

Plain Folk and Slavery

When in the 1830s activists began to attack the institution of slavery, they alleged that it degraded white workers as much as it injured blacks by making work contemptible. According to abolitionists, the South had only three classes of people: the planter aristocracy, slaves, and white trash. Ironically, the higher levels of the southern elite sometimes felt the same way about the people who shared their race but not their status. The letters and diaries of many planter aristocrats offer ample evidence of their contempt for ordinary white people. Yet as historian James Oakes has demonstrated, the statistical "average slaveholder" was not a planter but a small farmer. As expensive as slaves were, their price was not out of reach for an ambitious small farmer. With the purchase of a young boy, a farmer could increase the acreage he planted in cotton or tobacco and thereby significantly increase his income. By buying a young girl, he could ease the workload carried by his wife and daughters. Purchasing a slave was a major investment to a small farmer; having made it, he defended his right to his property.

Small farmers who did not own slaves still had reason to support the institution of slavery and were reminded of those reasons by southern politicians at every election during the tense years leading up to the Civil War. First, racially based slavery raised the status of all whites: the social contract worked out in colonial Virginia held into the 1860s. Second, slavery acted as a mechanism for race control. Plain folk feared that slaves set free would enact in the South another Haitian Revolution. Further, they believed that the rich would then withdraw from the region, leaving them alone to defend their families in a race war.

The vast majority of southern whites, rich or poor, supported slavery. This has led some historians to conclude that the planters so dominated the region that other classes deferred to their leadership as feudal peasants deferred to their lords. Other historians note that planter politicians had to carefully court the votes of the supposed peasants. Moreover, prewar southern politics featured many clashes between hill-country whites and the plantation flatlanders. Plain folk knew that planters had more money and power than they did, but they also believed that in political terms, all white men had been created equal. Any politician who said derogatory things in public about the common man paid a high price at the polls.

The Ties That Bind: Southern Religion

Northern visitors to the South often noticed that the region was missing the kind of community life typical of small towns in New England and the Midwest. There volunteer groups performed civic functions ranging from fund-raising for schools to putting out fires to organizing for political reform. Volunteer activists existed in the South as well but were much less common. The geography of southern life worked against the creation of such civic institutions. Living on isolated farms and plantations, southerners might see only household members for weeks on end. People met in churches.

Religion in the South united people across class and racial lines and provided a common vocabulary shared by planter, yeoman farmer, and slave. Although whites north and south went to the same denominations, the presence of blacks in southern congregations slowly changed the southern style of worship. By the end of the antebellum period, religion had become a major component of southern culture, as it is today. Southern religious style had become biracial, and although blacks and whites stopped worshiping together after the Civil War, each had taken from the other distinctive elements composing a southern way of faith.

From Preaching Liberty to Preaching Order

The roots of the southern religious order lay in the colonial period. Most settlers in the former English colonies were Protestants, but that did not mean that they all belonged to one unified church. Anglo southerners belonged to different religious groups that often had little in common other than their opposition to Catholicism. All thirteen of the original English colonies had "established," or tax-supported, churches. In the southern colonies the Anglican (present-day Episcopalian) Church was the established church. In the rebellion against Catholicism, Anglicans had not gone as far as other Protestants. They still had priests and a hierarchical organization headed by the Archbishop of Canterbury in England.

Other Protestant groups in the South rejected anything that reminded them of Catholicism, preferring much more simple and egalitarian forms of worship and church structure. Among such groups were Presbyterians, Baptists, and an Anglican reform movement that eventually became the Methodist Church.

Although Methodists and Presbyterians differed from Baptists in some points of doctrine and church structure, they shared a belief in the importance of conversion (what similar groups today would call "getting saved" or being "born again"). Without the conversion experience, attending church had no meaning. Religious groups who emphasize conversion also emphasize the necessity of carrying the Word to the unconverted, or evangelizing; therefore, they are labeled "evangelical Christians." Evangelical preaching, with its emphasis on brotherly love, the equality of believers, and the necessity of living a strictly moral life, offended the gentry. In essence, the evangelical message was that the lowliest Christian—even a slave—could be higher in the Kingdom of God than the biggest planter in Virginia. Concerned that Christianity would subvert slavery, most planters before the Revolution forbade ministers of any religious group to attempt to convert their slaves. By preaching to any crowd that gathered regardless of its racial and class composition, evangelicals subverted the social order and broke the law. In Virginia, only ministers licensed by the state were supposed to preach. A 1771 diary gives a glimpse of gentry reactions to the Baptist message:

> Brother Waller Informed us . . . about 2 Weeks ago on the Sabbath day down in Caroline County he Introduced the Worship of God by Singing. . . . While he was Singing the Parson of the Parish would Keep Running the End of his Horsewhip in [Waller's] Mouth, Laying his Whip across the Hym Book, &c. When done Singing [Waller] proceeded to Prayer. In it he was Violently Jerked off of the Stage, Caught him by the Back part of his Neck Beat his head against the Ground . . . they Carried him through a Gate that stood some Considerable Distance, where a Gentleman Give him . . . Twenty Lashes with his Horse Whip . . . Then B[rother] Waller was Released, Went Back Singing praise to God, Mounted the Stage & preached with a Great Deal of Liberty.
>
> (Isaacs, *Transformation of Virginia*)

The experience of religious persecution made Baptists the nation's most fervent advocates of the separation of church and state. After the Revolution, they supported Thomas Jefferson's bill to establish religious freedom in Virginia, lobbying to have the Anglican Church "disestablished," that is, cut off from state financial support. Although Americans today take for granted the separation of church and state, the United States was the first country in the world to make religion voluntary, and the southern states led the way. Conservatives worried that unless the state forced people to support churches, religion would wither. Instead, it flourished in America as never before.

Evangelicals in particular took advantage of the new religious scene. Although most of the old tidewater families remained faithful to the Episcopalian Church, evangelical preachers won thousands of converts on the southern frontier, beginning with the great Cane Ridge Revival in Kentucky in 1803.

Concerned that many frontier settlers had no religion, a group of young evangelical ministers sent out invitations to a meeting to be held at Cane Ridge to pray for conversion. The ministers were stunned when an estimated 15,000 people showed up, camped out in an open field, and waited nightly to hear them preach the Word by the light of bonfires. Thousands repented their sins in tears and groans of remorse, or shouted their joy at conversion; overcome in religious ecstasy, some danced, sang, laughed, or jerked convulsively. Cane Ridge was the first southern camp meeting, and the model used for similar events throughout the south to this day. From Cane Ridge the camp meeting and revival spread throughout the South. By the 1840s the evangelical denominations had swept the field. The Methodists and Baptists were the two largest religious bodies in the United States.

Cane Ridge Offshoots

The Cane Ridge Revival sparked the creation of at least two new Protestant religious groups. Discontented with the conservatism of the east coast Presbyterian authorities, revival ministers split away to form the Cumberland Presbyterian Church, most active today in Tennessee and

Kentucky. Others, wanting to restore what they contended was the original simplicity of the Christian faith, insisted that Christians could unite by following the Bible rather than denominational creeds. Led by Alexander Campbell and Barton Stone, this Restoration movement led to the creation of the Disciples of Christ. In the early twentieth century conservatives withdrew from the increasingly liberal Disciples and designated themselves as members of the Church of Christ. Churches of Christ are now most numerous in Tennessee and Texas.

Slaves and slaveholders attended revivals together, prayed together for God's grace, sang together, and shouted together their joy in God's mercy. Although many religious historians believe that the style of revivalism owes a great deal to African religious forms, which feature shouting and dancing as a part of worship, it may be more important to note that blacks and whites recognized each other as equals in religion: equally sinners and equally redeemed. Many of the evangelical churches that sprang up after revivals were biracial, with whites and blacks sharing in the leadership of the congregation. Both races were subject to church discipline. In some cases the preacher who led church services might actually be a slave. Influenced by religion, some Baptists and Methodists began to suggest that slavery was incompatible with the spirit of Christianity, and they called for gradual emancipation.

Although the Baptists and Methodists grew as outsider churches ministering to the poor, the discipline and hard work that the churches preached helped their members rise in the world and made the churches more attractive to the regional elite. By the 1820s, evangelical churches boasted as members some of the wealthiest men in the South, particularly in the western states. Owning slaves gradually changed evangelicals' attitudes toward the institution. In 1822, Richard Furman, a leading Baptist minister in South Carolina, explained to that state's governor that South Carolina's Baptist convention believed that owning slaves was "clearly established in the Holy Scriptures, both by precept and example." Furman expressed developing evangelical thought when he said that Christians had a duty to bring religion to their slaves and to care for them with kindness and justice: "though they are slaves, they are also men; and are with ourselves accountable creatures, having immortal souls and being destined to future eternal reward." However, Furman said, freeing the slaves "would not, in present circumstance, be for their own happiness, as a body; while it would be extremely injurious to the community at large in various ways." Furman expressed a hope that eventually Africans might be ready for freedom but suggested that the time would not be soon.

Southern evangelicals' acquiescence to slavery grew in part out of their pessimistic view of human nature. Unlike northern evangelicals, who came to believe that human beings could be reformed and society perfected, southern evangelicals clung to older concepts of the sinful nature of man and of Divine Providence, the power of God to order men's lives in ways not always clear to them. As southern evangelicals saw it, God had assigned roles to masters and slaves, just as he had to husbands and wives and to fathers and children. To reject these roles was to reject the will of God. As a southern woman wrote to her brother in 1836, "*Duty* plainly calls you to the station of a 'Planter' & a planter here is the *Master of slaves.* God knows I would gladly make them *freemen*, if I could. But in his Providence we are called to their care now & of course, their government."

The correct thing was to fulfill one's assigned role in a Christian manner: to be a good master, husband, and father. As southern white Christians saw it, only the irresponsible would give over authority to those clearly not designed by God to have it, such as women, children and slaves. Southern evangelicals were appalled, but not surprised, when the antislavery movement led to a parallel movement for women's rights. They condemned both as unbiblical and un-Christian. As northern churches became increasingly opposed to slavery, southerners withdrew from national assemblies into their own regional meetings. In 1844 southern Methodists formed the Methodist Episcopal Church, South, and in 1845 Baptists in the region stopped going to meetings in the North and formed their own Southern Baptist Convention.

In the 1840s and 1850s, southern whites and blacks continued to worship together, but preachers increasingly tailored their message along racial lines. Masters were told to temper firmness with kindness; slaves were told to obey. However, blacks knew that Christianity also contained a message of liberation: Jesus had come to set free the captives, just as Moses had delivered the children of Israel from Egyptian bondage. As white churches turned to preaching obedience, blacks clandestinely formed their own congregations.

Many masters tried to shut down religious meetings in the quarters, preferring that slaves worship God only under white supervision, especially after the Turner rebellion. However, the desire to control slaves warred with the need to be a good Christian and a good master, and others found that they could not in good conscience tell their slaves not to sing and pray together. Whites recognized the spirituality of black Christians, respected their beliefs, and learned from them. As one Virginia planter wrote in 1836, "This . . . is a Christian community.' Southerners read in their Bibles, 'Do unto all men as you would have them do unto you'; and this golden rule and slavery are hard to reconcile."

Some historians contend that by the 1830s the South had become a "slave society," so dominated by the institution and so committed to its defense that the Civil War thirty years later was all but inevitable. Others point out that slavery was only one of a series of issues dividing North and South in the early nineteenth century. For decades, politicians had managed to smooth over the differences and preserve the unity of the young nation. The Civil War broke out when politics failed.

Suggestions for Further Reading and Viewing

AFRICAN-AMERICAN MOSAIC, EX-SLAVE NARRATIVES, Library of Congress, http://lcweb.loc.gov/exhibits/african/afam015.html

IRA BERLIN, *Slaves without Masters: The Free Negro in the Antebellum South* (1992)

JOHN W. BLASSINGAME, *The Slave Community: Plantation Life in the Antebellum South* (1979)

CATHERINE CLINTON, *The Plantation Mistress: Woman's World in the Old South* (1982)

CHRISTIE ANNE FARNHAM, ED., *Women of the American South: a Multicultural Reader* (1996)

JEAN FRIEDMAN, *The Enclosed Garden: Women and Community in the Evangelical South, 1830- 1900* (1985)

HENRY LOUIS GATES, ED., *The Classic Slave Narratives* (1987)

ELISABETH FOX-GENOVESE, *Within the Plantation Household : Black and White Women of the Old South* (1988)

Eugene Genovese, *Roll, Jordan, Roll: The World the Slaves Made* (1972)

KENNETH S. GREENBERG, *Honor and Slavery: Lies, Duels, Noses, Masks, Dressing as a Woman, Gifts, Strangers, Humanitarianism, Death, Slave Rebellions, the Proslavery Argument, Baseball, Hunting, and Gambling in the Old South* (1996)

PETER KOLCHIN, *American Slavery, 1619–1877* (1993)

DONALD MATHEWS, *Religion in the Old South* (1979)

STEPHANIE MCCURRY, *Masters of Small Worlds: Yeoman Households, Gender Relations, and the Political Culture of the Antebellum South Carolina Low Country* (1995)

MELTON A. MCLAURIN, *Celia, a Slave* (1991)

CHRISTOPHER MORRIS, *Becoming Southern: The Evolution of a Way of Life, Warren County and Vicksburg, Mississippi, 1770–1860* (1999)

JAMES OAKES, *The Ruling Race: A History of American Slaveholders* (1982)

FREDERICK LAW OLMSTEAD, *The Slave States,* ed. Harvey Wish (1959)

FRANK OWSLEY, *Plain Folk of the Old South* (1982)

U. B. PHILLIPS, *Life and Labor in the Old South* (1929)

ALBERT J. RABOTEAU, *Slave Religion : The Invisible Institution in the Antebellum South* (1980)

KENNETH STAMPP, *The Peculiar Institution: Slavery in the Antebellum South* (1956)

BERTRAM WYATT-BROWN, *Southern Honor: Ethics and Behavior in the Old South* (1982)

3

Defending "Our Way of Life": Southern Politics to 1860

Southern political leaders dominated the early history of the United States. Having (as they thought) created the United States, white southerners then watched aghast as economic development, population growth and social reform changed their country into a place where they no longer felt welcome. When the white southern political leadership took their states out of the federal Union in 1860–61, they did so because they felt that the Union, as represented by the northern and western states, had already left them.

Southern secession provoked the worst war that the United States has ever suffered. The generation that fought the Civil War and every generation after have puzzled over the event: what caused Americans to divide so bitterly? Was Lincoln right when he said that the war was caused by slavery? Or were the southern leaders correct when they insisted that the war was fought to defend treasured concepts of states' rights and local autonomy? On the other hand, some observers thought that the war was caused by economic and social differences between North and South; were they correct? Since the war is the historical event that molded the modern

United States, Americans will probably continue to ask, "What caused the Civil War?" and to look for answers in the political history of the nation from the 1790s to 1860.

The struggle between North and South began in the halls of the U.S. Congress, in conflicts over the most basic questions of government: what is the role of the national government, and in whose interests shall the nation be governed?

Defending an Agrarian Republic: Jefferson, Jackson, and Calhoun

In 1860 Americans, North and South, were so angry at each other that they went to war. Because we know that the Civil War came, we tend to see all of the nation's political history from 1789 to 1861 as if it led inevitably toward war. This is mistaken. Even though North and South were different from the start, intense consciousness of those differences (labeled "sectionalism" by historians) did not develop until the 1830s, almost two generations after the Revolution. Sectionalism did not become a major factor in the nation's politics until the 1840s. Up until that time, southern and northern white men worked together in politics and government, respecting each other's differences and exhibiting a willingness to compromise issues when needed for party unity.

A careful observer of American politics in 1820 would have noticed that white southerners, as a group, tended toward a certain set of political ideals, which included a preference for small, decentralized governments and a profound devotion to liberty. Therefore, southern whites were more likely to vote for politicians who expressed those ideas, such as Thomas Jefferson and Andrew Jackson. However, both Jefferson and Jackson had many followers in the North and West as well, and neither can be seen as a strictly sectionalist leader. That distinction belongs to John C. Calhoun, the South Carolina politician who, more than any other, helped provide the ideological foundations for secession. To this day, aspects of southern politics reflect the ideas of Jefferson, Jackson, and Calhoun.

Jefferson and Agrarianism

The first American political parties, the Federalists and the Republicans (no relation to the present-day party), emerged in the early 1790s in conflict over national economic policy. Federalists supported Treasury Secretary Alexander Hamilton's ambitious plans for American economic development, which he outlined in a plan proposed to Congress in 1790–91. Hamilton proposed that the federal government consolidate federal and state debts and then refinance the debt, issuing bonds to pay it. The new bonds would be handled by a specially created Bank of the United States, which would use federal deposits as a basis for issuing bank notes: paper money backed up by U.S. government guarantees. Finally, Hamilton planned to stimulate industrial development, arguing that the nation needed to be able to supply its own industrial needs rather than being dependent on shipments from overseas.

Although Hamilton's plan was designed to accelerate the development of capitalism, the Federalists did not support modern concepts of social equality, believing instead in a highly structured class society led by the well-born. The Federalists' social conservatism appealed to some members of long-established planter families, but the party's economic platform drew most support from the wealthy merchant families of the Northeast.

Opposition to Hamilton's program centered around Secretary of State Thomas Jefferson and his fellow Virginian James Madison, then serving in the House of Representatives. Although the Virginians disapproved of Hamilton's debt funding plan, they agreed not to oppose it in exchange for Hamilton's support for locating the nation's new capital in the South, on the border between Virginia and Maryland. Jefferson, Madison, and their friends in Congress also opposed the creation of the Bank of the United States on the grounds that the Constitution did not give the federal government power to create any such institution. With President Washington's support, Hamilton won that battle but failed to get through Congress legislation strongly supporting industrial development.

In their opposition to Hamilton, Jefferson and Madison first articulated the concept of "strict construction," a doctrine of limited federal power that would reverberate through southern political history even into the twenty-first century. Put simply, strict constructionists believed that the federal government had only the powers specifically given to it by the Constitution. All other powers belonged to the states or to the people.

As the 1790s passed, Jefferson and Madison became leaders of their own political faction, the Republicans. Ancestors of the present-day Democratic Party, the Republicans of the 1790s declared themselves the defenders of the people's liberties against Federalist would-be aristocrats. Jefferson's vision of America's future differed radically from that of Hamilton. An advocate of agrarian interests, he believed that farmers were "the chosen people of God." Owning land made men self-sufficient and independent, therefore invulnerable to politically motivated economic pressure. Believing as he did that only landowning farmers were really free, Jefferson looked with horror on Hamilton's proposals to transform America into an industrial, urban country. He was also appalled by Hamilton's attempts to strengthen the powers of the central government. Jefferson's understanding of republican political theory led him to think that all governments tend toward tyranny, especially those central governments far removed from everyday contact with the governed. Jefferson believed that strict construction of the Constitution could keep the federal government from becoming too strong. Vesting most power in state governments was safest, Jefferson thought, but even there, "That government is best which governs least."

In the late 1790s Federalists and Republicans struggled for political dominance. Although both parties had members throughout the nation, Jefferson's Republicans appealed most to white southerners because his ideas expressed their social reality. As they saw it, the South was the republic of landowning, independent farmers Jefferson envisioned and defended.

In political terms, Jefferson was the founding father of the South, and his ideas have echoed through southern politics ever since. Of these ideas, none was to have more significant impact on southern history than the concept of states' rights. Like strict construction, states' rights doctrine emerged out of the political conflicts of the 1790s.

In 1796 John Adams, a Federalist, was elected president. Facing stiff opposition from the Republicans, in 1798 the Federalists pushed through Congress the Sedition Act. In violation of the First Amendment, the Sedition Act allowed the federal government to imprison its critics. Jefferson and Madison wrote resolutions for the Virginia and Kentucky legislatures evoking the right of the state to protect its citizens against the federal government. These resolutions suggested that states could declare federal legislation unconstitutional. The state legislatures' protests became moot in 1800 when Jefferson was elected president, and the Sedition Act was repealed. However, the concept of states' rights would be used again and again by southern politicians for the next 150 years.

Jefferson's presidency ushered in a long period of economic and geographic expansion. Through his purchase of the Louisiana Territory from France in 1803, Jefferson acquired for the nation what he called "an empire of liberty": as he saw it, enough land to ensure that America would be an agrarian republic for hundreds of years. To protect that empire, Jefferson and his successor, James Madison, tried to steer the United States clear of entanglements in European affairs. This was not an easy thing to do. From 1795 to 1815, the British and the French fought a series of wars for European dominance. Although both sides interfered with American trade, white southerners felt that British policies injured the nation's honor. Led by young Kentucky congressman Henry Clay, a group of southern and western representatives known as the "War Hawks" eventually pushed Madison to declare war on the former mother country again, in 1812.

This small war, which was settled by a treaty returning U.S.-British relations to the "status quo ante bellum" (meaning that neither side had lost or gained anything), was to have fateful consequences for the South. First, it raised to prominence a backwoods militia general from Tennessee, Andrew Jackson, who successfully fought campaigns against British-allied Indian tribes in the southeast and defended New Orleans from British attack in 1815. The war's impact on national expansion proved to be even more significant. In the southern states, the war opened up Indian lands for white settlement. In the northern states, the war spurred economic development. Merchants whose wealth derived from overseas trade found themselves temporarily out of business. Seeking for places in which to invest their idle capital, they turned from trade to manufacturing, bringing the Industrial Revolution to America.

From 1815 on, industrialization and urbanization transformed the northeastern states. While the states of the Old Northwest (the present-day Middle Western states) remained predominantly agricultural, their farmers came to produce mostly foodstuffs for the Northeast's growing cities. Thus industrialization linked northern and western states into one market system, tied together by a system of roads, canals, and railroads. By 1860, the southern economy had expanded geographically from the East

Coast all the way to Texas, but it was still based upon agricultural production of tobacco, rice, sugar, and cotton, and still tied to slave labor. While the economic basis of the southern way of life remained the same, the North had changed.

Economic Policy and the Emergence of Sectionalism

On the national level, politics from 1815 to 1845 revolved around the proper role of the federal government in the economy. Should the government sponsor economic development or stay aloof from it? The ways in which Americans answered the question spotlighted increasing regional differences. People in the Northeast and in parts of the Middle West wanted high taxes on imported goods. These taxes, or tariffs, would protect developing industries from overseas competition. They also wanted government aid for "internal improvements" such as roads and canals.

Southern politicians often opposed both tariffs and internal improvements. Geographically blessed with many navigable rivers, southerners did not need as much federal aid for transportation. Moreover, high tariffs raised the price of manufactured goods bought by southern farmers. Many white southerners saw no reason why they should pay to subsidize economic development in New England.

Even as early as 1820, the developing economic differences between North and South had an impact on national politics. Significantly, American politicians very quickly began to roll up all the differences into one: the southern states allowed slavery, the northern states did not. Thus debates over slavery were also debates over economic policy. Slave states wanted low tariffs; non-slave states tended to support tariffs. Slave states opposed internal improvements; non-slave states supported them. This is an oversimplification, since some white southern leaders wanted tariffs (for example, on sugar, to protect Louisiana's crop from overseas competition); some also supported internal improvements. Conversely, rural residents of the Midwest often agreed with their farming cousins down south about the tariff. Nonetheless, the association between support for slavery and opposition to federal sponsorship of economic development became stronger and stronger in the public mind, fixed there by a series of debates that began in 1820 with the crisis over Missouri.

The Missouri Compromise

As the North's population grew, so did that region's power in the House of Representatives. However, all states regardless of size have two votes in the Senate. With the admission of Mississippi in 1817 and Alabama in 1819, the Senate represented eleven slave and eleven free states. Then in 1820 Missouri applied for admission to the Union as a slave state.

The resulting controversy awoke southern white politicians like "a fire bell in the night," to use Thomas Jefferson's words. Missouri had been settled mostly by white southerners, a small minority of whom owned slaves. Northern leaders in the House of Representatives demanded, as the price of admission to the Union, that slavery in the territory be gradually abolished. The Senate, where white southerners held an equal number of seats, voted to admit Missouri as a slave state.

The debates in both chambers were vicious, exposing regional differences that had long been glossed over in the interests of national unity. Northern politicians believed that the Founding Fathers had tolerated slavery only because they thought the institution was on the verge of dying out.

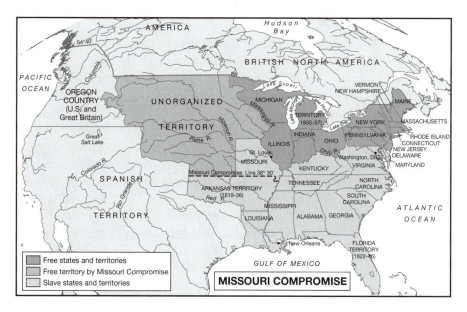

The Missouri Compromise.

If slavery were allowed to spread into the West, free labor would not be able to compete, nor would industry develop. White southerners were most shocked to hear northern leaders say that no slave state should be admitted to the Union because slavery was incompatible with republican forms of government. This suggested that northern leaders considered the state governments of the south illegitimate and not really part of the American union.

Facing disunion, Kentucky Congressman Henry Clay, then Speaker of the House, put together a compromise balancing the admission of Missouri as a slave state with Maine, a free state. The Missouri Compromise also contained a provision barring slavery from the territory of the Louisiana Purchase north of the 36° 30′ parallel.

Although the compromise kept the Union intact, the damage to relations between North and South was done. From 1820 on, southern white politicians would scrutinize all national legislation for potential danger to regional interests.

The Rise of Andrew Jackson

Henry Clay, a congressman from the slave state of Kentucky, nonetheless thought of himself as a nationalist. In the wake of the Missouri crisis he put forth an economic program, the "American System," designed to bind the nation together through internal improvements, including federal aid for highways. Clay's plan also included protective tariffs. In 1824 he ran for the presidency, joining a field of candidates, all Republicans, that included John Q. Adams of Massachusetts, John C. Calhoun of South Carolina, William Crawford of Georgia, and Andrew Jackson of Tennessee.

Jackson appalled the nation's northeastern elite. A Scotch-Irish frontiersman risen to the status of planter and militia general, Jackson owned slaves, gambled on horses, and fought duels. The "Hero of New Orleans" was imperious by nature, quick-tempered, and so tough that his soldiers nicknamed him "Old Hickory," after that almost indestructible wood. All these characteristics endeared him to southern plain folk, who thought of the general as what they would be if they were heroes.

Jackson's reputation as a war hero won him the popular vote in 1824, but since he did not receive a majority of the electoral votes, the election went to the House of Representatives, Clay's stronghold. To block

Andrew Jackson.

Jackson's victory, Henry Clay swung his House supporters behind John Quincy Adams, who had come in second in popular vote. (William Crawford, the choice of the party congressional caucus, came in third in popular vote but was incapacitated by illness.) Adams then named Clay his secretary of state. Jackson denounced this arrangement as a "corrupt bargain," and his supporters in Congress made Adams's presidency a one-term misery. In 1828 Jackson swept into the presidency at the head of a faction of the Republican Party called the "Democratic Republicans," soon to be known simply as the Democrats. (Thus was the present-day Democratic Party born.)

Jackson thought that as president he had the right and duty to act in behalf of "the people," whose elected representative he was. He became the most powerful president the United States had seen to that date, using his office to attack men and policies that he thought threatened liberty. He also paid back his political enemies, vetoing a Clay-sponsored bill to fund road construction in Kentucky on the grounds that federal funding of "internal improvements" was unconstitutional. He opposed high tariffs and began the process of Indian removal discussed in the previous chapter by urging Congress to pass the 1830 Indian Removal Act.

After his reelection in 1832, Jackson took out after the Bank of the United States. He insisted that as a private institution outside direct federal control, the Bank held too much power over the nation's economy. When the bank's charter came up for renewal, Jackson vetoed it in the name of the "humble members of society—the farmers, mechanics and laborers." Believing that the bank unfairly aided the rich, Jackson removed federal deposits from the institution, thereby destroying it, and placed federal funds in state banks instead. This action set off a period of acute instability in the nation's developing economy. Jackson's stand won him additional support among his primary constituents, white farmers in the South and West and laborers in East Coast cities, who agreed with him that the bank's policies had been too hard on debtors. However, his behavior as president was so high-handed that his opponents began calling him "King Andrew the First." They took for themselves the traditional name of the antimonarchical English party, the Whigs.

From Jackson's election in 1828 through the 1840s, the Democrats and the Whigs sparred over national policy. Like the earlier Federalists and Republicans, these parties were not sectionally based. There were Whigs and Democrats on both sides of the Mason-Dixon line. Still, the Democratic Party advocated policies that appealed more to southern than to northern voters. Although individual Democrats often modified their principles to serve the interests of their constituents, in general the Democrats stood for "laissez-faire" government that did not intervene in the economy for or against the interests of any faction, a stance appealing to antitariff white southerners. The Democrats' support for limited government resonated with southerners loyal to Jeffersonian concepts; moreover, a laissez-faire government would be less likely to meddle with the institution of slavery.

The Jacksonian Democrats' most lasting contribution to the South, and to the nation, may have been electoral reform. Insisting that all white men were politically equal, the Jacksonians demanded that property qualifications for voters be dropped. In the South, the trans-Appalachian southern states quickly adopted universal white manhood suffrage. By the end of the 1850s the more conservative eastern seaboard states had done so as well. The result was a transformation in the style of politics. Gone were the calm tones and stately sentences of the revolutionary generation. The new politicians had to appeal to voters who were barely literate and often ignorant of the subtle points of economic or foreign policy.

To win votes, leaders had to entertain as they educated. Taught by Jefferson and Jackson to fear concentrated, centralizing power, southern politicians passed on to their constituents a powerful message: liberty is always threatened and must be defended. White southern politicians of both parties found that the surest way to win elections was to promise to defend the people's freedom against all threats foreign and domestic; they adopted an exaggerated rhetoric that demonized their opponents and on occasion risked destabilizing the political system.

Calhoun and Nullification

In the 1830s South Carolina political leaders came close to causing a civil war when they refused to comply with a federally enacted tariff designed to protect developing industries in the northeast. Many of South Carolina's leaders condemned high protective tariffs as unconstitutional. They charged the federal government with attempting to boost the economy of one region of the country at the expense of another. If Congress could pass tax policies against the interests of a state, they asked, what prevented Congress from enacting laws directly targeting state or regional institutions like slavery? In 1828, when Congress passed a high protective tariff (the "Tariff of Abominations," according to Carolinians) they called upon John C. Calhoun, then serving as Adams's vice president, to give words to their protest. At their requestion, Calhoun wrote the South Carolina Exposition. (Calhoun had withdrawn from the 1824 presidential race to run for vice president; in 1828 he was reelected to that office, this time as Jackson's vice president.)

In the Exposition, Calhoun tried to grapple with two difficult

John C. Calhoun of South Carolina as a young man.
Library of Congress.

questions: First, how could a state protect itself from the tyranny of the federal government? Second, how could states' rights, or sovereignty, be upheld without destabilizing the entire federal union? His answer was ingenious. Calhoun said that the states had created the federal government through the Constitution. Therefore, each state had the right to declare laws unconstitutional. Once a state had nullified a law, Calhoun suggested, the law should be submitted to a similar process in all the states. If a majority of the states voted the law constitutional, the original nullifying state had the choice of submitting to the law or of seceding from the Union.

Mrs. Jackson and Mrs. Eaton

In 1828, Andrew Jackson's political enemies added to their list of epitaphs—gambler, slaveholder, man of blood—one more insult. They labeled Jackson an adulterer.

As a young man just moved to Nashville, Tennessee, Jackson fell in love with the daughter of a prominent family. Unhappily married, Rachel Donelson had moved back into her parents' house when Jackson met her. Hearing that Rachel's husband had obtained a divorce, Jackson and Rachel Donelson eloped from Nashville to Natchez, Mississippi, then part of the Spanish territory of Louisiana. They were married there and lived together for several years before finding out that Rachel's husband had not, in fact, obtained a divorce at the time they were wed. They remarried immediately, but the damage to Rachel's reputation was already done. Technically, she had been a bigamist, married to two men at the same time.

For all of his life, Jackson remained fiercely loyal to Rachel. He believed that the mud slung at their marriage during the 1828 campaign shortened Rachel's life. She died before his inauguration in 1829.

This personal history helps explain why Jackson fell out with Calhoun. When one of Jackson's cabinet, John Eaton, married a barmaid with a reputation for sexual adventuring, Mrs. Calhoun led the wives of the cabinet in a social boycott of the Eatons. Jackson defended Peggy Eaton, insisting that she had been unjustly accused of cheating on her first husband. Caught between his president and his wife, Calhoun chose domestic tranquillity, and consequently slid out of Jackson's confidence.

Calhoun hoped to win Jackson's support for the doctrine of nullification. But relations between the two men chilled after a falling out over a social matter. Moreover, for all his defense of liberty, Jackson was a nationalist, a soldier who had shed blood in defense of the United States. In 1830, the political differences between Calhoun and Jackson became public at a dinner in honor of Thomas Jefferson. Jackson rose to make a toast, and staring directly at his vice president, said challengingly: "Our Federal Union, it must be preserved." Calhoun answered, offering a toast to "The Union—next to our liberty most dear. May we always remember that it can only be preserved by distributing equally the benefits and burdens of the Union." In 1832, Calhoun resigned from the vice presidency and went home to lead the South Carolina opposition.

When Congress passed another high tariff bill in 1832, South Carolina nullified it. State leaders mobilized the militia and threatened to secede. They hoped to spark a regionwide resistance. Instead, South Carolina found itself out on a limb, alone. Although most white southerners agreed that the tariff was unfair to regional interests, no other state legislature in the region joined South Carolina in nullification.

President Jackson disapproved of high tariffs but disliked threats of disloyalty and secession even more. He got Congress to pass a "force bill" affirming that the president could use the military to enforce federal laws in the states, and growled that if the Carolinians persisted, he would personally lead an army to the state and hang Calhoun.

Facing the possibility of civil war, Henry Clay and Calhoun pushed through Congress a compromise tariff that gradually lowered import taxes. This gesture gave the South Carolina leadership a way to back down without too much humiliation. In 1833 South Carolina rescinded its tariff nullification but nullified the force bill, a last bit of defiance that Jackson ignored.

Jefferson, Jackson, and Calhoun left a profound impact on southern political thought. Many regional political leaders took suspicion of concentrated power and a commitment to states' rights into congressional debates in the 1830s. However, the party structure required compromise, since Whigs and Democrats alike had to draw upon voters from both sides of the Mason-Dixon line in order to win elections.

Compromise on regional issues became increasingly difficult when a sizable minority of people in the North began to campaign against the evils of slavery.

From Necessary Evil to Positive Good: the Proslavery Defense

The generation that fought the American Revolution felt deeply uneasy about the institution of slavery. Southern Founding Fathers like Jefferson and Washington publicly expressed hopes that slavery would gradually fade away. Meanwhile, southern leaders said, slavery was not their fault. It was an institution inherited from previous generations, and since it could not safely be done away with abruptly, it had to be tolerated as a necessary evil. In the North, where slavery was not essential to the economy, the evil was not so necessary. In the generation after the Revolution, northern state governments abolished slavery within their borders. However, northern politicians agreed with their southern colleagues that slavery was a state rather than a federal matter. During the 1830s and 1840s a series of events occurred that cast doubt on that proposition.

The Emergence of Abolitionism

In the early 1800s, revivals made thousands of converts to evangelical Christianity. These new Christians found that their faith required them to reconsider all social institutions. In the South, the revivals led to a campaign to evangelize the slaves and demands from ministers that slaveowners live up to the biblical criteria for good masters. But in the North, many new Christians decided that slavery was sinful because it took from slaves the God-given free will to make moral choices, including the one to strive for salvation. As midwestern antislavery lecturer Theodore Dwight Weld explained, "he who robs his fellow man of this tramples upon right, subverts justice, outrages humanity, unsettles the foundations of human safety, and sacrilegiously assumes the prerogatives of God." Believing slavery to be a sin so great that tolerating it might cause the wrath of God to fall upon the entire nation, Weld and others called for the immediate abolition of the South's peculiar institution, and the acceptance of freed blacks as part of the American community.

Free Blacks in the Free States

In 1860, about 250,000 free blacks lived in the northern states. Proslavery southerners used their condition as an example of northern hypocrisy.

At the start of the century, free blacks had been found in skilled trades throughout the North. But as white immigrants poured into the nation, they forced blacks out of those jobs and down the employment ladder to its lowest rungs. Irish immigrants fought battles with black men for control of jobs on the docks in northern coastal cities. Working-class whites repeatedly attacked blacks in a series of urban riots. By 1860, most black men worked at day labor and menial service jobs that white men would not take.

Northern law segregated blacks, forbidding them entry to most places of amusement, restaurants, and public facilities. Most northern public schools were also segregated by law. In urban areas, blacks lived crowded into slums—the only areas where they were allowed to rent.

Blacks were denied the right to vote in most of the northern states. (Only New England had liberal policies in this regard.) The new states of the West had even more restrictive policies. The constitutions of Indiana, Illinois, Ohio, Michigan and Iowa, simply forbade free blacks to settle there at all.

Abolitionists knew that most people in the North, let alone the South, did not consider slavery morally wrong. They therefore set out to evangelize the North, preaching antislavery as revival preachers had salvation. In many northern locales, angry white mobs attacked abolitionist speakers. The leading abolitionist newspaper editor, William Lloyd Garrison of Boston, was at one point paraded around that town with a rope around his neck, an unsubtle hint to shut up about slavery. Garrison came close to sharing the fate of Elijah P. Lovejoy, an abolitionist editor killed by an Illinois mob in 1837. Northern businessmen thought antislavery agitation would widen sectional differences, damage trade, and ultimately destroy the Union; working-class northern whites thought that freed slaves would compete with them for jobs. Despite years of trying, abolitionists were unable to convince a majority of northerners that slavery should be ended. They did, however, provoke a strong reaction from southern political leaders.

In the mid-1830s the American Anti-Slavery Society, then the leading abolitionist organization, took advantage of new printing technologies to inundate the nation with antislavery propaganda. Historians estimate that in 1835 the society distributed 1.1 million pieces of abolitionist literature, much of it sent out to the public through the U.S. mail. Southern white political leaders protested bitterly that the abolitionists would cause a slave rebellion like that led by Nat Turner only a few years previously. Federal postmasters refused to ship abolitionist literature south, with President Jackson's tacit approval.

In 1836 antislavery people targeted slavery in the District of Columbia, which was the only part of the nation under the direct control of the federal government. When petitions calling for the abolition of slavery in the district began to pour into Congress, Democrats joined with southern Whigs to have the petitions permanently "tabled." By these actions, southern political leaders in Congress and in the Jackson administration protected slavery, but at a high cost. Northerners who were indifferent to slavery expressed outrage over this de facto violation of First Amendment rights to free speech, press, and petition.

To win support for abolition, antislavery writers depicted the South as a snake pit of immorality and violence. Since many northern Christians found it hard to believe that their fellow Methodists and Baptists could be so evil, abolitionists made extra efforts to describe the hypocrisy and brutality of Christian slaveholders. One white abolitionist leader said that there was more morality in the average house of prostitution than in the Methodist Church, which tolerated slavery. Abolitionist writers also charged that slavery corrupted women of both races: black women because they were prey to the bestial lusts of white southern men, and white women because they were forced to tolerate their husbands' infidelity. Slavery destroyed families, abolitionists said, by separating mother from child, husband from wife. Finally, the abolitionists made a point more convincing to the average northern citizen than any evocation of morality: slavery retarded economic development. Abolitionist writers described the South as uncivilized and backward, lacking the railroads, factories, and cities that marked progress in the North. They warned that slavery destroyed upward mobility for whites, since no free worker could compete against slave labor.

In the late 1830s a faction of the abolitionist movement decided that ending slavery could not be accomplished through preaching and petitions. Forming the Liberty Party, they carried the abolition message into politics. Members of the Liberty Party agreed that slavery was immoral, but they put increasing emphasis on the ways in which slavery harmed whites by closing off opportunity for upward mobility. By the early 1840s the Liberty Party was strong enough in some northern states to influence presidential elections.

The Proslavery Defense

Abolitionist preaching did not bring the white South to repentance. Their institutions, families, religion, and personal characters under attack, southern white leaders retaliated by defending the peculiar institution in stronger terms than ever before. Slavery was not evil, they argued, but a positive good, and the foundation of liberty for white men.

In 1837 Calhoun made a speech to the Senate that contained the major themes proslavery writers would elaborate upon for the next quarter century. The South Carolina senator explained that slavery could not be destroyed without a race war that would end in the extermination of the losers. Nor was there any reason to destroy an institution that had been beneficial to both races; Calhoun said that southern slavery raised Africans from a "low, degraded and savage condition" and introduced them to civilization. Slavery had been good for southern whites as well, the senator said, and offered in evidence American history: "I ask whether we have not contributed our fair share of talents and political wisdom in forming and sustaining this political fabric; and whether we have not constantly inclined most strongly to the side of liberty, and been the first to see and first to resist the encroachments of power." To the argument that slavery retarded economic development, Calhoun retorted that tariffs, not slavery, kept the South down.

Finally, Calhoun pointed out that all civilized societies divide wealth unequally, with the laboring classes receiving less than the people at the top. He suggested that southern slavery compared favorably with the European free labor system, which left old, worn-out workers to the poorhouse. Slavery in contrast was "direct, simple and patriarchical," Calhoun said, sheltering the slave in sickness and old age. Moreover, slavery "forms the most solid and durable foundation on which to rear free and stable political institutions."

Other proslavery writers filled in Calhoun's outline, producing by 1860 a body of literature defending the South, slavery, patriarchy, white supremacy—and liberty for white men only. In the process, proslavery southerners wrote some of the most trenchant criticism of emerging capitalism ever published.

White Christian ministers cited texts from the Bible to prove that God approved of slavery. Did not the apostle Paul tell slaves, wives, and children to be subject to their masters? (Proslavery writers were not shocked when abolitionist women began agitating for women's rights; they considered abolitionism a slippery slope that would lead inevitably to the destruction of all natural and godly authority.) In the 1840s southern Baptists and Methodists withdrew from the national denominations and formed their own regional associations, the Southern Baptist Convention and the Methodist Episcopal Church, South. Thereafter, Sunday services often featured proslavery sermons. By 1860, on the very eve of secession, Presbyterian minister Benjamin M. Palmer, of New Orleans, assured his congregation that abolitionism was "atheistic" and that the South's cause was more than just:

> To the South the highest position is assigned, of defending, before all nations, the cause of all religion and of all truth. In this trust, we are resisting the power which wars against constitutions, and laws and compacts, against Sabbaths and sanctuaries, against the family, the State and the church; which blasphemously invades the prerogatives of God, and rebukes the Most High for the errors of his administration, which, if it cannot snatch the reins of empire from his grasp, will lay the universe in ruins at his feet.

The Scriptures

Proslavery ministers found ample support for their views in the Bible. From Genesis, they derived support for racially based slavery, arguing that Africans were the children of Ham, son of Noah, who for his sins was cursed to serve his brothers. The Israelites held slaves, as did all ancient societies, and ministers sometimes quoted Leviticus in sermons concerning the proper relationships between slave and master. However, the bulk of southern proslavery sermons came from the New Testament, from the Epistles of the Apostle Paul. Among the texts most often used were Ephesians 5:22–6:9 and Colossians 3:18–5:1. These passages treat slavery as a domestic matter. Paul tells wives, children, and slaves to be submissive and obedient, while instructing husbands, fathers, and masters to treat their dependents with proper care and affection. Although no southern denomination today uses these texts in support of slavery, they are widely quoted by conservative Christians in support of male dominance within the family.

Many southern political leaders, including Calhoun, thought that abolition was a British plot to sabotage American unity. Although the British had freed the slaves in their colonies and had used the British navy to suppress the trans-Atlantic slave trade, proslavery writers charged the British with hypocrisy. They pointed out that supposedly free workers in British coal mines and textile factories were treated worse than some southern slaves. Southern writers argued that capitalism produced "wage slaves." In the 1850s Virginian George Fitzhugh's two books, *Sociology for the South* and *Cannibals All,* summed up this vein of proslavery argument. Fitzhugh said that free society reduced men to economic cannibals, fighting constantly for survival:

And now Equality where are thy monuments? And Echo answers where! Echo deep, deep from the bowels of the earth, where women and children drag out their lives in darkness, harnessed like horses to heavy cars loaded with ore. Or, perhaps, it is an echo from some grand, gloomy and monotonous factory, where pallid children work fourteen hours a day, and go home at night to sleep in damp cellars. . . .

In contrast, Fitzhugh said, southern planters cared for their slaves as for their children, and southern society, founded on slavery, was rock-steady: "We have no mobs, no trades unions, no strikes for higher wages, no armed resistence to the law . . . we are totally exempt from the torrent of pauperism, crime . . . and infidelity which Europe is pouring from her jails and alms houses on the already crowded North."

Proslavery writers denied that the institution hurt poor whites. Instead, they said, slavery made it easier for poor whites to rise in the world and guaranteed that they met the richest white men in the South as political equals. Writing in the late 1850s, J. D. B. DeBow, editor of the most widely circulated southern magazine, *DeBow's Review,* summarized this argument. According to DeBow, skilled white workers in the South received higher wages than their counterparts in the North; they did not have to work in crowded cities, "with remorseless and untiring machinery," nor did they have to compete with "foreign pauper labor." In the South, DeBow said, the poor white man "preserves the status of a white man, and is not regarded as an inferior or a dependent." Southern whites did not work as servants, and all whites met as equals. Indeed, DeBow said, the poor white knew that he could purchase a slave and through slavery, move up in the world: "The large slaveholders and proprietors of the South begin life in great part as non-slaveholders." So did the South's politicians, according to DeBow, and he cited the examples of Andrew Jackson and Henry Clay to prove his point.

Most southern writers were willing to rest their defense of slavery on the Bible, political economy, and social tradition, but some southern scientists tried to find a scientific basis for racially based slavery. In the 1850s Dr. Josiah Nott, a physician from Mobile, published *Types of Mankind,* in which he argued that the races were in fact separate species. Although this argument troubled religious southerners, who stood by the biblical account of Creation, Nott and other southern students of "natural history" (biology) used pseudoscience to argue the inferiority of blacks and their suitability for servitude. Scientific racism justified slavery by literally dehumanizing blacks. Nott's theories marked a new stage in the evolution of racism, and would be influential in the South, and indeed throughout the nation, well into the twentieth century.

Uniting to defend slavery, white people who had previously thought of themselves as Virginians or Texans began to think of themselves as Southerners. As they saw it, abolition threatened the most basic liberties of white men, including the right to own property and to be secure in one's own home. Abolitionist leaders were professed Christians, and many avowed pacifism, but they openly supported slave revolts. In an 1844 congressional debate about the gag rule on abolitionist petitions, a southern congressman asked John Quincy Adams, who had returned to the House after his tenure as president, about a statement he had made in a speech to free blacks at Pittsburgh. Was it true, the Alabama congressman asked, that Adams had said abolition might come peacefully or through blood, but either way, "Let it come"? Adams responded, "Though it cost the blood of millions of white men, let it come. Let justice be done, though the heavens fall." The knowledge that a sizable minority of northern men and women cheerfully looked forward to the slaughter of southern whites made southern political leaders talk publicly about leaving the Union. However, secession talk was muted, for the most part, until the 1850s, and even then most southern political leaders dismissed the southern radicals advocating regional independence as "fire-eaters," too extreme to be taken completely seriously.

The Road to War

In 1845 the United States government provoked a war with Mexico so that the United States could take Mexican lands in the Southwest and in California. Northerners and southerners alike supported the war for the spoils it would bring but argued bitterly over the division of the lands taken from Mexico. Northern political leaders wanted those new lands to be "free," that is, open only to free labor. Southern leaders considered northern attempts to exclude slavery from the West both insulting and unconstitutional. Congressional quarrels over the Mexican Cession both illuminated and deepened sectional divisions, leading finally to the Civil War.

The Constitution and the Territories

The abolitionist attempt to move slavery onto the national agenda in the 1830s failed in part because of the structure of the American governing system. Most Americans saw slavery as a state, not a federal, issue. They believed that the federal government could act for or against slavery only in areas under its direct control. In addition to the District of Columbia, the federal government administered frontier territories prior to statehood. By long precedent, Congress controlled the status of slavery in the territories, prohibiting it in some and permitting it in others. The Northwest Ordinance of 1787 had prohibited slavery in the territories that became Ohio, Indiana, Illinois, Wisconsin, and Michigan. In 1820, Congress had allowed slavery in Missouri but had prohibited it in most of the rest of the territory acquired through the Louisiana Purchase. When the abolitionists began their antislavery campaign, no further territorial acquisitions looked likely. The Southwest and California belonged to Mexico, and the British claimed the Pacific Northwest. When the United States expanded geographically, slavery became a subject of national debate.

In the 1840s leaders of the Democratic Party won popular support for American expansion to the West. One party leader stated that the United States had a "manifest destiny" to create an empire for democracy that stretched from sea to sea. Manifest Destiny became the campaign slogan for American expansionists such as James K. Polk, a Tennessean and a protégé of Andrew Jackson who was elected president in 1844.

Manifest Destiny appealed to North and South alike, but northern voters became suspicious when Polk negotiated a treaty with Britain giving up half of American claims in the Northwest for a clear title to the Oregon territory. Was it possible, they wondered, that he was most interested in acquiring territory from Mexico, territory that would be south of the Missouri Compromise line and therefore open to slavery? When Polk provoked a war with Mexico, northern suspicions were confirmed.

The Mexican War

Polk caused a war with Mexico so that the United States could take California, long coveted by American expansionists for its great natural harbors on the Pacific. To get California, Polk used the situation in

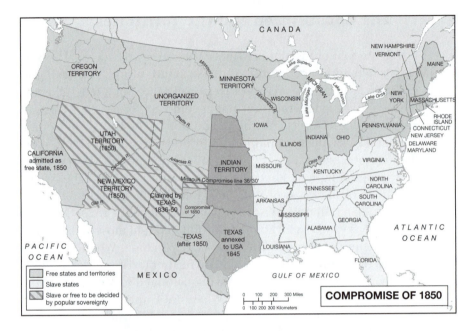

The Compromise of 1850.

Texas. In the early 1800s southern slaveholders had migrated into eastern Texas, then part of the Spanish-held colony, Mexico. When Mexico won its independence, the Anglos living there became Mexican citizens, although they remained culturally, religiously, and politically distinct. When the Mexican government declared slavery illegal in 1829, the Anglo settlers in Texas refused to comply. Tensions between the government in Mexico City and its recalcitrant province grew until, in 1836, the Texans rebelled. Led by Sam Houston, another Jackson protégé from Tennessee, they fought a war with Mexico and won their independence. They then applied for annexation to the United States. President Jackson was personally sympathetic, but he knew that asking Congress to admit Texas to the Union would reopen the slavery issue and possibly cause a war with Mexico. Rebuffed by Jackson, the Texans declared themselves an independent republic.

During his campaign for the presidency in 1844, Polk promised to annex Texas. Before Polk was inaugurated in 1845, Congress acted on this promise, annexing Texas by joint resolution. However, the new state's borders were not clear. The Texans claimed as their southwestern border the Rio Grande. The Mexican government insisted that the border of Texas had always been 130 miles north and east, at the Nueces River.

Polk used this border dispute to start a war with Mexico. In 1846 he sent General Zachary Taylor into the disputed territory. When Mexican troops fired on an American patrol, Polk announced that Mexico had "shed American blood upon the American soil." In May 1846, he pushed through Congress a declaration of war against Mexico.

In the Mexican War, young Americans who would later lead opposing armies fought for national expansion. Robert E. Lee, William T. Sherman, George Meade, and Ulysses S. Grant, all in the regular Army, served in Mexico, as did Jefferson Davis, as an officer of the Mississippi militia.

Although the Mexican forces defended their country valiantly, they were poorly led, and the United States brought the fighting to an end in 1847 with the capture of Mexico City. In 1848 the war officially ended with the treaty of Guadalupe Hidalgo. By this treaty the United States se-cured the disputed territory in Texas, the Mexican lands in the Southwest (currently Arizona, New Mexico, Utah, and Nevada) and the sought-after prize, California.

Most of these new lands fell below the 36° 30′ parallel designated in the Missouri Compromise as the dividing line between slave and free states. Southern political leaders had wholeheartedly supported the Mexi-can War. No wonder, said many northern leaders: it was fought to acquire territory for the expansion of slavery.

For their part, southern political leaders agreed that expansion was essential for both political and economic reasons. To protect slavery, southern leaders needed votes in Congress to balance those from the North. Adding new slave states would help keep the sectional balance. Slaveholders also needed new territories as outlets for their surplus slave property. If the supply of slaves exceeded the demand, the value of slaves would drop. Proslavery propagandists warned poor whites that when slaves cost more to maintain than they earned for their masters, the masters would abandon them and remove themselves and their wealth to safer climes. Poor whites would be left alone to fight the race war that southern leaders assumed would follow emancipation.

In 1846 northern Democrats walked a difficult political tight-rope. Their constituents were perfectly willing to support a war to grab land from Mexico but wanted to keep that land for people like themselves: non-slaveholders. Pennsylvania Congressman David Wilmot thought he saw a way to have the land without the slaves. He offered to Congress a "proviso," or amendment, to a military appropriations bill. The Wilmot Proviso declared that slavery would not be permitted in the territories taken from Mexico. Unwittingly, David Wilmot set off the chain of events leading to the Civil War.

First, the proviso destroyed party unity. Southern Whigs joined with southern Democrats in opposition to the proviso, while northern Whigs and Democrats voted for it. The North's greater population gave it the majority in the House of Representatives, but in the Senate southern politicians held the balance of power. For four years, from 1846 to 1850, anti-slavery congressmen reintroduced the proviso, the House passed it, and the Senate voted it down. By 1850 both houses of Congress had divided bitterly along sectional lines.

Northerners who wanted to keep slavery out of the Mexican Cession were not necessarily abolitionists. In fact, many did not care at all about the evils of slavery. Instead, "free soil" men wanted to make sure that the West would be a "white man's country," where white men could work and move up in the world without competition from slaves or free blacks. On the other hand, abolitionists also opposed the expansion of slavery, believing that if the institution were confined to the South, it would eventually die. Free-soil men and abolitionists made common cause in 1848, forming the Free-Soil party to resist the spread of slavery into the territories.

Zachary Taylor, a Whig, was elected president in 1848. A hero of the Mexican War, the old general was a Louisianan and a slaveholder, all characteristics that appealed to the southern wing of the Whig Party. But Taylor's actions as president quickly alienated southerners. Hoping to end the territorial controversy, Taylor encouraged California and New Mexico to draw up state constitutions and apply for admittance to the union. Both would come into the Union as free states. Southern leaders saw this as a betrayal and a violation of the Missouri Compromise. Infuriated, southern fire-eaters invited delegates from the slaveholding states to gather at a convention in Nashville in June 1850, to consider secession.

In January 1850, Henry Clay, the architect of the Missouri Compromise, came through with one last plan to save the Union. Clay's Compromise of 1850 contained provisions concerning the Texas debt, the borders of New Mexico, and other items of critical interest to people in those locales. More important, it called for the admission of California as a free state, an end to slave trading in the District of Columbia, and a stronger fugitive slave law that would allow slaveholders to retrieve runaways from northern states. For the rest of the Mexican Cession, the New Mexico Territory, Clay proposed a solution previously suggested by northern Democrats: popular sovereignty, under which the settlers who moved into the territories would decide for themselves whether the lands would be slave or free.

The compromise occasioned intense debate. Calhoun rose from his deathbed and, wrapped in a blanket, sat in the Senate chamber to hear a colleague from Virginia read to the body his last speech: "I have, Senators, believed from the first that this agitation of the subject of slavery would . . . end in disunion." According to Calhoun, disunion grew from northern aggression. He cited antislavery agitation, the North's refusal to share newly acquired territories with the South, and the North's system of tariffs as factors in destroying the Union. Calhoun said that as a result, "the North has acquired a decided ascendency over all the powers of the system. . . . What was once a constitutional federal republic is now converted, in reality, into one as absolute as that of . . . Russia, and as despotic in its tendency as any absolute government." To save the Union, Calhoun said, the Senate had to enact measures to reassure the Southern states. He suggested that a constitutional amendment be passed guaranteeing the balance of power between free and slave states. Otherwise, he warned, the South would secede.

In 1850 other southern leaders were not yet willing to follow Calhoun down that road. They looked for help to the party system. Despite Clay's leadership, the Whig Party was deeply divided over slavery. Northern Whigs opposed the compromise. To put through the compromise, Clay had to turn to a young Democratic senator from Illinois, Stephen Douglas. An ambitious man, Douglas knew that he would need southern support to fulfill his dream of becoming president. He rallied northern and midwestern Democrats and pushed Clay's compromise through Congress, with some modifications, section by section. Although no one faction supported all of the compromise, its passage defused the crisis. In the summer of 1850, the southern convention in Nashville fizzled out without seriously proposing secession, and political observers praised Clay and Douglas for saving the Union.

Although Douglas and Clay managed to avert a civil war, the conflict focused public attention on sectional differences. During the debates over the compromise, northern Whig Senator William Seward had stated that a "higher law" than the U.S. Constitution mandated that slavery be kept out of the Mexican Cession. Even southern moderates worried about such a statement, which suggested that northern morality mattered more to the senator from New York than the law of the land.

The new, strict federal Fugitive Slave Act further exacerbated sectional divisions. When slaveholders or their agents used the law to recover their runaway human property from northern communities, the meaning of chattel slavery was forcibly brought home to northern whites. People who had been only abstractly involved in the issue watched appalled as blacks who had been living as free men were dragged back to the South in chains. The fact that southern slave hunters sometimes mistook free northern blacks for runaways did not help matters. While some free blacks armed themselves and prepared for resistance, others simply gave up on the United States and migrated to Canada.

Public anger led to legislative action. Northern states passed "personal liberty laws," which denied that the federal government had the right to intervene in the states to enforce the Fugitive Slave Act, thus taking a states' rights position. Ironically, southern whites at this point became advocates of federal power, applauding as President Franklin Pierce (a northern Democrat) sent federal troops into Boston to retrieve a runaway slave and shipped the man back south on a U.S. navy vessel.

When northerners protested against the Fugitive Slave Act, southern whites realized that many northerners did not believe that slaves were legitimate property, deserving of legal protection just like any other form of property. Like Senator Seward, they seemed to believe in a "higher law" than that of the United States.

This higher-law concept also figured heavily in the most successful work of propaganda ever published in the United States, Harriet Beecher Stowe's *Uncle Tom's Cabin*. Published in 1851, it became one of the greatest best-sellers of the nineteenth century, not only in the United States but throughout the world.

Stowe's book played off of new northern concepts of family, womanhood, and religion, describing the evils of slavery in domestic rather than political terms. Stowe showed how slavery destroyed black families, separating husband from wife and mother from child. Her hero, Uncle Tom, a perfect Christ-like figure, died to protect the lives and virtue of enslaved women. Her message was simple: slavery was morally wrong, no matter what the law of the land said.

Condemned throughout the South, *Uncle Tom's Cabin* was nonetheless widely read there. Several prominent southerners penned attacks on the novel, explaining how unlikely it was that any slaveholder would act the way Stowe's white southerners did. Others published anti-Tom novels describing the essential goodness of the southern slave system. To no avail: Mrs. Stowe's work swept the field, creating stereotypes of slaves and white southerners that would last for generations.

The Failure of Politics

Political parties channel and contain conflict. During the 1830s and 1840s, northerners and southerners worked together in political parties, putting aside sectional disagreements in order to achieve common goals. In the 1850s the party discipline that had enabled Clay and Douglas to save the Union disintegrated. The Whig Party was the first to go. When the Democrats fell apart in 1860, southern Democrats led their section out of the Union.

The Whig Party, already weakened by internal divisions over slavery, disintegrated in the early 1850s. For a brief time it appeared that the American, or "Know-Nothing," Party would replace the Whigs. The Know-Nothings were nativists, opposed to immigrant political power and most especially to Catholics. They had almost no following in the South but briefly dominated state politics in the Northeast.

Catholics and Jews in the Antebellum South

The slave South, so conservative in many ways, was one of the less prejudiced regions of the country when it came to Catholics and Jews.

In the 1840s, Irish immigrants poured into the North, seeking refuge from a devastating famine and from British oppression. At the same time, German immigration increased. The Irish and many of the Germans were Catholic. Up until that time, most citizens of the United States (outside Louisiana) had been Protestants. Many northern Protestant clergymen reacted with fear to the Irish and German immigration. Some talked about a papal conspiracy to take over the United States. Protestant mobs in several northern cities attacked Catholic churches. This anti-immigration, anti-Catholic feeling found political expression in the Know-Nothing (American) Party of the 1850s. The Know-Nothings proposed to make it harder for immigrants to attain citizenship. This party found very little support in the South, and southern politicians in Congress made speeches defending Catholics as good citizens. (The fact that most Catholics voted Democratic probably had something to do with southern attitudes as well.)

The Jewish population of the antebellum South was quite small. At that time predominantly an urban people, Jews rarely farmed or owned plantations. Immigrant German Jews usually settled in the north, where opportunities for business were better. However, the old coastal cities of the South did have small Jewish communities, some dating back to colonial days. This was the background of the most successful Jewish American politician of the early nineteenth century, Judah Benjamin of Louisiana. A resident of New Orleans, a lawyer, and a plantation owner, Benjamin was elected U.S. senator in the 1850s and went on to serve the Confederacy in multiple cabinet posts.

By the 1850s white southern political leaders understood that their power in Congress was diminishing. Calhoun's analysis had been correct: the free states dominated the House, and as more came into the Union, they would dominate the Senate. Southern political leaders also understood that no southerner could be elected president. However, within the Democratic Party southern interests still mattered. The Democrats were not as strong in the North as their opponents. To carry the presidency, a Democratic candidate needed southern votes. Within the Democratic Party, southern political leaders acted as kingmakers, assuring that Democratic nominees for the presidency were favorable to southern interests.

"Doughfaces," they were called: "northern men with southern principles." Thus in 1852 southern Democrats rallied to elect Franklin Pierce and took leading positions in his government.

In 1854 Senator Stephen Douglas of Illinois shattered the relative peace that had followed the Compromise of 1850. Douglas, one of the architects of the compromise, coupled nationalism with a pragmatic disdain for slavery as a moral issue. Convinced that blacks were inferior and incapable of surviving in freedom, Douglas also thought that northerners who worried about the spread of slavery into the West were being silly: why would masters even want to bring slaves into a climate where cotton would not grow? As far as he was concerned, the whole territorial issue was bogus. However, he knew that southern political leaders did not feel that way. They felt that southern honor had been insulted by attempts to restrict the expansion of slavery.

Southern leaders complained that California was closed to them, as was the Oregon territory; under the principle of popular sovereignty they could take their slaves into New Mexico, but no one thought the institution would prosper there. The last remaining unsettled lands were in the old Louisiana Purchase. The Nebraska territory ran from Missouri to the Canadian border, but all of it was north of the Missouri Compromise line. Needing southern support for a transcontinental railroad project, Senator Douglas offered southern white leaders a deal: in exchange for their votes in Congress, he would introduce legislation organizing the Nebraska territory, with the slavery issue to be settled by popular sovereignty.

Southerners in both houses of Congress helped pass Douglas's Kansas-Nebraska Act. They were stunned when the act provoked a firestorm of criticism. Many people in the North saw the act as a betrayal of the Missouri Compromise, which had reserved the Kansas and Nebraska lands for free soil. In vain southern leaders pointed out that northern leaders had already repudiated the Missouri Compromise in 1850 when they refused to extend the 36° 30′ line through California. Furious at what they saw as a capitulation to the "Slave Power," former Whigs and rebellious northern Democrats joined to form an "anti-Nebraska" party. Joined by Free-Soil men and Know-Nothings, this new party took the name "Republican."

There were no southern Republicans. Although previous parties had regional power bases, the Republicans were the first (and so far, only) party in the nation's history to be completely sectional in nature. Free of southern influence, the Republicans took up the old Whig prodevelopment economic policies and combined them with the Free-Soil Party's opposition to the expansion of slavery into the territories. This stance appealed to abolitionists, who hoped that containing slavery in the South would eventually destroy it, and also to northern white racists who wanted to keep the West a white man's country. The new party grew rapidly.

Republican leaders charged that southerners and their allies in the national government had created a "Slave Power conspiracy" that endangered all American liberties. According to Republicans, doughface northern politicians were but puppets for their southern masters. As evidence, Republicans cited efforts by southern politicians in the late 1850s to manipulate the nation's foreign policy in the interests of the South.

In 1854 a group of southerners serving as American diplomats in Europe issued a statement, the Ostend Manifesto, urging the United States to buy or take by war with Spain the island of Cuba, where slavery was still legal. Although nothing came of this, it proved to Republicans that the Slave Power was willing to drag the entire nation into war to extend its own territory.

Some white southern leaders did think that extending American territory into the tropics would help solve the problem of slavery. Lured by the possibility of earning big profits growing cotton, sugar, and tropical crops, slaveholders would migrate even further south, leaving the temperate zones for white settlers. In 1854 a small group of southerners founded the "Knights of the Golden Circle" to promote the expansion of the American slave system into a "golden circle" through Mexico, Central America, northern South America, and back through the West Indies. This empire for slavery would bring twenty-five new slave states into the union. Alternately, promoters suggested, the Golden Circle could declare independence and form its own country. As producers of cotton, tobacco, sugar, and coffee, the slave empire would be one of the richest nations in the world. Although this vision never appealed to the average southern white voter, it gave Republicans more evidence of the Slave Power conspiracy.

Kansas

By the mid-1850s the Democratic Party was the last strand holding the nation together. The Republicans openly campaigned against the

South. The nation's major religious groups had split into northern and southern branches, and ministers on either side denounced the other in thundering sermons. Only within the Democratic Party did politicians from North and South work together. The Kansas issue destroyed the unity of the Democratic Party, and with it the last hope for national unity.

The Kansas-Nebraska Act had organized two territories, Nebraska and Kansas, the latter just west of Missouri, a slave state. The status of slavery in Kansas would be settled by popular sovereignty, or as people called it at the time, "squatter sovereignty": the side that moved quickly to get the largest number of settlers to Kansas would win. Southern political leaders, spurred on by Missouri Senator David Atchison, urged proslavery settlers to go to Kansas; abolitionist and free soil men in the North did the same for their side. Meanwhile, apolitical Americans from North and South poured into the new territory to take up farms on the new land.

Democratic leaders like Stephen Douglas knew that Kansas would be a test of popular sovereignty, which they saw as the only way to avoid sectional conflict over the slavery issue. Unfortunately, popular sovereignty failed in Kansas. When proslavery settlers rigged elections to make sure that Kansas became a slave state, antislavery settlers boycotted the entire process. Eventually the new territory had two "governments," one for slavery and one against. A series of governors appointed by President Pierce could make no headway toward settling the issue. Believing that the law was on their side, proslavery and antislavery forces fortified their positions and prepared for armed conflict.

In 1856 proslavery forces, equipped with grand jury warrants allowing them to arrest antislavery leaders, raided the antislavery "capital" at Lawrence. They shot up the town and burned the Free State Hotel, which they claimed (with good evidence) had been constructed as a fort.

In retaliation for the "sack of Lawrence," in which no antislavery men had been killed, abolitionist John Brown mounted a night attack on the homes of three Southern families. Brown and his men pulled the men of the families from their cabins and used guns and broadswords to execute them in their own front yards. Ironically, none of the men so butchered owned any slaves.

After these massacres, the conflict in Kansas broke out into guerrilla warfare. Abolitionist newspapers trumpeted that in "Bleeding Kansas," southerners used violence and political chicanery to deny free-soil settlers their rights.

Meanwhile, Massachusetts Senator Charles Sumner used the sack of Lawrence as occasion for a vicious attack on slavery, the South, and southern representatives in Congress. Sumner singled out Senator Andrew P. Butler of South Carolina for special attention, making fun of his "loose expectoration" in speech. (Butler was an old man who had suffered a stroke.) Over in the House of Representatives, Butler's kinsman Preston Brooks determined that Sumner's insult could not go unpunished. Arming himself with a cane, Representative Brooks found Sumner at his desk in the Senate Chamber. He announced that Sumner had insulted his state and Senator Butler, then proceeded to beat Sumner over the head with his cane until the implement broke. Brooks left the Massachusetts senator lying bleeding on the Senate floor.

While Republicans made "bleeding Sumner" a symbol of southern barbarism, southerners rallied to the support of Preston Brooks. Ousted from the House of Representatives, he was quickly reelected by his South Carolina constituents. Southerners shipped him hundreds of canes to replace the one he broke over Sumner's head, accompanied by suggestions that he target other Republican leaders in Congress. Perhaps most notable was the silver-headed cane from Charleston engraved, "Hit him again."

In the course of events leading to the Civil War, many things happened that seem to be more important than Brooks's caning of Sumner. Yet the episode illustrates very well how culturally different North and South had become by 1856. As Sumner's New England constituents saw it, Brooks was a criminal, just the kind of violent man likely to be produced by a slave society. They were appalled that he had brought his violence into the very halls where laws were created.

For their part, southerners did not distinguish much between fighting words and actual fighting. They could not understand why the Yankees thought verbal abuse, such as perpetrated by Sumner, was more morally acceptable than physical abuse. The Richmond Whig editorialized, "The only regret we feel is that Mr. Brooks did not employ a horsewhip or cowhide against his slanderous back instead of a cane." Even the use of a cane had symbolic import to southerners: it was the kind of implement used on inferiors, such as children and slaves. Had Sumner been a man of honor, Brooks could have challenged him to a duel. However, all southerners knew that men from Massachusetts disdained duels. Mistaking principle for cowardice, many southerners believed that "Yankees won't fight," a misapprehension that would have fatal consequences later.

The Impact of *Dred Scott*

In 1856 and 1857 a series of events occurred that gave southern political leaders cause for guarded optimism about their region's safety in the Union. James Buchanan of Pennsylvania, a Democrat, won the presidency with the strong support of the South: 119 of his 174 electoral votes came from the slave states. The ultimate doughface, Buchanan did everything he could to favor southern interests. At his inauguration he announced that the Supreme Court was about to issue a decision that should settle the question of slavery in the territories. This was the famous *Dred Scott* decision, like Buchanan's election a stunning victory for the South.

Scott, a slave who had traveled with his late master into Illinois, a free state, and into Wisconsin territory, where slavery had been prohibited by the Missouri Compromise, sued his master's estate for his liberty, stating that his brief residence in free territory made him a free man. The case dragged on in state and then federal court for years, before reaching the Supreme Court in 1856. In 1857, just after Buchanan's inaugural, the court issued its verdict: Dred Scott was not free. The court split on the reasons why, and all nine justices wrote separate opinions. However, public attention focused most on the opinion written by Chief Justice Roger Taney, a Marylander.

Taney's decision was more pro-South than southern leaders could ever have hoped for. The Chief Justice ruled against Scott, then explained his reasons at elaborate length. First, Taney said, as a black man and a slave Scott could not sue in federal court. The rights guaranteed in the Declaration of Independence were for whites only, Taney said, because the Founding Fathers had considered blacks too inferior for national citizenship and fit only to be slaves. The Chief Justice wrote that blacks "had no rights which the white man was bound to respect." Second, Taney said that Scott's residence in Wisconsin Territory did not make him free because Congress had no constitutional right to prohibit slavery in the territories in the first place: it was an unjustifiable federal violation of individual property rights. With this ruling, Taney made impossible all federal efforts to stop the spread of slavery into new lands. Finally, Taney said that if the federal government could not designate territories as free states, neither could territorial governments, as subsidiaries of the federal government. By the time Taney finished, it appeared that southerners were free to take their slaves into any territory of the Union and to maintain slavery there until the territory outlawed slavery at the time it became a state, if it chose to do so. Southern leaders were jubilant: the right to slave property had been upheld by the Supreme Court.

Later in the year, President Buchanan urged Congress to admit Kansas as a slave state. Northern Democrats, led by Stephen Douglas, protested that the proslavery constitution supported by Buchanan was a fraud, passed without the votes of the majority of Kansas settlers. A coalition of northern Democrats and Republicans blocked the admission of Kansas, but at great cost to Democratic Party unity and to Douglas's political fortunes. He had hoped to run for the presidency in 1860 with southern support, but after the fight over Kansas he found that support dwindling.

Douglas could no longer satisfy voters in the North, who wanted slavery's expansion halted, and voters in the South, who wanted the liberty to take their slaves wherever they pleased. Douglas's political problem typified the dilemma of the entire Democratic Party, by 1858 the only force still unifying North and South.

Douglas's opponent in the 1858 senatorial race in Illinois spotlighted the Democrat's problem. Abraham Lincoln asked Douglas to explain: in the light of the *Dred Scott* decision, how can popular sovereignty work? Douglas repeated his position on this point, stating that people in the territories could keep slavery out by refusing to enact laws protecting slave property. Douglas's answer suited the voters of Illinois, who sent him back to the Senate, but not his fellow Democrats in the South. Southerners were aghast to hear Douglas say that territories could just refuse to protect their property, and geared up to oppose his nomination on the Democratic ticket in 1860.

John Brown and the Crisis of Fear

In October 1859, abolitionist John Brown and a small band of followers seized the federal arsenal at Harper's Ferry, Virginia. The local authorities surrounded Brown's forces, who had holed up in a railroad engine house, and called for help. The federal government sent a detachment of troops, led by Lieutenant Colonel Robert E. Lee, U.S. Cavalry, and his aide, Lieutenant J. E. B. Stuart. The professionals quickly overwhelmed Brown's tiny amateur army and took Brown prisoner.

Brown's raid aroused intense national interest, especially when investigations revealed that Brown had planned to set off a slave insurrection, with the full support and funding of a group of New England abolitionists. He had hoped to take the arsenal, announce an insurrection, and arm the slaves, who would rally to the banner of freedom. No slaves joined Brown's abortive "rebellion," but his raid evoked the South's deepest fears of slave insurrection and race war. While northern observers suggested that Brown was insane, the governor of Virginia, Henry Wise, considered Brown a dangerous terrorist (to use our present-day word) and described him as "a man of clear head, of courage, fortitude, and simple ingeniousness. He is cool, collected, and indomitable." Wise thought Brown's courage and sincerity only made him more deadly. The state of Virginia indicted Brown for treason, murder, and inciting insurrection.

At his trial, Brown gave one of the most famous speeches in all of American history, justifying his crimes in the name of God: "Now, if it is deemed necessary that I should forfeit my life for the furtherance of the ends of justice, and mingle my blood further . . . with the blood of millions in this slave country whose rights are disregarded by wicked, cruel and unjust enactments—I submit; so let it be done!" When Brown was hanged for his crimes, northern sympathizers rang church bells in his honor. Although Republican leaders cautioned that Brown's means were wrong, many applauded his goals.

For many southerners, this was the last straw. The governor of Florida called for "eternal separation from those whose wickedness and fanaticism forbid us longer to live with them in peace and safety." Jefferson Davis, then serving as senator from Mississippi, said that Brown's mission had been to "incite slaves to murder helpless women and children." One of the women so targeted, Margaretta Mason (wife of Virginia Senator James M. Mason) wrote that Brown had intended "to incite the horrors of a servile war—to condemn women . . . to see their husbands and fathers murdered, their children butchered, the ground strewed with the brains of their babes." A South Carolinian wrote, "Every village bell which tolled its solemn note at the execution of Brown proclaims to the South the approbation of that village of insurrection and servile war." Virginia fire-eater Edmund Ruffin arranged that each southern governor would receive a pike from the store brought by Brown to Harper's Ferry to arm the slaves. All over the South, newspapers noted a transformation in public opinion. People who had before scoffed at the notion of secession were now openly advocating disunion.

In 1860 the Democratic Party, long the venue in which sectional differences were resolved, could no longer play that role. At a convention held in Charleston, southern delegates demanded that the party support proposals for a federal slave code to protect slave property in the territories. Southern delegates threatened to bolt the party unless the provision was enacted, while northern delegates promised to walk out if it was. Southern fire-eater William Lowndes Yancey, a delegate from Alabama, urged the northern delegates to save the Union by supporting slavery, while insisting that the South could not back down: "Ours is the property invaded; ours are the institutions which are at stake; ours is the peace which is to be destroyed; ours is the honor at stake." When the proslavery platform failed to pass, the delegations from Alabama, Georgia, Arkansas, Mississippi, Louisiana, South Carolina, Florida, and Texas bolted the convention, which then disintegrated. The party leadership announced a second convention to be held at Baltimore in June. At Baltimore, the majority nominated Stephen Douglas for the presidency. At that, the Upper South states, led by Virginia, left the convention. Joining with the fire-eaters led by Yancey, the bolting southern delegations nominated vice president John C. Breckinridge for the presidency. Thus the Democratic Party entered the 1860 election fatally divided.

The situation was complicated further when former Whigs from Virginia, Kentucky, and Tennessee formed the Constitutional Union party and nominated John Bell for the presidency. "The Old Gentlemen's Party," as it was derisively referred to, wanted above all to bury sectional divisions before those divisions brought on disunion. Although the Constitutional Unionists had no clear platform, standing vaguely for the Constitution and law and order, the party achieved a surprising popularity in the Upper South.

The Republicans nominated Abraham Lincoln for the presidency. Although Lincoln was a moderate Republican, committed to containing slavery but not to abolition, southern political leaders denounced him as a black abolitionist (an ambiguous phrase that impugned Lincoln's politics, motives, and ancestry). Fire-eaters, long stigmatized by other southerners as radicals, finally took leadership roles, promising that if Lincoln were elected, the South would leave the Union. Yancey took this message into the northern states, proclaiming that the South would secede before being reduced to the status of "hewers of wood and drawers of water." Despite these warnings, Lincoln and other Republicans discounted the possibility of southern secession.

Born in Kentucky to a family of poor white migrants from Virginia, married to a belle from a prominent Kentucky slaveholding family, Lincoln did not share the hatred for southerners so often exhibited by Republicans from New England. He had southern friends, including the former Whig congressman from Georgia, Alexander Stephens. Lincoln thought that the southerners who promised secession were just bluffing. Had they not promised secession in the 1830s over nullification, and in the 1840s over the territorial question? He believed that the majority of the southern population was still loyal to the union, and in the long run they would prevail.

Lincoln won the presidency in 1860 with no votes from the southern states; his party did not even bother to campaign there. Breckinridge carried the Deep South, and Bell the Border South. Stephen Douglas, the only candidate on the ballot throughout the nation, came in second to Lincoln in the popular vote but lost badly in the electoral race, winning only Missouri and three electoral votes in New Jersey.

With the election returns in, southern white political leaders realized that the South had just become irrelevant in national politics. Their last weapon, the ability to swing a presidential election in favor of a doughface, was now, apparently, gone. The House of Representatives had long been in the hands of northern interests. Southern leaders had been able to maneuver in the Senate to block antislavery legislation passed by the House, but they knew those days were numbered: as more free states came into the Union, the balance in the Senate would swing against them. Fire-eaters called for immediate secession. Southern unionists counseled patience, reminding the region that the Republicans had promised to leave slavery alone in the South. Yes, said the secessionists, but how long would that promise hold? Perhaps Lincoln might keep his word, but would the next Republican president do so? Why should the southern states wait until Republican legislation destroyed their economies and endangered slavery? Would it not be more honorable to leave the Union now, and take the consequences, rather than leave the issue to be resolved by the next generation?

By 1860, even normally calm southern white politicians, men who had scorned fire-eaters previously, had become secessionists. They believed that their cause was just—as righteous a cause as that of the revolutionaries in 1776. In essence, secessionists believed that they were the true children of the American Revolution, whose promise had been stolen and betrayed by the northern states. By seceding from the Union, they would reestablish the nation the Founding Fathers intended.

Just as the Republicans had discounted the possibility of secession, secessionists discounted the possiblity of war. Believing that secession was perfectly legitimate under the Constitution, and believing also that the North lacked manhood and valor, the secessionists thought that they would be allowed to depart in peace.

On December 20, 1860, South Carolina left the Union. By February 1861, Mississippi, Florida, Alabama, Georgia, Louisiana, and Texas had followed. Frantically, border state politicians tried to find a compromise that would avert war, but their efforts failed. The Republican Party refused to drop its opposition to the extension of slavery, which was after all the reason for the party's formation in the first place.

James Buchanan, serving out the last months of his presidency, did not intervene as southern state authorities took over federal installations in the region (mostly post offices) in the name of the new southern Confederacy, formed in February 1861 at Montgomery, Alabama. By the time Lincoln took office on March 5, 1861, only two forts, Pickens in Florida and Sumter in South Carolina, remained in federal hands.

Decision for War

The federal commander at Fort Sumter, Major Robert Anderson, was from Kentucky and had a good bit of sympathy for the southern position, but when South Carolina authorities asked him to surrender the fort to them, he refused. Anderson fortified his position at Sumter, a fort located on an island in Charleston Bay. Provisioned with enough food to last four months, the major awaited his orders.

Jefferson Davis, newly elected president of the Confederacy, understood that attacking the fort might mean war. Still, the new Confederacy could not allow the Union to maintain an outpost in Charleston Bay, at the very heart of southern nationalism. Davis sent General P. G. T. Beauregard to take command of state forces at Charleston. Beauregard asked again for Anderson's surrender. The federal commander refused, despite knowing that his supplies were running low.

Up in Washington, Lincoln faced a momentous decision. If he sent provisions to Sumter, he would signal to the Confederacy that his gov-

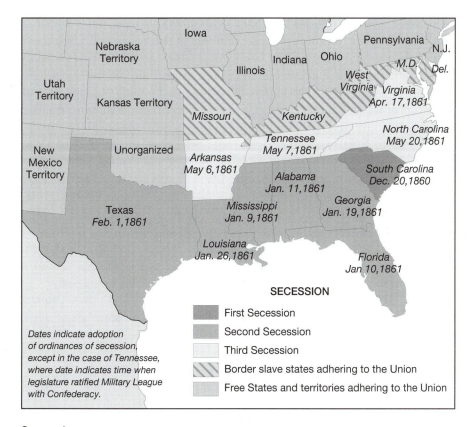

Secession.

ernment planned to maintain the fort. Wishing to avoid the appearance of starting an armed conflict, Lincoln sent a letter to the governor of South Carolina stating that he would reprovision Anderson but would not send in additional troops or arms. The Confederate authorities did not want the situation in Charleston Bay prolonged. Knowing that the federal fleet was on its way, Confederate authorities fired on Sumter at 4:30 a.m., April 12, 1861. The Civil War had begun.

President Lincoln called for the states to send him troops to put down the rebellion of "combinations too powerful to be suppressed by the ordinary course of judicial proceedings, or by the powers vested in the marshals by law," language carefully chosen to avoid the impression that states, rather than individuals, had seceded. (Lincoln still held out hope that southern unionists would win political power in the South and bring their states back into the Union.) The border states then faced a choice: send in their militias to help put down the rebellion or become rebels themselves. Tennessee Governor Isham Harris defiantly proclaimed, "Tennessee will furnish not a single man for the purpose of coercion, but fifty thousand if necessary for the defense of our rights and those of our Southern brothers." Virginia, North Carolina, Arkansas, and Tennessee joined the Confederacy, although not without controversy. The western counties of Virginia so wanted to remain loyal to the Union that they seceded from the Old Dominion and were ultimately admitted to the Union as West Virginia. East Tennessee remained a stronghold of unionism throughout the war.

A West Tennessee farmer probably captured the feelings of many people in the South when he wrote in later years, "I was for the Union as long as there was any hope of our remaining in it with peace and honor. When Lincoln issued his proclamation calling for 75,000 troops to whip . . . the Seceded States, I was satisfied that day had passed, and now—though not what you'd term a regular Secessionist—I am the most uncompromising *rebel* you ever knew."

Suggestions for Further Reading

THOMAS ABERNATHY, *The South in the New Nation, 1789–1819* (1961)

WILLIAM L. BARNEY, *The Road to Secession* (1972)

IRVING H. BARTLETT, *John C. Calhoun* (1993)

JOHN BOLES, *The Great Revival, 1787–1895* (1972)

STEPHEN CHANNING, *A Crisis of Fear: Secession in South Carolina* (1970)

WILLIAM J. COOPER, JR. *The South and the Politics of Slavery, 1828–1856* (1978)

DAVID BRION DAVIS, *The Problem of Slavery in the Age of Revolution,* 1770–1823 (1975)

JOHN D. EISENHOWER, *So Far from God: The U. S. War with Mexico 1846–1848* (1989)

GEORGE FITZHUGH, *Cannibals All! Or, Slaves without Masters* (1857) Available through the University of North Carolina's *Documenting the South* web project at http://metalab.unc.edu/docsouth/fitzhughcan/fitzcan .html

LACY K. FORD, JR., *Origins of Southern Radicalism: The South Carolina Upcountry 1800–1860* (1988)

WILLIAM W. FREEHLING, *The Road to Disunion: Secessionists at Bay, 1776–1854* (1990)

MICHAEL HOLT, *The Political Crisis of the 1850s* (1978)

ERIC MCKITRICK, ED., *Slavery Defended: The Views of the Old South* (1963)

WILLIAM LEE MILLER, *Arguing about Slavery: The Great Battle in the United States Congress* (1996)

DAVID M. POTTER, *The Impending Crisis, 1848–1861* (1976)

ROBERT REMINI, *Andrew Jackson and the Source of American Freedom* (1981)

MITCHELL SNAY, *Gospel of Disunion: Religion and Separatism in the Antebellum South* (1993)

J. MILLS THORNTON III, *Politics and Power in a Slave Society* (1978)

ERIC WALTHER, *The Fire-Eaters* (1992)

GAVIN WRIGHT, *The Political Economy of the Cotton South* (1978)

4

War and Defeat, 1861–1865

The men who formed the Confederate States of America in 1861 considered themselves the heirs of the American Revolution, rebelling like their fathers had against an oppressive government. They believed that their rebellion was constitutional, since the states, having formed the Union, had the right to leave if necessary to protect their rights. Satisfied with southern society as it then existed, the Confederate leaders proposed a revolution to maintain the status quo. Instead, they provoked the worst war in American history and brought down upon their people devastation, poverty, and despair. The Confederacy was founded to protect states' rights and slavery, but the demands of war forced the Confederate government toward centralized national power and forced them to consider freeing the slaves. Too late: the war swept away slavery and the way of life based upon it.

In the history of the South, the Civil War is the event from which things are dated. Before the war is the "Old South," and after it, the New. What follows is a brief survey of the history of the war, presented from the Confederate perspective and focusing on some of the perennial questions debated by historians of the conflict. Given the enormous population and industrial advantages possessed by the Union, why did it take the forces of the federal government four years of the hardest fighting in the nation's history to put down the rebellion? When defeat came for the Confederacy, was it because of battlefield losses, or because of the fragile new nation's internal divisions? How did slavery affect the ability of the Confederacy to wage war? Ultimately, did the federal armies free the slaves, or did the slaves free themselves?

Facing War

In 1861 Jefferson Davis became the president of the new Confederate States of America. His administration took office first in Montgomery, Alabama, and then, with the secession of Virginia, moved to Richmond, that state's capital, only 100 miles from Washington. The Confederate government chose Richmond in recognition of Virginia's traditional leadership role in the region, and also because the city contained most of the South's industrial base in the form of the Tredegar Iron Works, the only plant in the region capable of manufacturing cannon.

Although the fire-eaters had promoted a southern revolution, the white voters of the South did not chose them to lead it. Davis was a southern moderate. Born in Kentucky not far from the birthplace of Lincoln, Davis had grown up in Mississippi. A West Point graduate and a veteran of the Mexican War, Davis served as secretary of war in the Pierce administration, and as senator from Mississippi. Although adamant in defense of southern rights, Davis held hopes that secession could be averted until the Republican victory in 1860 convinced him otherwise. Alexander Stephens, the Georgia politician chosen as Confederate vice president, was a former Whig and a friend of Lincoln's. Other members of Davis's cabinet included many prominent Democrats but few of the men who had roused the region to secession.

In their forms of government, as in their choice of personnel, the Confederates indicated a strong conservatism. The Confederacy adopted the United States Constitution as its own, making only a few changes designed to clarify the protected status of slavery and states' rights.

FRANK LESLIE'S

ILLUSTRATED

NEWSPAPER

Entered according to the Act of Congress, in the year 1861, by FRANK LESLIE, in the Clerk's Office of the District Court for the Southern District of New York.

No. 277—Vol. XI.]   NEW YORK, MARCH 16, 1861.   [PRICE 6 CENTS.

THE HON. JEFFERSON DAVIS, PRESIDENT-ELECT OF THE NEW SOUTHERN CONFEDERACY, ADDRESSING THE CITIZENS OF MONTGOMERY, ALA., FROM THE BALCONY OF THE EXCHANGE HOTEL, ON THE NIGHT OF FEBRUARY 16TH, 1861, AND PREVIOUS TO HIS INAUGURATION.—FROM A SKETCH BY OUR SPECIAL ARTIST.—SEE PAGE 258.

The structures of government—Senate, House, presidency, and courts—in the Confederacy did not differ significantly from those in the United States.

The Confederacy was born in war, and Davis knew that his first and most important task was to maintain the new nation's independence on the battlefield. With hindsight, historians have pointed out just how daunting that task was. The population of the Union, including those slave states remaining loyal, was 20.7 million. The Confederacy's population was 9.1 million, of which 3.5 million were African-Americans, mostly slaves.

Eventually about three-quarters of all military age (18–45) white men in the South served in the Confederate armies, an estimated 850,000 men. Although the Confederate contention that every able-bodied white man capable of carrying a gun went to war is not technically accurate, it must have seemed so to the aged men, women, and children left at home. The Union could field many more men, approximately 2.1 million, without sending more than half of its military-age men to service. Moreover, the southern states had only the most minimal industrial base.

The Confederate leadership thought that the Confederacy's assets offset its liabilities. First, its war aims were simple: hold out until the Union recognized Confederate independence. The Confederacy would be fighting a defensive war, on its own territory, and nations, like sports teams, have a home-court advantage. In contrast, the federal government's war aim in 1861 was to preserve the Union by putting down the rebellion. Some Confederate leaders thought that the Lincoln administration did not have the will or the courage necessary for this arduous task. Many Confederates also believed that the Yankees were a nation of cowardly, pasty-faced, urban clerks unlikely to make good soldiers. Although men like Davis who had served with northerners in the Mexican War knew better, some white southerners sincerely thought that one rebel soldier could "whip" four Yankees.

The Confederacy counted among its assets a tradition of martial prowess. The southern states had always sent a disproportionate number of men to the U.S. Army's officer corps. When Lincoln called for troops to put

Jefferson Davis addressing a jubilant crowd after his inauguration as president of the Confederacy, Montgomery, Alabama, March 1861. From *Leslie's Illustrated Weekly.* Library of Congress.

down the rebellion in 1861, 313 southern officers, among them men considered the best the U.S. military had, resigned their commissions and returned to the South to join the Confederacy. Moreover, many southern men then in private life had attended military schools. Virginia maintained its own officer training school, the Virginia Military Institute, and other states had similar military academies. President Jefferson Davis was himself a graduate of West Point and had studied military science. By contrast, the commander in chief of the federal armies, Abraham Lincoln, sent to the Library of Congress for books on strategy and tactics and studied them late into the night for insight into his unexpected role.

The Confederates also remembered that the revolutionaries of 1776, fighting for their independence against greater odds, had found allies in Europe. The Confederate government looked for help to Britain and France, both of which had textile industries that depended largely on southern cotton. It was true that both nations had repudiated slavery, and that it would be politically difficult for them to side with a slaveholding republic against one that promised to set slaves free. But as the British government noted in 1861, Lincoln had made no such promises. In 1861 the federal government fought to save the Union, not free the slaves, and the Union, containing four slave states, Maryland, Delaware, Kentucky, and Missouri, was morally no different than the Confederacy in the eyes of British abolitionists.

Not about Slavery?

For generations, people on both sides of the Mason-Dixon line have revered the military leaders of the Confederacy, seeing men like Stonewall Jackson and Robert E. Lee as exemplars of the best of America. However, very few Americans find it easy anymore to stomach slavery. Therefore, people who want to think well of the Confederate army try to split the war off from its political causes, or to deny the existence of those causes. Thus neo-Confederates prefer to insist that the war was not fought for slavery, but for states' rights. They point out that many Confederate leaders had but lukewarm support for the peculiar institution, and that many common soldiers owned no slaves—all true. It is also true that men sign up to fight wars for all kinds of reasons. A man may join up because he supports the cause, or to get away from home, to go adventuring with friends, or (the classic reason) because his girlfriend broke up with him. But the reasons of common soldiers are not the reasons of state.

The southern states seceded because they thought the Republican Party threatened slavery. In a public speech on March 21, 1861, the vice president of the Confederacy assured his listeners that secession had ended all agitation on that topic, and added that the cornerstone of the Confederacy was "the great truth that the negro is not equal to the white man; that slavery, subordination to the superior race, is his natural moral condition." Nor were all soldiers reticent on the subject. General Nathan Bedford Forrest, a slave trader, was asked about the Cause after the war. He reportedly replied, "Hell, I fought to keep my niggers." The leaders of the Confederacy, for all their sins, were not hypocrites, and would no doubt be puzzled at their present-day supporters' attempts to deny the importance of slavery to the conflict.

Davis sent diplomats to Britain to angle for British recognition of Confederate independence. This, the Confederate leadership thought, would bring a declaration of war from the United States against Great Britain. In such a war the Confederacy would be allied with the most powerful empire on the planet. The British navy would make short work of the much smaller American navy, supplies would pour in from British munitions factories, and the new nation's independence and success would be assured. Davis and his government were elated when the British acknowledged that a state of war existed between the Union and the Confederacy in 1861. To the British government, recognizing belligerency was only recognizing fact. But to the Confederacy and the Union, it seemed a first step toward the world's acknowledgment of the Confederacy as a true, independent nation.

In the long run, Confederate dreams of a British alliance failed to come true. Cotton provided less leverage than Davis had hoped. The cotton harvests in the late 1850s had been much bigger than average, and British and French textile firms had stocked up on the fiber at bargain prices. When the war began, they had enough cotton to keep going for several years. By the time their southern supplies ran out, the British had ready other sources of cotton in Egypt and India. Nonetheless, until 1863 both Lincoln and Davis thought such an alliance was possible, and this possibility conditioned decisions both men made about the conduct of the war.

Raising an Army

The American Civil War was not fought by regular, professional armies, because neither side had one. In 1861 the United States Army consisted of only about 16,000 men, mostly stationed in the western territories. Americans believed that in time of danger, the nation should call upon its men for defense. Manhood and honor required them to respond. Therefore, both Lincoln and Davis sent messages to the governors of their respective states, requesting volunteers for service. In the Confederacy, volunteers poured in so quickly that Davis's government, unable to provide them with arms, sent thousands home.

Soldiers volunteered to serve with their friends and neighbors, trained together, and went into battle together. Towns, counties, and states formed troops, often sending them into service with parades, speeches, and regimental flags lovingly sewn by "the ladies." Regiments outfitted themselves, usually wearing homemade uniforms dyed "butternut" brown, while officers strove for a stylish "cadet gray." Prominent men could also form their own troops. Wade Hampton, an extremely wealthy South Carolina planter, went into battle like a feudal lord at the head of a cavalry troop he recruited and equipped at his own expense. In contrast, a hard-bitten West Tennessee slave trader, Nathan Bedford Forrest, raised one of the conflict's most famous cavalry units by putting up posters in Memphis inviting men to come ride with him and kill Yankees. Serving with friends and neighbors made for high morale among the troops. On the other hand, the practice of sending all the young men from a community into battle at once had horrific effects back home. One disastrous frontal charge could make widows and orphans of an entire community.

The down-home quality of the Confederate army led to discipline problems. Though the Confederate government chose its generals, lower-ranked officers were elected by the men with whom they served. Confederate soldiers notoriously refused to take military spit-and-polish seriously. They often neglected to salute, referred to officers by their first names, and generally behaved in ways that demonstrated their ingrained belief that all white men were equal. Officers who had served in the regular army quickly found that these volunteer troops could not be easily commanded, but they could be led. The result was a historical anomaly: it was more dangerous to be a Confederate officer than a common soldier. Eighteen percent of the Confederacy's generals died in battle, as compared with 12 percent of the enlisted. The Union army had similar problems, but to a lesser degree, and with greater resources could better afford them. When Confederate officers were killed, they could not easily be replaced by men of similar capabilities.

Strategy, Tactics, Logistics

In 1861 the Confederate strategy, or long-term plan for victory, was simple: hold out until the Yankees gave up. This strategy was defensive, and also (like all military strategies) informed by politics. The Confederates wanted to win their independence with their society intact. Confederate armies fought to protect their homeland and their property, including their slaves. Therefore, the Confederate leadership did not even seriously consider alternative strategies, such as fighting the kind of guerrilla/partisan war that had worked well for the rebels of 1776. They fought a conventional war because it was the kind of war most compatible with their war aims.

The Union strategy was also conventional: throw a naval blockade around the Confederate coast, encircle the rebel nation, take control of the Mississippi valley, and advance on the rebels from all sides, squeezing them into submission. This "Anaconda Plan," first proposed by Union General Winfield Scott in 1861, required the Union to mount offensives into Confederate territory, but made good use of the federal advantages: greater manpower, greater industrial capabilities, and a strong navy. When Scott first proposed his plan, other Union officers were incredulous. Blockades, encirclement—all that would take years! Most of the federal leadership thought that the war would be over in a few months, perhaps brought to an end by a rapid capture of the Confederate capital at Richmond. Then the southern Unionists would rise up, take command, and bring their states back into the Union. The federal government seriously miscalculated southern support for the rebellion. When federal leaders' optimism proved unfounded, they fell back on Scott's plan, drawn to it by its inherent logic, and followed it, with modifications necessitated by unfolding events.

Down in Richmond, the Confederates also adjusted their strategies in response to the demands of war. When events indicated that the Union would not give up quickly, the Confederacy moved from a simple defensive strategy to an "offensive-defensive." They would carry the war into the northern states, hoping that southern victory on northern soil would convince the Yankees to give up their effort to force the southern states back into the Union. To this end, Confederate generals timed incursions into northern territory so as to influence northern congressional and (ultimately) presidential elections.

During the Civil War, both sides used tactics, or methods of warfare, that were old-fashioned. Generals on both sides had been taught during their student days at West Point that a frontal charge could often break an enemy's lines and achieve victory. The frontal charge actually had worked well in previous wars, when soldiers were armed with smoothbore muskets. Smoothbore muskets were inaccurate past 80 yards. Soldiers waited until one volley had been fired, then raced to close with the enemy before they could reload, often finishing a battle in hand-to-hand combat with bayonets. However, during the Civil War rifled muskets, or rifles, replaced the old smoothbores. The new rifles were accurate at 400 yards. Men who charged into rifle fire were cut down long before they reached the enemy lines. As a result, hand-to-hand combat was rare; soldiers joked that the main use of bayonets was to roast meat over fires. In the Civil War, the defenders of a well-entrenched position had a decided advantage over the attackers. Yet generals on both sides continued to order charges, and their men died in inordinately large numbers.

While the Confederate strategy was rational, and their tactics no worse than the other side's, Confederate logistics were a nightmare. Logistics is the art and science of military supply, getting arms and food to the armies in the field. In 1862 Davis put Josiah Gorgas, a Pennsylvanian who had married a southern woman, in charge of the Confederate Ordnance Bureau. Gorgas worked miracles, building powder and ammunition factories throughout the South, forging cannon out of church bells and distilling niter—a key component of gunpowder—out of urine contributed by Confederate civilians. The Confederates actually sent squads out after battles to pick up used bullets for recycling. As a result of Gorgas's genius for organization, the Confederacy never ran out of munitions, although severe supply problems sometimes led to momentary shortages.

Instead, it ran out of food, clothing, and shoes. At first glance, it is hard to see why armies from a farming region should lack food. The answer is partly political, partly social. First, the Confederate Commissary General was a friend of President Davis, who overlooked his incompetence. Second, the big farms of the Confederate states grew nonfood staple crops for export. Though plantations usually supplied their own food requirements, they specialized in cotton, rice, sugar, or tobacco, not beef and wheat. Third, small farmers who specialized in family subsistence had relatively little food to market, especially after the Confederacy took most of the young male labor force to the army. Finally, the Confederacy had difficulty transporting the food they did have to the armies in the fields. Southern railroads were limited to begin with and deteriorated rapidly during the war. As for uniforms and shoes, the Confederates did not have enough factories to supply the armies' needs. Confederate women sewed and knitted constantly for the soldiers; even Mrs. Robert E. Lee sent packages of stockings to her general husband for distribution to the troops. While the Union troops were so well supplied that they often tossed away packs during quick marches, Confederates scrounged for food, stripped corpses for shoes and uniforms, starved, and stood picket duty barefoot in the snow. Photographs from the last years of the war show Confederate troops as ragged, gaunt skeletons, still glaring defiance.

The War at Sea

When the war began, the Confederacy had no navy. Shipbuilding was a speciality of the New England region, not of the South. The Union had a good navy and used it well. In 1861 President Lincoln ordered a naval blockade of the Confederate ports designed to keep the rebels from trading cotton for supplies from Europe. At first ineffective, the blockade got better and tighter as the war proceeded, becoming a major factor in eventual Union victory.

Desperate to break the blockade, the Confederates became technological innovators. In 1861 Confederate forces at Norfolk took a captured Union ship, the *Merrimack,* covered it with armor, and set it out into the federal blockade at Hampton Roads. The *Merrimack,* renamed the *Virginia,* was one of the first ironclad ships in naval history. Cannon shot bounced off her, as the Union crews at Hampton Roads discovered to their dismay. The *Virginia* wreaked havoc among the blockade ships for one day, before being stopped by the *Monitor,* a newly designed Union ironclad, which fought the Confederate vessel to a standstill. When the Confederates withdrew from Norfolk in May 1862, they scuttled the *Virginia.*

Confederate innovations continued, driven by desperation. The Confederacy became the first nation to use a submarine in warfare. It lost three crews in testing the *H. L. Hunley,* but the combat submarine did succeed in destroying a Union blockade ship off the coast of Charleston before it sank in 1864.

Unable to break the Union's stranglehold, the Confederacy depended on blockade runners, swift ships that smuggled goods through the Union naval lines into southern ports, and on "commerce raiders." These were ships that roved the oceans, destroying Union merchantmen wherever they encountered them. The most famous raider was the *Alabama,* built in England, crewed by British seamen, and commanded by Captain Raphael Semmes. Setting sail in 1862, the *Alabama* sank sixty-two Union merchant ships and one U.S. naval vessel before being destroyed by the U.S.S. *Kearsage* off the coast of France in 1864. Fleeing from the *Alabama* and other Confederate raiders, American shipping companies transferred their registries to other nations so that they would not have to fly the flag of the United States. After the war, the U.S. government demanded that the Brit-ish pay for damages caused by commerce raiders constructed in British ports; eventually the British government paid $15.5 million in "*Alabama* claims."

The Course of War, 1861–1864

The Confederacy won the first battle of the Civil War. Eager to capture the Confederate capital at Richmond, federal forces advanced

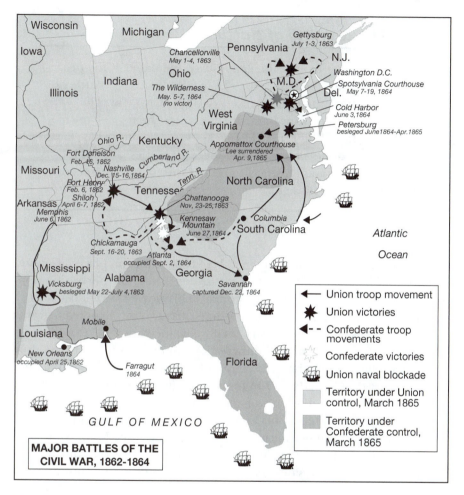

The Civil War.

upon Confederate forces at Manassas in northern Virginia. On July 21, 1861, congressmen who had ridden out from Washington to observe the battle watched aghast as the Union troops crumbled under a Confederate counterattack, turned tail, and ran back to the federal capital. The Confederates were jubilant, confirmed in their suspicion that the northerners would not fight.

The Naming of Battles

In naming battles, the Union used the name of the nearest river. Thus the first battle of the Civil War is the Battle of Bull Run in the official records of the Civil War. The Confederate army named battles after the nearest town; therefore, Bull Run is Manassas. As a rule, historians have followed the Union pattern for most battles, although those writing military history from the Confederate perspective tend to use those terms.

In the aftermath of First Manassas, Lincoln placed General George McClellan in command of the Union forces in the Washington-Maryland area, the Army of the Potomac. This proved very lucky for the Confederacy. Although McClellan saw himself as a young Napoleon, he was a timid, cautious commander, perpetually convinced that the Confederate armies he faced had him outnumbered. Assuming command in late July 1861, McClellan reorganized his army and trained his men but did not advance against the Confederates in force again until the spring of 1862.

The continuous chess match between Confederate and Union forces in Virginia riveted public attention from 1861 through the end of the war, obscuring the significance of events taking place in the West. The western war was not about capturing capitals. Instead, it took a much more modern turn, with both sides concentrating on controlling transportation routes, particularly rivers.

In February 1862, the federal army and navy forced coordinated successful attacks on Fort Henry, on the Tennessee, and Fort Donelson, on the Cumberland. When these two forts fell to Union forces led by U.S. Grant, the federal armies gained river access to the heart of the mid-South. Nashville surrendered to the Union by the end of the month and remained under federal occupation through the end of the war.

While the Confederates regrouped at Corinth, Mississippi, an important railroad junction, the federal forces under Grant's command followed them south down the Tennessee River and established a base camp at Pittsburgh Landing, Tennessee. Convinced that the Confederates were demoralized after their springtime losses, the Union troops were unprepared for a massive Confederate attack on their lines on April 6. Led by General Albert Sidney Johnston, the Confederates pushed the Union forces to the banks of the Tennessee River on the first day of the Battle of Shiloh, but had to withdraw when Grant brought in reinforcements for the second day. The Confederates limped away to Corinth, their retreat covered by Nathan Bedford Forrest's cavalry. Exhausted and shocked by the carnage—at least 1,700 men were killed on each side at Shiloh, among them General Johnston, and about 16,500 were wounded—the Union army allowed the rebels to slip away. By the time that Grant's superior, General Henry Wagner Halleck, reached Corinth, the Confederates had escaped to fight again another day.

Meanwhile, the Union navy, under command of Admiral David Farragut (ironically, a Tennessean) took New Orleans on April 29, then advanced upriver to Baton Rouge and Natchez, both of which surrendered. Further north, the Union navy took Memphis. By the end of June, 1862, the Confederates held only a 200-mile stretch of the Mississippi, dominated by the fortified city of Vicksburg, Mississippi. Federal attempts to take Vicksburg failed, leaving the Confederates with one last tenuous connection through which supplies and men could be sent from the Southwest.

Confederate losses in the West shocked the southern population in the spring of 1862. Shiloh proved that the Yankees could and would fight. Memphis and Nashville, centers of the South's meager industrial base, were in federal hands, and New Orleans, the largest city in the Confederacy, suffered under Union occupation. From England, Confederate diplomats sent pessimistic messages: each Confederate loss made British recognition less likely.

Conscription, Liberty, and States' Rights

Volunteers had flocked to the Confederate army in the spring of 1861, signing up for one year in service. Many planned to go home in the spring of 1862. Facing the possibility that the Confederate armies would melt away, the Davis government instituted a military draft. The Confederate conscription law required the men whose enlistments were expiring to remain with the army for three more years and allowed the government to call upon all men aged 18 to 35 for three-year terms in service. The law allowed for various occupational exemptions (clergymen, civil servants). In addition, the law exempted men on plantations with twenty or more slaves. Wealthy conscripts could also hire substitutes to go fight in their place. Confederate authorities justified what poor whites sarcastically called the "twenty-Negro law" on the grounds that white supervision was necessary to maintain control of the slaves and to prevent insurrections. To non-slaveholders, that made no difference. Saying that the conflict had become "a rich man's war, but a poor man's fight," many resisted the draft; many already in service deserted. As a white Alabama farmer wrote about the region's upper class, "All they want is to get you pupt up and go to fight for their infurnal negroes and after you do there fighting you may kiss there hine parts for o they care."

Citizens on both sides of the Civil War thought conscription violated their liberties. When the Union instituted its own draft in 1863, riots broke out in New York City. However, the southern conflict over conscription highlights a problem, already faced by the Confederate government in 1862, that became ever more pressing as the years passed. As the common white folk of the South saw it, the Confederate government was fighting a war to protect their liberties and to preserve states' rights. Yet to win that war, the Confederate leadership had to do things that violated individual liberties and trampled on states' rights. Georgia Governor Joseph E. Brown spoke for many when he denounced the conscription act: "No act of the Government of the United States prior to the secession of Georgia struck a blow at constitutional liberty so fell as has been stricken by this conscription act." Brown did everything he could to impede conscription in his state, and other southern governors followed suit.

Although conscription alienated many white southerners, the Confederate government thought it was worth the price. The draft kept men in the army and allowed the government to replenish the ranks. Eventually about 120,000 conscripts served the Confederacy, while about 70,000 came in as hired substitutes.

General Lee

Early in 1861 President Lincoln asked the aging commander of the United States Army, General Winfield Scott, who should be put in charge of federal forces in the imminent crisis. Scott had only one suggestion: United States Army Colonel Robert E. Lee, whom Scott considered best qualified for command in the entire regular army. Lee was descended from one of the "first families" of Virginia, with a heritage that went back in the state for 200 years, but he had never lived the life of a planter aristocrat. His father, a hero of the Revolution, died in debt and disgrace, leaving Lee and his mother to the charity of her wealthy relatives. Lacking land or money, Lee trained to be a professional soldier. He went to West Point, where he trained to be an army engineer, and married a descendant of Martha Custis Washington, whose family's great house at Arlington became Lee's off-duty home. By 1861 he had served with distinction in the Mexican War and had been commandant at West Point. Lincoln offered him command of the U.S. forces.

Then Virginia seceded from the Union, and Lee decided to go with his state, writing to his sister, "With all my devotion to the Union, and the feeling of loyalty and duty of an American citizen, I have not been able to make up my mind to raise my hand against my relatives, my children, my home. I have therefore resigned my commission in the Army, and save in defense of my native state . . . I hope I may never be called on to draw my sword." However, the government of Virginia called upon him to assume command of state forces. Lee first saw action in unsuccessful campaigns against federal forces in western Virginia, where he earned the contempt of his green troops by ordering entrenchments: the "King of Spades," they called him, and "Granny Lee," too old and timid to command young men. (Lee was 54, and going gray.) By July 1861, he was acting as Jefferson Davis's military adviser in Richmond.

In the spring of 1862 McClellan finally moved the Army of the Potomac out of Washington. The Federals transported their troops down the Chesapeake Bay to the coast of Virginia. The plan was to march up the peninsula from Yorktown to Richmond and attack the Confederate capital from the rear, while a smaller army guarded Washington against any attack from Confederate forces further west in the Shenandoah Valley. The Confederate forces on the peninsula numbered 16,000; the invading federal army, 112,000. Yet McClellan hesitated to attack, convinced that the Confederates actually outnumbered him.

The Confederates took advantage of McClellan's hesitancy to bring in reinforcements, and on May 31 they attacked the Army of the Potomac at Seven Pines. The Confederate commander, General Joseph E. Johnston, was wounded in the battle. President Davis appointed Lee to replace him in command of the forces Lee named "the Army of Northern Virginia." Good, said McClellan: Lee was "too cautious and weak. . . . Personally brave and energetic to a fault, he . . . is likely to be timid and irresolute in action." Nonetheless, McClellan asked Lincoln to send him more troops.

Meanwhile, out in the Shenandoah Valley, General Thomas "Stonewall" Jackson was tearing up three federal armies. Jackson had gained his nickname for steadfastness at First Manassas. A math instructor at the Virginia Military Institute, Jackson was a devout Presbyterian, convinced that the Confederate cause was the cause of God. His victories in the valley thrilled the Confederacy, and he became the first hero of the war. Lincoln refused McClellan reinforcements, keeping back troops to guard Washington against an assault from Stonewall's men.

Taking command in Virginia, Lee ordered Jackson's army to reinforce his troops blocking McClellan's path to Richmond. The combined Confederate forces then attacked. In the Battle of Seven Days (June 25– July 1) Lee drove the Army of the Potomac back down the Peninsula to Yorktown, where it was evacuated by the Union navy. Lee then turned the Army of Northern Virginia northwest and defeated Union forces in central Virginia at the second battle of Manassas. His way open, Lee pushed on into Maryland in the early fall, carrying the war for the first time into a state still in the Union.

Casualties, Kills, and Medicine

When historians say that both sides suffered thousands of casualties in a particular engagement, that does not necessarily mean that thousands died. The term "casualties" refers to the number of men killed, so seriously wounded as to be out of action, missing, or taken prisoner. (In effect, casualties are "out of the game.") Today, wounded soldiers have a good chance of survival, thanks to advances in battlefield medicine. During the Civil War, military science had created methods of injuring people faster than medicine had invented ways to patch them up. Civil War doctors did not yet understand germ theory, so they operated on wounded men with dirty instruments, bound them up with filthy rags, and then amputated limbs that became infected. To kill the pain, they dosed patients with morphine and sent them home addicted.

Wounded Civil War soldiers on both sides had slightly better chances of survival in hospitals staffed by women. Just as ignorant as the doctors about the causes of disease and infection, women had nonetheless been taught to keep things clean.

McClellan's Army of the Potomac pursued Lee's forces, and finally caught them at Antietam Creek near Sharpsburg, Maryland, on September 17. The ensuing battle resulted in 25,000 casualties and at least 5,000 dead. Neither side won a conclusive victory, and Lee slipped back to Virginia. Finally fed up with McClellan's perpetual "slows," Lincoln relieved him of duty in November.

The second summer of the Civil War ended in stalemate. In the West, Confederate armies moved up through eastern Tennessee to invade Kentucky in the spring and summer of 1862, only to withdraw back to Chattanooga by autumn. As the armies of the Union and Confederacy moved into winter quarters, however, Lincoln made a move that would transform first the war, and then the nation. The Union president had realized the truth of an argument made strenuously by abolitionists and African-American leaders in the North from the first day of the conflict: to end the war and save the Union, he would have to attack slavery, the basis of the rebels' economic system. Using the quasi-victory at Antietam as occasion, Lincoln issued the preliminary Emancipation Proclamation.

Emancipation and the War

Slaves grew the Confederate armies' food. Slave labor battalions, conscripted despite their masters' protests, dug fortifications for the Confederacy. Slaves worked in southern war industries and served the armies in many noncombatant auxiliary positions, from cook to teamster to nurse. Yet the fact that slaves worked for the Confederacy did not mean that they

During the Civil War thousands of slaves fled for freedom to the Union army. The Emancipation Proclamation gave them further encouragement. This illustration originally appeared in *Harper's Weekly* in February 1863. The original caption reads, "The effects of the Proclamation—freed Negroes coming into our lines at Newbern, North Carolina."

supported the Confederacy. To the contrary: long before whites on either side would admit it to themselves, enslaved and free blacks throughout the United States had grasped the war as a way to gain freedom for their race.

Black Confederates?

In recent years southern heritage advocates, in their continual effort to deny that slavery was the cause of the Civil War, have insisted that black southerners served in the

Confederate army. As proof, they have offered pictures of blacks in construction battalions. These men were slaves, conscripted as labor, and their service to the Confederate army is no evidence that they supported its cause.

Another source of the "black Confederate" mythology lies in the tendency of rich Confederate officers to bring their slave body servants with them to the army. These black men followed the rebel army throughout the war. Such loyalty attracted attention, since it was evidenced at a time when literally hundreds of thousands of slaves were running for freedom to the Union lines. However, we should not confuse personal loyalty to a man with political support for the Confederacy. (We should also remember that the officers in question usually owned the servants' entire families, surely a factor that helps explain the servants' behavior.)

Ironically, the neo-Confederates are correct in supposing that at least some people of color supported the Confederacy. In the Deep South, in Louisiana and along the Gulf Coast, free peoples of color often owned slaves. Moreover, colored Creole communities had long supported militia units. When Louisiana seceded, leaders of the New Orleans colored militia unit offered their services to the Confederacy and were turned down. The same happened to similar units elsewhere. In 1861 the Confederacy and the Union agreed on one thing: the coming conflict was to be a white man's war. By the time that the Union changed its mind in 1863, members of the Louisiana black militia had changed theirs as well. Many mustered in as soldiers for the Union, serving in the Louisiana Native Guards.

As Union armies marched into southern territory, slaves ran away from nearby plantations and (as southerners said bitterly) "deserted" to the Yankees. Whole families followed in the wake of Union armies. Along the Georgia and Carolina coast, slaves even sailed boats out to take refuge with the Union blockade. Nonplussed Union officers did not know what to do with these people. The rules of war required that Union officers respect the property of Confederate civilians, and slaves were property. Therefore, some Union officers sent runaways back. Other officers found this highly unsatisfactory, for both political and military reasons. As racially prejudiced as their southern cousins, Union officers were nonetheless moved by the intensity of the slaves' desire for freedom. "It is all humbug about Slaves liking to stay with their masters," one Union soldier concluded, while a Massachusetts lieutenant wrote, "I will never be instrumental in returning a slave to his master. . . . I'll die first." Other officers sheltered runaways for practical reasons: why strengthen the Confederacy by returning to it the means of making war? This was the stance of General Benjamin Butler, commanding federal troops on the Virginia coast, who in 1861 began to call runaway slaves "contrabands of war," items of property that could legitimately be liberated from Confederate use.

By the summer of 1862, tens of thousands of contrabands had joined the Union cause, working as they had for the Confederacy in non-combat auxiliary positions. As one Illinois soldier wrote from Mississippi in 1862, "every regt [regiment] has nigger teamsters and cooks which puts that many more men back in the ranks. . . . It will make a difference in the [regiment] of not less than 75 men that will carry guns that did not before we got niggers." The contrabands made it impossible for the Union to ignore the connections between the war and slavery.

Today, when every schoolchild thinks that the Union fought the Civil War to free the slaves, it is sometimes hard to grasp that in 1861 the Lincoln administration had no such intention. Northern white soldiers enlisted in the Union army to save the nation, not to liberate a race many of them considered hopelessly inferior and incapable of freedom. Determined to keep the war a white man's fight, Union authorities did not allow free northern blacks to join the Army. Even within the Republican Party, only a minority initially supported a war of liberation. Lincoln himself was not an abolitionist. He thought that slavery should be put on the path to extinction by confinement in the South, but he expected that it might take as long as a century to phase out the institution. Doubting that blacks and whites could live together as equals, Lincoln favored colonization of former slaves to Africa. As late as August 1862, Lincoln met with leaders of the free black community in the North to urge them to support such a plan; they indignantly refused.

Meanwhile, the contrabands continued to force the issue, making their way by the hundreds to the Union lines. By the end of 1862, approximately 100,000 former slaves had freed themselves. Black leaders in the North and their abolitionist allies urged Lincoln to put these people to good use: allow blacks to join the Union army, and "the sable arm" would save the union.

Gradually, Lincoln came to believe that emancipation was necessary for the Union war effort. In September 1862, he announced that at of January 1 all slaves in states still in rebellion would be "then, thenceforward, and forever free." As critics noted, the proclamation was worded in such a way as to exempt from emancipation the slaves in states loyal to the Union and those in territories then occupied by Union armies. Lincoln hoped to give border state slaveholders time to pass state bills gradually emancipating their human chattel, but he warned that no one should be oblivious to the signs of the times: a Union victory would bring an end to slavery in the United States. On January 1, 1863, Lincoln issued an official Emancipation Proclamation.

Emancipation was designed to hurt the Confederacy, and it succeeded. The proclamation authorized black enrollment in the Union army. Eventually about 180,000 African-American men did military service, and many more men and women worked for the federal armies as manual laborers. The proclamation also destabilized slavery. As word of the proclamation spread through the South, slaves awaiting Union victory became recalcitrant and hard to manage. The proclamation finally destroyed any serious Confederate hope of a British or French alliance. In the moral climate of nineteenth-century Europe, the Emancipation Proclamation made the United States the hero, and the Confederacy the villain, of an epic of liberation.

Soldiers of the Cross

During the Civil War the former slaves now in blue uniforms added a new verse to the old spiritual, "Climbing Jacob's Ladder," which describes the hard struggle to salvation: "Don't you think I make a soldier, Soldier of the Cross." Over 100,000 former slaves joined the Union army. Even more remarkably, almost every able-bodied man in the free black communities of the North enlisted. For African-Americans, the Civil War had become a battle for liberation, manhood, and citizenship.

The Confederacy denied that black Union troops were really soldiers and instead considered them to be similar to slaves in revolt. The Confederate government threatened to kill or enslave any captured blacks, but modified its policy when Lincoln promised to retaliate against captured southern soldiers in northern prisoner of war camps. When Confederate troops clashed with units containing black troops, they often fought more fiercely and sometimes refused to take prisoners, or killed black soldiers after their surrender. Some captured black troopers were sent back to their former masters, and others became, in effect, the slaves of the Confederate army, while still others who had been free before the war were treated much the same as white prisoners. However, the Confederate government refused to exchange black Union prisoners, prompting the federal government to halt the repatriation of Confederate prisoners. The result was serious and deadly overcrowding in POW camps on both sides by 1864.

High Tide of the Confederacy

In a series of battles from December 1862, to July 1863, Robert E. Lee proved himself to be anything but timid and indecisive. As a friend commented about Lee, "His name might be audacity." From Fredericksburg, in December 1862, to Chancellorsville in May, Lee outmaneuvered, outbluffed, and overawed a series of Union generals, winning battle after battle against great odds. He took dangerous risks, but all his gambles paid off. However, Lee's losses were high. At Chancellorsville, Lee's army suffered 13,000 casualties to the Union's 17,000. Stonewall Jackson, Lee's right-hand man, was one of the men killed at Chancellorsville. Unlike the Union, the Confederacy could not easily replace the fallen. Nonetheless, Lee's men well-nigh worshiped him for the victories he won. For his part, Lee came to believe that his army could do anything he asked of it.

In May 1863, Davis, Lee, and other Confederate leaders met to consider strategy for the coming summer campaign season. Always an aggressive commander, Lee proposed to invade the North, striking into Pennsylvania. Victories on northern soil would further demoralize "those people," as Lee called the enemy. If he could capture some northern city—perhaps Harrisburg, with its important railroad junctions, or Philadelphia—then surely the northern people would give up the war. The government approved his plan, and in June he marched the Army of Northern Virginia across the Mason-Dixon line into Pennsylvania.

Always low on supplies, the rebel army stocked up in the rich farmland of southern Pennsylvania, taking food and livestock from farms and liberating shoes and clothing from merchants in the towns. (They gave the Pennsylvanians receipts promising payment in Confederate money.) The Army of the Potomac, under the command of General George Meade, pursued them north. The two armies clashed at Gettysburg.

After two hard but inconclusive days of fighting, Lee decided on a dangerous gambit. He would send three divisions, or 13,000 men, into a frontal charge into the very center of Meade's line. At three o'clock on July 3, the third day of battle, the divisions, led by General George Pickett, began to advance across a long meadow, directly into the federal guns. The Federals watched quietly until the Confederates came into range, then opened up on them with artillery and rifle fire, mowing down soldiers like wheat in the open field. Only a few made it all the way to the federal guns, where they were killed or captured. The charge was broken. Half of the men who began it lay dead or wounded on the field; the survivors limped back to the Confederate lines. Lee rode out to meet them, calling to them, "It is all my fault," and asking for their help to rally the army.

At Gettysburg Lee's long string of gambler's luck ran out. Only General Meade's caution stood between the Army of Northern Virginia and total defeat. Lee and his generals expected Meade to follow up the debacle of Pickett's charge with an attack of their own. In such an attack, the Army of Northern Virginia could have been destroyed, and the war in the East brought to an end. However, Meade, like many Union generals before him, held back. Much to their own surprise, the Confederates were allowed to retreat to Virginia. The war continued, but the Army of Northern Virginia was broken. Lee lost one-third of his army at Gettysburg, and with those casualties also lost the ability to take the war to the enemy. From Gettysburg on, Lee would fight on the defensive.

Vicksburg to Chattanooga

High on bluffs 200 feet over the Mississippi, Vicksburg held the river for the Confederacy. The Union had failed to take it in 1862 and had sent General Ulysses S. Grant and his subordinate, William Tecumseh Sherman, to try again. In a series of battles, Grant coordinated his land forces with the river navy commanded by Admiral David Porter. The Union commanders assaulted Vicksburg; that failed. They tried to find a way around Vicksburg; that failed, too. During the winter of 1862–63 Grant fought a series of battles that forced the Confederate troops in the region to pull back into Vicksburg itself. He then attacked them there but was unable to break through Confederate defenses. Finally, in late May, Grant settled down for a siege. By July, the garrison and civilians at Vicksburg had been reduced to eating rats. The soldiers petitioned their commander: "If you can't feed us, you had better surrender." Vicksburg surrendered on July 4, one day after Lee's defeat at Gettysburg. The Confederacy had been cut in half. From 1863 on, the Confederate state governments and armies west of the Mississippi would fight their own war, unable to send support to the East.

In the late summer of 1863, Union forces in the West continued their victories, pushing into eastern Tennessee. There the fighting focused on Chattanooga, a small city in southeastern Tennessee. Chattanooga was a railway crossroads and the gateway to Georgia. By taking Chattanooga, the Union hoped to drive a wedge between the Confederate armies in the Deep South and Lee's forces in northern Virginia, splitting the Confederacy yet again. The Confederate commander at Chattanooga, General Braxton Bragg, allowed the Union armies under the command of General Rosecrans to flank his defenses. Realizing that he could not defend the city, Bragg evacuated Chattanooga on September 9, and the federal troops moved in. Bragg retreated to northern Georgia and the Confederate government pulled troops away from the Army of Northern Virginia to reinforce him. On September 20, this reinforced Confederate army dealt a severe defeat to Rosecrans's army at the Battle of Chickamauga; the federal general himself joined a panicked retreat to Chattanooga, and the Confederates laid siege to the city.

Chickamauga was the last significant Confederate victory of the war. Lincoln replaced Rosecrans with U.S. Grant, fresh from his summer victories in Mississippi. Grant opened up new supply lines that allowed the Union forces in Chattanooga to be reprovisioned and reinforced. In November, Grant's forces drove the Confederates out of their positions surrounding the city. With the fall of Chattanooga, the Union army had an open road to the Deep South, with only the remains of Bragg's army left to oppose them. For the Confederacy, even more ominous news followed. In March 1864, Lincoln appointed Grant general-in-chief of all the Union armies. While coordinating all Union military efforts, Grant would also assume command of the Army of the Potomac in the next spring campaigns.

The Confederate Home Front

By 1864 many southerners could not make up their minds whom they hated most, Abraham Lincoln or Jefferson Davis. To have any chance of winning the war militarily, the Confederate government had been forced to take actions that alienated a large portion of the southern white civilian population. The war heightened political and class divisions among the southern white population. Some historians argue that the Confederacy lost the war on the home front before it lost on the battlefield.

Southern Unionists

Deceived by postwar propaganda that glorified the "Lost Cause," many southerners today believe that the region was unified in defiance toward the federal government. In fact, many white people living in the Confederacy remained loyal to the United States. Some of the federal government's most famous military leaders, such as Admiral David Farragut and General George Thomas, were natives of the South, and thousands of southern white men, many of them from border states like Tennessee, fought with the Union army.

Throughout the region, prominent white men and women, many of them members of the defunct Whig Party, had opposed secession. When it came, they maintained low profiles and waited for the Union to deliver them from the rebels. When federal forces took Memphis in 1862, one man wrote, "I thank God and the union army that I am once more permitted to Express and write my feelings freely. . . . My prayers have at last been answered and now Treason gives way to Justice and truth."

Unionism was especially strong in the southern hill country, where the plantation economy and slavery had never completely taken hold. As noted earlier, western Virginia split off from the Old Dominion as a result of secession and was admitted to the Union as the new state of West

Virginia. East Tennessee opposed secession, remained loyal to the Union, and sent thousands of men to join the federal army. Unionists in east Tennessee and in other hill-country regions formed guerrilla bands to resist the Confederacy and to protect their communities from similar bands formed by rebel sympathizers. For years, Union and Confederate guerrilla forces fought each other in the southern hills. When federal troops moved into northern Alabama, they found Unionists hiding from Confederates in caves and hollow logs, living in indescribable suffering. One woman, visiting a federal army camp, asked to see the Union flag. A soldier recorded, "Some of our boys brought her a Flag—she took it and geathered it up in her hands and kissed it while the tears rolled down her cheeks." The bitterness provoked by guerrilla warfare lingered long after the war and gave rise to many postwar feuds.

Class and Gender on the Home Front

Although southern whites united to maintain racial privilege, class tensions remained just below the surface. While the southern elite had continually assured poor whites that all white men were equal, Confederate war mobilization proved the contrary. The burdens of war did not fall equally upon all southerners. To a large extent, class determined how a person experienced the war. This was true especially for women.

Plantation Ladies and the War   When a plantation owner went off to war, he did so voluntarily; Confederate conscription laws gave exemptions to men supervising slave labor forces of twenty or more. The planter could also rest assured that his family would not starve. The slaves would continue to do the farm work for which they had been originally purchased, replenishing plantation storehouses with grain, vegetables, and meat. Few planter families went hungry in the early years of the war. The richest families found the war an inconvenience that deprived them of luxuries, not of necessities. Mary Chesnut, wife of a prominent Confederate politician, kept a diary of the war years in Richmond that chronicles rounds of parties, balls, and social festivities. Although the sons of the southern elite rallied to the Confederacy, and willingly gave their lives for the cause, they did so without immediate risk to their families.

Women of the southern upper class varied in their response to the war. Plantation mistresses, trained to defer and submit to their husbands, found it hard to manage the workforce, who were less subservient to "Missus" than to "Master." Used to a privileged and protected status, some plantation women went through a kind of psychological crisis when that status was threatened. The resulting introspection led many to question the basic tenets of southern upper-class society, including the propositions that slavery was a positive good and that white men were superior to blacks and white women. For this small number of upper-class women, the Civil War proved to be a mentally liberating, if painful, experience.

Most elite southern women, however, rallied to the cause. In September 1863, Mary Jones, the elderly widow of a Presbyterian minister in coastal Georgia, wrote to her soldier son:

> Do not . . . suppose that my spirit quails beneath the dark clouds which appear to curtain our political horizon on almost every side. No. I believe we are contending for a just and righteous cause; and I would infinitely prefer that <u>we all</u> perish in its defense before we submit to the infamy and disgrace and utter ruin and misery involved in any connection whatever with the vilest and most degraded nation the face of the earth.

Wherever federal armies occupied Confederate territory, federal officers noted the defiance of southern women. Confident that Yankee officers would not retaliate against women, rebel girls denounced them on the streets, spat in their faces, and generally embodied the region's defiance. The ladies of New Orleans were especially outspoken. When Admiral Farragut and the commander of the army occupation forces, General Benjamin Butler, went walking through the town's narrow streets, a woman emptied her chamber pot onto the admiral's hat. After that, Butler proclaimed that any New Orleans woman who insulted a federal soldier would be considered a "woman of the town," or prostitute, and treated as such. Shocked, southern patriots denounced "Beast Butler"—but New Orleans ladies stopped harassing federal troops. However, Butler's action foretold an ominous turn in the conduct of the war. Defiant southern civilians convinced some officers, including most notably General William T. Sherman, that the war could not be won through conventional military encounters: it would be necessary to break the spirit of the civilians as well.

Plain Folk   When the Confederate authorities conscripted a common white farmer, they stripped his family of their essential means of support. Farm wives typically had no slaves to do heavy labor. Many women found it difficult, if not impossible, to do traditionally male chores and to carry on their normal heavy workload as well. While wealthy women wrote to husbands in service complaining about the difficulties of labor management, white women of the plain folk often wrote pathetic illiterate letters to their men describing families on the verge of starvation: "We haven't got nothing in the house to eat but a little bit o meal. . . . If you put off a-coming, twont be no use to come, for we'll all hands of us be out there in the garden in the grave yard."

Pushed to the economic edge by the removal of male labor, common folk faced further depredations at the hands of Confederate mobilization. To feed the army, the Confederate government in 1863 passed an impressment act that authorized Confederate authorities to seize food and supplies from civilians. Technically, army officers who seized a farmer's livestock and corn "paid" the farmer with a receipt; however, everyone knew by 1863 that Confederate money and receipts based upon it were so much wastepaper. Embittered farmers hid their supplies and often refused to put out crops at all. Southern common folk had supported secession to protect their liberties, but it was the Confederate government, not the Union, that took the food right out of their mouths. Resentment toward Davis's government grew. In September 1863, the women of Miller County, Georgia, wrote to the Confederate government:

> But little . . . of any sort to Rescue us and our children from a unanamus starveation. . . . An allwise god ho is . . . without Respect of persons and full of love and chairty that he will send down his fury and judgement in a very grate manar [on] all our leading men and those that are in power ef thare is no more favors shone tothose the mothers and wives and of those hwo in poverty has with patrootism stood the . . . Battles.

Some farm women left the countryside to take up jobs in Confederate war production factories, only to find that hunger had followed them to town. Even Richmond, the Confederate capital, suffered as the federal blockade, the occupation of much prime agricultural land by Union forces, and the difficulties of farming during wartime combined to reduce food supplies throughout the South. Prices soared, and poor people starved. In 1863 the working-class women of Richmond rioted for food. Shouting "Bread or Blood," they marched into the center of town before being dispersed by Jefferson Davis, who appealed to their patriotism and, that failing, threatened to have them shot. The Richmond riot was replicated in towns all over the South, to no avail.

Common folk noticed with resentment that the rich did not seem to be sharing their suffering. Some bided their time and took revenge with the help of the Yankees. A federal officer in Virginia reported that southern poor whites were "always willing to show where the rich ones have hidden their grain, fodder, horses &. Many of them tell me it is a great satisfaction to them to see us help ourselves from the rich stores of their neighbors." Others made class resentment the pretext for desertion: "I got tired of fighting for a lot of old Rich Planters. . . . Here I was fighting to save their negroes and property and them remaining at home, living in all the luxuries of li[f]e," said one deserter at Memphis.

Habits of Rebellion

Many years ago a historian of the Civil War commented that the Confederacy's tombstone should read, "Died of States' Rights." Having rebelled against the supposed tyranny of the federal government, the Confederate government faced severe criticism whenever it took measures threatening to infringe upon states' rights or individual property rights. Davis felt that such measures as conscription, impressment, the suspension of habeas corpus, and high taxes were all essential for the war effort. Many southern politicians disagreed, denouncing the Confederate president as incompetent at best and tyrannical at worst.

The Confederacy lacked a functioning political party system that would have allowed Davis or his enemies to mobilize support or channel dissent. Instead, Davis's supporters and his detractors formed small, squabbling groups as much concerned with their own ambitions and egos as with the fate of the Confederacy. Several of the most prominent fire-eaters, angered by Davis's refusal to accord them the power they thought they deserved, turned against Davis's government all the powers of invective they had previously used against the federal government. William L. Yancey accused Davis of violating the people's liberties. Louis Wigfall, senator from Texas, supported the Confederacy's most severe war measures, but despised Davis personally and denounced him in drunken speeches delivered in Richmond bars.

Some of the most significant opposition to Davis came from the Confederate state governments. Most of Georgia's political leadership, from Governor Brown to former senator Alexander Stevens, the vice president of the Confederacy, joined in criticism of Davis's conduct of the war. Brown thwarted conscription by placing thousands of his political supporters in draft-exempt offices. Brown and Governor Zebulon Vance of North Carolina both stockpiled supplies for their own militia troops, holding back uniforms, shoes, and guns at a time when Confederate soldiers in Virginia needed them.

Davis's own personality became a factor in his government's unpopularity. An able, honest, and intelligent man, Davis was also hypersensitive and unable to tolerate criticism. Sure of his own correctness, he rarely solicited advice from other politicians. Congressional delegations who visited him complained that while his manner was perfectly polite, he clearly did not take them or their suggestions seriously at all. Davis surrounded himself with men who would not challenge his leadership. His cabinet was a collection of mediocrities, with one major exception: Judah P. Benjamin, former senator from Louisiana, who became so essential to Davis that he made him in turn attorney general, secretary of war, and secretary of state. Benjamin managed to be good at his job without threatening the president, a feat also accomplished by Robert E. Lee. However, Davis resented other able men such as General P. G. T. Beauregard, while favoring incompetents like General Braxton Bragg for their loyalty.

Davis's faults as a leader aside, historians have wondered whether any politician could have satisfied the Confederate revolutionaries. Having spent most of their careers in opposition, few Confederate politicians had experience with building up rather than tearing down.

The Year of Jubilee

According to the Bible, the ancient Israelites were told by God to celebrate every fifty years the "Year of Jubilee," during which the leaders proclaimed liberty to the entire land and set free all the Israelite slaves. For American slaves, the Union army brought the Jubilee in its wake. With joy and with courage, black southerners took their new liberties into their hands and before the war ended had begun to work out the meaning of freedom.

For two generations before the Civil War white southerners justified slavery by arguing that emancipation would inevitably lead to a race war. They pointed to the Haitian revolution as their worst-case scenario and charged that abolitionists wanted to see the South drenched in the blood of white women and children. In the end, no such thing happened. White men went to war leaving their wives and children on isolated plantations, sometimes surrounded by hundreds of slaves. There is no instance in the historical record of any slaves rising up to take vengeance on the defenseless. Instead, black men behaved as *men,* by the standards of their own culture and that of southern whites: they joined the Union army. A generation after the war, *Atlanta Constitution* editor Henry Grady memorialized the black man who fought for freedom: "To his eternal credit let it be said that whenever he struck a blow for his own liberty, he fought in open battle." Instead of attacking their former masters, freedmen and women negotiated with whites a new way of living. It was not an easy transition for either side.

Freedpeople often tested their new liberties by the simple expedient of walking away from the old plantation. Many joined the Union army, while others worked for the Union cause in noncombatant positions. Many took to the roads to search for family members sold away previously. Some left just to prove that they could, drifting from place to place among the tide of refugees sweeping across the South by 1864. Others congregated around Union garrisons in southern cities, forming the nuclei of post-war urban black communities.

For some former slaves, freedom meant the ability to defy the master and get away with it. One southern girl recorded an encounter that must have been replicated all over the region. Her brother, recently returned from the army, gave an order to a former slave. When the man did not jump to obey, his former master hit him, only to have the ex-slave knock him down. The girl noted that her brother was very depressed these days. Many former masters shared similar, if less violent, awakenings. Some who had prided themselves on their kindness and paternalism toward the slaves were shocked to be repaid in "disloyalty." Slaves, it turned out, did not necessarily love their masters, even the "good" ones. Many who ran away to the Union army looted their plantation before leaving, while others who stayed appropriated to themselves items of the master's property as a kind of back pay.

Some freedmen anticipated that the Yankees would crown emancipation by confiscating the rebels' lands and giving them to the former slaves, whose unpaid work over the years had earned them title. Trained in agricultural labor, most freedmen had aspirations very similar to those of common white folks. With forty acres and a mule, they could be economically independent. In the last months of the war, many former slaves walked the old plantation with a proprietary eye, contemplating which part of the property might ultimately be theirs. As one Virginia freedman told his former mistress, "Der ain't goin' ter be no more Master and Mistress, Miss Emma. All is equal. I done hear it from de cotehouse steps. . . . All de land belongs to de Yankees now, and dey gwine to divide it out 'mong de colored people." When the division came, the man said, he would take the kitchen, since he helped build it. One former slave flustered his ex-master by offering to sell back to him the share of the plantation he expected to receive from the federal government. The freedmen's belief that they were about to receive land grants from the federal government was not based upon fantasy. In fact, several proposals to redistribute traitors' lands were considered by Congress during the Civil War, and the issue was by no means settled by the time the war ended.

Nor was the status of the former slaves themselves. Even after the Emancipation Proclamation and the enlistment of freedmen in the Union army, large numbers of northern voters continued to oppose emancipation and especially any steps to make blacks equal with whites politically and socially. "Peace Democrats" used racial slurs in campaigns against the Republicans in 1864, coining the term "miscegenation" to denote the kind of race mixing they opposed. As late as August 1863, Lincoln had to defend emancipation to Illinois Republicans, his former constituents and strongest supporters. Aware that many white northerners would cheerfully trade away blacks' liberty for peace, Lincoln made the passage of a constitutional amendment outlawing slavery in the United States part of his 1864 election campaign. Congress passed the Thirteenth Amendment in January 1865, and all but three Union states (New Jersey, Kentucky, and Delaware) ratified it. This amendment assured the freedom of African-Americans but did not give them citizenship or political rights.

The Long Road Down, 1864–1865

In the spring of 1864 Lincoln put Ulysses S. Grant in charge of the Union war effort. Grant worked out a coordinated plan for attacking the Confederacy and moved his headquarters to the field, taking command of the Army of the Potomac. Grant understood the brutal arithmetic of the Civil War: the Union had more men and more guns than the Confederacy. Previous federal generals, appalled by casualties, had lacked the will to use their greater resources. Grant would not make that mistake. Although his 1864 campaigns shocked the Union public and earned him the nickname "Butcher Grant," Grant ultimately marshaled the Union's resources and brought overwhelming force to bear on the Confederate armies. By 1865 he had destroyed the Confederate government's ability to make war.

Lee vs. Grant in Virginia

In May 1864, Grant began a campaign in Virginia designed to deny Lee the mobility he had used to such great effect in the previous two summers. Lee had to defend Richmond, through which came most of his army's supplies. By striking toward Richmond, Grant would draw Lee to battle and keep him tied down. From May 5 to June 3, the Union and Confederate armies clashed in three major battles, at the Wilderness near Chancellorsville, at Spotsylvania, and at Cold Harbor. At the Battle of the Wilderness, Lee and his men once again outfought the Union forces, inflicted high casualties, and slipped away. Previous Union generals had retreated after being similarly bloodied. This time, Grant ordered his troops to pursue Lee's army. The Federals chased Lee to Spotsylvania, where another battle occurred, equally inconclusive and with equally high casualties. Lee again slipped away and moved south, to be caught again by Grant at Cold Harbor. The following battle cost the Army of the Potomac 7,000 casualties, most lost in a hopeless frontal charge against entrenched Confederate lines. In mid-June the Army of Northern Virginia joined other Confederate troops behind the fortifications at Petersburg, a small city that guarded one of the approaches to Richmond. Repeated federal attacks failed to dislodge Lee, and Grant settled down to a siege that lasted until March of 1865.

By 1864, the Confederate army in Virginia could no longer take the war into the enemy's territory. Once known for quick and daring movements, Lee fell back upon entrenchment and forced the Union army to attack. The result was very high casualties for the Union: 64,000 from March to June. However, Lee had lost half of his remaining army in the spring campaigns, and by the end of the summer he was trapped in Petersburg.

At this point, the only thing the Confederacy had going for it was the North's war weariness, amplified by the enormous casualties suffered in Grant's spring campaign. With Lincoln running for reelection in November, the Army of Northern Virginia could only hope that a Republican defeat might bring a negotiated end to the war.

Total War

In the spring of 1864 William T. Sherman, in command of the Union's main western army just south of Chattanooga, began his march toward Atlanta. An important center of Confederate manufacturing and railroad transportation, Atlanta had become a symbol of Confederate resistance. Sherman hoped that capturing Atlanta would aid the Union cause psychologically as well as militarily. Joe Johnston's much smaller Army of Tennessee blocked Sherman's way. Always stronger on the defensive, Johnston fought a shrewd, slow retreat into the Georgia interior, making Sherman pay for each foot of ground all the way south to Atlanta. Although most military historians give Johnston high marks for making the best of what he had to fight with, his defensive tactics angered President Davis and much of the Confederate public. As they saw it, Johnston was letting Sherman penetrate deep into the heartland of the South. On July 16 Davis replaced Johnston with John Bell Hood, a commander noted for aggressiveness. Hood attacked Sherman's army at the edge of Atlanta but failed to drive the Yankees away. Sherman laid siege to Atlanta and finally in early September took the city, while Hood's army slipped away. This victory, coming as it did only shortly before the 1864 election, heartened the Republican Party and the Lincoln administration.

A conservative with deep doubts about the feasibility of racial equality, Sherman was an unlikely person to put into effect the Union's new policy of total war. Personally, the general liked southerners. He had served as commandant of a Louisiana military academy before the war and had enjoyed the experience. Yet by 1864 Sherman and other Union officers had come to the conclusion that the war would never end until the spirit of the southern people had been broken. To do that, the Union army proposed to make war on civilians. As Sherman said, "We cannot change the hearts of those people of the South, but we can make war so terrible . . . that generations would pass away before they would again appeal to it."

To convince Confederate civilians to stop the war, Sherman proposed a daring campaign. He would cut loose from his supply lines and take his army east across Georgia to Savannah on the coast, then north through the Carolinas and on up into Virginia. Lee would be trapped between two federal armies. However, the chief significance of the campaign was the march itself through undefended Confederate territory. Sherman proposed to take his men "through Georgia, smashing things to the sea" and to "make Georgia howl!" As he told Grant, this might not be war, but it was statesmanship. The march would demonstrate to the Confederates and the world that the Davis government was unable to defend the southern heartland. The Lincoln government gave its approval.

On November 15, Sherman's men torched everything of military value in Atlanta and marched east out of the burning city, singing "John Brown's Body." Sherman's March, as it came to be known, endures in southern memory to this day. Charged with "foraging" for food, crews of "bummers" scoured the Georgia countryside, carrying off anything edible. Since the purpose of the march was to demoralize civilians, officers let the men invade private homes, terrorize families, steal personal belongings, vandalize private property, and burn down anything they chose, from plantation houses to small towns. A sixty-mile-wide swath of destruction appeared in the wake of Sherman's army. While southern white women wept in the ruins of their burned-out homes, thousands of slaves followed in the wake of Sherman's troops, often suffering terribly in their attempt to keep up with the army.

Sherman reached Savannah at Christmas, then moved north into South Carolina. There his men poured vengeance upon the people of the first state to secede from the Union. On February 18 Charleston surrendered to the white colonel of a black regiment, whose troops then marched in triumph through the birthplace of secession, greeted with cheers by the black population of the city. Sherman's men burned, looted, and pillaged north through the state. They left Columbia, the state capital, in flames in mid-February and moved on into North Carolina, reaching Goldsboro by April 1865.

Meanwhile, Hood had attempted to distract Sherman by taking his Army of Tennessee north from Georgia into middle Tennessee. (Sherman scoffed, saying that if Hood would ride to the Ohio River, he would provide him rations.) There Hood's aggressive tendencies led to disaster. At the Battle of Franklin on November 30, he ordered a frontal charge against federal entrenchments with predictable results: 6,300 Confederate casualties, among them twelve generals. The federal forces at Franklin retreated to Nashville but on December 15 came out to attack Hood's army and to drive it back southward. Disgusted with Hood, soldiers deserted by the dozens and welcomed the return of Joe Johnston to command with a sad rewrite of the "Yellow Rose of Texas:"

And now I'm going southward, for my heart is full of woe;
I'm going back to Georgia to find my Uncle Joe.
You may talk about your Beauregard and sing of General Lee,
but the gallant Hood of Texas played hell in Tennessee.

Johnston took back an army less than one-third the size of the one he had turned over to Hood in July. He led the army north into the Carolinas to slow, as best he could, Sherman's march toward Virginia in April.

The Last Days

In September and October of 1864 things went exceptionally well for the Union. Sherman took Atlanta. General Philip Sheridan destroyed the Confederate forces guarding Virginia's breadbasket, the Shenandoah Valley, then proceeded to follow Grant's orders to strip the valley of anything of use to the Confederacy. Heartened and encouraged, northern voters returned Abraham Lincoln to the presidency, rejecting the Democrats, their peace plans, and their candidate, former general George McClellan. With Lincoln as commander in chief, there would be no negotiated peace settlement giving the Confederacy its independence.

The common Confederate soldier understood that the war was lost long before his leaders acknowledged defeat. Soldiers knew that they could not save the Confederacy, but if they went home they could, perhaps, rescue their families from starvation and preserve their own lives. All during the fall of 1864 the Confederate desertion rate grew, and it became a torrent in the early months of 1865. Lee wrote that his troops, "who have acted so nobly and borne so much," were deserting by the hundreds every night.

Backs to the wall, the Confederate leadership considered freeing the slaves and arming them to fight the Union. First broached by General Patrick Cleburne early in 1864, the concept of enlisting slaves gained the support of many Confederate politicians, journalists, and military men, including General Lee, who suggested that men who volunteered to fight for the Confederacy should be given their freedom. The proposal also drew heavy criticism from some southern politicians, who thought it dishonorable and impractical. Howell Cobb of Georgia, member of a prominent slaveholding family, protested that "if slaves will make good soldiers our whole theory of slavery is wrong."

Cobb's statement illustrated the connections between southern concepts of race and gender. Enslaved males had never been accorded the respect due to men but had instead been treated as, and even called, "boys." For southern white men, soldiering was a requisite of manhood. If slaves could be soldiers, that implied that they were men, and that upset not only the "theory of slavery" but the racial concepts underlying white supremacy as well. Despite planters' protests, in March 1865, the Confederate Congress passed a bill authorizing the enlistment of black soldiers, leaving the question of their status after service ambiguous.

By the time the Confederacy was willing to trade slavery for independence, it was too late. In January 1865, the last major port under Confederate control, Wilmington, North Carolina, fell to Union forces, thus cutting Lee's supply lines to Petersburg. Davis sent a delegation including Vice President Stephens to see if peace terms could be obtained. Stephens met with his old friend Lincoln on a Union ship at Hampton Roads, Virginia, but the negotiations came to a quick and, for the Confederacy, unsatisfactory conclusion. With Union forces closing in on the Confederacy on all fronts, Lincoln insisted that any peace settlement had to include terms for reunion of the states and emancipation. The Confederate leadership rejected these terms as the equivalent of surrender. From January to March the hopelessness of the Confederacy's situation became more and more obvious, especially to the common soldiers, who deserted in droves. By early April Davis and other Confederate leaders were talking about the nation's last hope, guerrilla warfare; failing that, they planned to die in the last ditch.

On April 2, Lee slipped out of Petersburg, hoping to join up with Johnston in North Carolina and fight one last desperate stand. The Confederate government blew up or burned everything in Richmond that might be of use to the Yankees and fled south. On April 3, Union soldiers marched into Richmond. Among them were black troopers, some of them runaways from Virginia. While whites hid behind closed doors, Richmond's slaves, now free men and women, cheered the black troops as returning heroes come to set their people free. On the following day Richmond blacks gave a liberator's welcome to Lincoln himself, who had come down to see the fallen city and to sit, for a moment, at Jefferson Davis's desk.

Grant pursued Lee's army through the countryside of central Virginia, inflicting severe casualties on that already greatly depleted force. When Union troops captured Lee's incoming rations and encircled his army at Appomattox Station, Lee knew he could not fight his way out. His army now numbered no more than 35,000 men, and Grant had 80,000. One of his officers urged him to take to the woods and fight on as the leader of a guerrilla band. Lee explained that guerrilla warfare would cause even more harm to the South: "We would bring on a state of affairs it would take the country years to recover from." On April 9 Lee surrendered to Grant at Appomattox. The Union general, moved by Confederate valor, made generous terms. In exchange for surrender, Grant allowed the Confederate troops to keep their horses to use in spring planting. Lee rode off through his cheering, weeping troops, head held high as tears rolled down his face. Grant ordered his celebrating troops to keep it quiet: gloating over a fallen enemy of this caliber seemed inappropriate. Then he sent rations over to feed the starving Confederate army.

In his second inaugural address, delivered in March 1865, Lincoln had put before the country his own view of the Civil War. In almost biblical prose, Lincoln had argued that slavery was a sin of which all Americans, North and South, were guilty, and for which all were paying in blood: "[I]f God wills that [the war] continue, until all the wealth piled by the bond-man's two hundred and fifty years of unrequited toil shall be sunk, and until every drop of blood drawn with the lash, shall be paid by another drawn with the sword . . . so still it must be said, 'the judgments of the Lord, are true and righteous altogether.'" Having collectively paid for the sin of slavery, Lincoln suggested, North and South could reunite and, "[w]ith malice toward none; with charity for all," rebuild the shattered nation. Lincoln had already made clear that his own terms for reuniting, or "reconstructing," the nation were quite liberal and flexible. On April 14, Good Friday, Lincoln was assassinated by a southern sympathizer, the actor John Wilkes Booth.

The last remaining Confederate commander in the east, Joe Johnston, surrendered to Sherman on April 18, and the remaining Confederate forces west of the Mississippi surrendered on May 26. Davis and members of his government made it all the way south to Georgia before being captured on May 10. While the pathetic remnants of the once proud Confederate army made their way back to their homes, the federal government imprisoned Davis; he remained in confinement for two years.

The Confederate soldiers came home to devastation. Throughout the Deep South, burned villages and plantation houses bore silent testimony to the passage of the Union armies, as did the mourning black clothing of southern civilians. Approximately 260,000 Confederate soldiers died in the war; one out of every three Confederate soldiers never came back home. No other American armies have ever suffered such high casualty rates. Nor have any other Americans ever suffered such a catastrophic defeat, losing not only a war but an entire way of life. Returning soldiers and civilians alike agreed: slavery was over, and with it the Old South. The New South would have to be created.

Defeated and embittered, Confederates remained defiant. In 1866 a new song became popular in the region:

> Oh, I'm a good old rebel, and that's just what I am
> For this Yankee nation I do not give a damn

I'm glad I fought against it, I only wish we'd won
And I'm not asking pardon for anything I done. . . .

. . .

I can't take up my musket and fight them now no more
But I ain't gonna love them, now that is certain sure
And I don't want no pardon for what I was and am
I won't be reconstructed, and I don't care a damn.

Suggestions for Further Reading and Viewing

STEPHEN V. ASH, *When the Yankees Came: Conflict and Chaos in the Occupied South, 1861–1865* (1995)

EDWARD AYERS ET AL., *The Valley of the Shadow: Two Communities in the American Civil War.* University of Virginia web site, http://jefferson.village .virginia.edu/vshadow2/

RICHARD E. BERINGER, HERMAN HATTAWAY, ARCHER JONES, AND WILLIAM N. STILL, JR., EDS, *Why the South Lost the Civil War* (1986)

GABOR S. BORITT, *Why the Confederacy Lost* (1992)

KEN BURNS, *The Civil War* (PBS Home Video, 1997)

CATHERINE CLINTON AND NINA SILBER, EDS., *Divided Houses: Gender and the Civil War* (1992)

E. MERTON COULTER, *The Confederate States of America, 1861–1865* (1950)

BURKE DAVIS, *The Long Surrender* (1985)

PAUL D. ESCOTT, *After Secession: Jefferson Davis and the Failure of Confederate Nationalism* (1978)

DREW GILPIN FAUST, *Mothers of Invention: Women of the Slaveholding South in the American Civil War* (1996)

SHELBY FOOTE, *The Civil War,* Vols I–III (1974)

DOUGLAS SOUTHALL FREEMAN, *Lee* (1934)

GARY GALLAGHER, *The Confederate War* (1997)

MARK GRIMSLEY, *The Hard Hand of War: Union Military Policy Toward Southern Civilians, 1861–1865* (1995)

ALAN T. NOLAN, *Lee Considered: General Robert E. Lee and Civil War History* (1991)

JAMES M. MCPHERSON, *The Battle Cry of Freedom: the Civil War Era* (1988)

————, *For Cause and Comrades: Why Men Fought in the Civil War* (1997)

ROBERT MANSON MYERS, ED., *The Children of Pride* (1984)

ROGER L. RANSOM, *Conflict and Compromise: The Political Economy of Slavery, Emancipation and the American Civil War* (1989)

EMORY THOMAS, *The Confederate Nation, 1861–1865* (1979)

————, *Robert E. Lee: A Biography* (1995)

UNITED STATES WAR DEPARTMENT, *The War of the Rebellion: A Compilation of the Official Records of the Union and Confederate Armies* (1880–1901)

WOODWARD, C. VANN, ED., *Mary Chesnut's Civil War* (1981)

5

Reconstruction, 1862–1877

The Civil War has become a hobby for many Americans. People enjoy reading about campaigns, visiting battlefields on summer vacations, and even dressing up as Civil War soldiers to reenact battles. For many people, the war is deeply romantic, an American epic. No one feels that way about Reconstruction, the period from 1862 to 1877 during which the shattered nation attempted to reunify and reconstruct itself. After the sweeping narrative and fascinating characters of the Civil War, Reconstruction is a historical letdown. Reconstruction is about politics, economics, and law, not items easy to dramatize in period costumes. Even worse, Reconstruction is not a story with a happy ending.

The major players in Reconstruction all wanted different things. Having lost the war, white southerners accepted defeat but wanted to come back into the Union without making serious changes in the South's social system. Black southerners, now free, wanted the accoutrements of true freedom under the American system: political and property rights. The federal government, then under the control of the victorious Republican Party, wanted the South to become more like its idealized vision of the North, a haven of free labor and entrepreneurial capitalism. These were not compatible goals. Understandably, then, Reconstruction was a time of intense political conflict in the South and in the national government. Reconstruction lasted three times as long as the Civil War itself. When the period came to an end, none of the major players had completely achieved their goals, and all had become disillusioned and tired of the entire process.

No period in American history has been the subject of more debate than Reconstruction. Even the people who participated in Reconstruction disagreed about what happened then. For generations after 1877, white southerners learned from their parents and grandparents that Reconstruction represented the wicked revenge of the victorious North upon the prostrate, defeated South. White southerners insisted that Reconstruction, not the Civil War, left a legacy of bitterness between North and South. Meanwhile, black southerners remembered Reconstruction as a brief, shining moment when true political, social, and economic opportunities seemed possible for them; after Reconstruction, that hope had to be deferred for a hundred years.

The Historiography of Reconstruction

History does not change: what happened in the past hap-pened. However, the way that historians interpret events often does change. Historians are influenced by the times in which they live, and they pick up on new ideas and concepts. Moreover, historians learn to use new techniques and technologies of research, thus changing the way they see the past. The way historians wrote about Reconstruction in 1920 is not the way they write about it today. The study of the evolution of historical writing is called *historiography*. Students working on doctorates in history spend at least as much time studying historiography as history, and sometimes more.

No field in American history offers a more dramatic historiography than that of Reconstruction, or one more revealing of American regional and racial attitudes. In the late nineteenth and early twentieth centuries, Columbia University professor William Dunning and his students created a "school" of history that condemned Reconstruction as harsh, punitive, and a tragic error. This interpretation held sway for fifty years and became part of American popular culture: it is the version of history found in films like *Gone with the Wind,* for example.

The members of the Dunning school wrote as they did in part because they accepted without much question concepts about race held by most educated white Americans of the time. They assumed that blacks really were inferior, incapable of governing themselves, and they pictured black politicians as the pitiful dupes of carpetbaggers and scalawags. Understandably, the first challenges to the Dunning school came from black historians, led by W. E. B. DuBois, who in 1935 published *Black Reconstruction in America, 1860–1880.* However, the racial climate in the nation as a whole meant that DuBois and his followers did not receive much of a hearing.

In the 1950s, as the Civil Rights Movement heated up, the idea that blacks did not deserve citizenship rights seemed less and less defensible. Historians began to look again at Reconstruction. They produced a series of works that now comprise the revisionist school of Reconstruction historiography. The revisionists insisted that Reconstruction had produced much that was good in southern life, including the region's first public school systems. They pointed out that corruption in the South was no worse than elsewhere in the nation at the time. They rehabilitated the reputations of carpetbagger leaders, noting that many were motivated by principle, not profit. They showed how whites had terrorized politically active blacks. Most of all, revisionists showed blacks as political actors in their own right, not puppets.

Since the 1970s, a new postrevisionist school of Reconstruction historiography has developed. Taking for granted the right of black people to participate in politics, this new school instead focuses more on the Republican

Party's mistakes during Reconstruction, both nationally and in the South.

Historians continue to debate the meaning of Reconstruction's modest successes and great failures, aware that within Reconstruction history lie the roots of the nation's current racial problems. Did the federal government fail at Reconstruction because it tried too hard to transform the South's social system? Conversely, did Reconstruction fail because the federal government lost its nerve and gave up on reforming the South? Did Reconstruction go too far, or not far enough?

If we see the Civil War and Reconstruction period as one long struggle from secession to reunification, then who won? Did white southerners lose the war but win the peace?

Reconstruction as National Policy

Reconstruction tied together in one tangled knot a number of difficult questions. First, the constitutional issues: Were the Confederate states really out of the Union, and if so, how could they be brought back in? Were white southerners citizens of the United States with constitutional rights that had to be respected, or were they defeated enemies with no rights that victors had to respect? Then, the racial issues: Under the Thirteenth Amendment, blacks had been permanently set free, but did freedom mean equality? What was the status of the freedpeople to be? Would black men be given the rights of white male citizens, including the right to vote, or would they be relegated to partial citizenship, like white women? Finally, the social and economic issues: Did the end of slavery mean that black southerners and whites would meet as social equals? Would black and white children attend the same schools? Would black men and women be paid wages for the labor they had hitherto done as slaves? Or would the planters' lands be confiscated and given to their former slaves?

Although most of these questions would be settled in the South, all of them had great relevance to the nation as a whole. Most important of all were the issues revolving around the postwar racial settlement. By making decisions about race in the South, the federal government effectively created a national racial policy that remained in effect until the 1960s.

Reconstruction during the War

In a very real sense Reconstruction began as soon as Union armies occupied southern states. By 1862 Louisiana and large parts of the Upper South were under federal control. Lincoln appointed military governors for those states. Then in 1863 Lincoln announced his own plans for postwar Reconstruction in his Proclamation of Amnesty and Reconstruction. Any Confederate supporter who swore future loyalty and promised to accept abolition would be pardoned of his treason. (Lincoln exempted top-ranked Confederate military and political leaders from the offer.) When 10 percent of the men who had voted in 1860 took the loyalty oath, they could then proceed to form a new state government. Lincoln required that the state governments formed under this plan write into their new state constitutions provisions abolishing slavery.

Significantly, Lincoln did not demand that the newly reconstructed states give freedmen any sort of political power. When representatives of Louisiana's sizable population of free people of color petitioned the president for the right to vote, Lincoln suggested to the governor of Louisiana that it might be appropriate to let African-American property owners and/or Union veterans participate in the upcoming state constitutional convention. As mild as this suggestion was, it was ignored; the new state governments formed under Lincoln's plan were for white men only. Indeed, many southern Unionists expressed with equal vehemence hatred for the "aristocrats" who had led the South into war and disdain for the former slaves.

Lincoln's 1863 Reconstruction plans should be seen as a part of his overall strategy for Union victory. His extreme leniency was designed to encourage southerners to give up the fight and rejoin the Union; he asked only that they agree to give up slavery. His plans also reflected his own interpretation of the Constitution. From the start of the war, Lincoln had denied that the Confederate states were, or even could be, out of the Union. If southerners were not out of the Union, then they had the same rights as all American citizens and could not be treated as conquered enemies. Finally, Lincoln's plan was based upon his acute understanding of American party politics. Himself a former Whig, Lincoln had friends and political acquaintances in the South, and he knew that many of them only half-heartedly supported the Confederacy. Through leniency, Lincoln hoped to encourage these men to support the Union, and, not coincidentally, the Republican Party.

In 1864, concerned that Lincoln's plan did too little to protect the former slaves, Congress passed the Wade-Davis Bill. This legislation would have required that a majority of the state's white males swear a loyalty oath to the Union before readmittance. In addition, the Wade-Davis Bill restricted voting for the new state constitutional conventions to men who could take an "Ironclad Oath" that they had never supported the Confederacy. Finally, the bill promised blacks equality under the law but not the right to vote. Lincoln refused to sign the bill, so it never became law. This angered some members of Congress, including the authors of the bill, who accused Lincoln of trying to dominate the Reconstruction process. Congress refused to seat the representatives of Lincoln's reconstructed southern governments, thus effectively keeping them out of the Union.

The controversy over the Wade-Davis Bill highlighted conflicts between Lincoln and some members of his own party over Reconstruction policy. While Lincoln favored reconciliation, some Republicans in Congress advocated punishment. Of that faction, the most outspoken was Pennsylvania Congressman Thaddeus Stevens, who argued that defeated and occupied areas of the South were "conquered territories," and that southerners were defeated enemies to whom the Constitution no longer applied. Congressmen who took this position argued that Reconstruction should do more than bring the southern states back into the Union. Instead, the victorious Union should sweep away the racial, social, and economic systems of the Old South and replace them with new institutions modeled on those of the North.

Like Lincoln, most Republican congressmen were not willing to go that far. Instead, they agreed with Massachusetts Senator Charles Sumner that the Confederate states had committed "state suicide" in seceding. Having destroyed their legitimate state governments, Sumner said, the Confederate states had reverted to territorial status and would have to be readmitted to the Union. According to the Constitution, the federal government could admit only those states with properly republican governments. Sumner and other Republicans took that to mean that the federal government had the right to reform southern state governments before readmitting the states to the Union. In 1864, this meant that all the readmitted states would have to agree to abolish slavery.

The Freedmen's Bureau

In March 1865, Congress passed and Lincoln signed the first major Reconstruction legislation, an act authorizing the creation of the Bureau of Refugees, Freedmen, and Abandoned Lands. The Freedmen's Bureau, as it was commonly called, was a new thing in American history, an agency whose functions included emergency relief management, welfare, and mediation. Between 1865 and 1870, bureau workers distributed approximately 22 million meals and provided shelter for thousands of refugees, many of them white. The bureau also acted as a welfare agency. To help the 4 million former slaves adjust to liberty, the Freedmen's Bureau ran schools. Having been denied literacy during slavery, freedmen, women and children flocked to these schools, often cosponsored by northern religious or philanthropic organizations. In addition, the bureau urged freedmen and their former masters to work out labor contracts and arbitrated conflicts between landowners and workers.

The bureau was also charged with settling former slaves on "abandoned" lands. Some members of Congress wanted to confiscate the lands of Confederate leaders and redistribute them to the former slaves. Although the Lincoln administration and Congress as a whole were not willing to go that far, the bureau and the army did sponsor some land redistribution, making it possible for a few former slaves to gain title to lands confiscated for back taxes. In addition, Sherman, encumbered by thousands of contrabands following his march through Georgia, had settled them on plots of land along the coast, with a promise to clear up the titles later. These resettlement efforts, taking place as they did in the last days of the war, convinced many freedmen that the federal government was going to give each family "forty acres and a mule," the requisites for self-sufficiency.

Reconstruction policy had not been finalized by the time of Lincoln's death in April 1865. Some historians, noting Lincoln's personal tendencies toward compassion and leniency, have suggested that Reconstruction history would have taken a very different course had Lincoln lived.

Richmond ladies going to receive government rations. The Freedman's Bureau fed thousands of refugees, regardless of color or politics. This drawing, which appeared in 1865 in *Harper's Weekly,* captures the disdain of upper-class Confederate women for the occupying Union army. The original caption reads, "Don't you think that Yankee must feel like shrinking into his boots before such high-toned Southern ladies as we!" Library of Congress.

Others have scoffed at this, pointing out that Lincoln's kindly nature had not prevented him from authorizing total war against Confederate civilians, or, indeed, from presiding over the bloodiest war in American history. These historians believe that Lincoln would have exhibited in Reconstruction the same characteristics he did as war leader: tough-mindedness, flexibility, and a shrewd sense of the politically feasible. Whether Lincoln's leadership would have made Reconstruction easier, or harder, for freed-people and for defeated white southerners is a question that can never be answered. What is certain is that Lincoln had much better political skills than his successor.

Johnson, Congress, and Reconstruction

Andrew Johnson was a southern Democrat, a Jacksonian from upper east Tennessee. Like Lincoln, Johnson had been a poor boy, raised without advantages or education in the backwoods. A small-town tailor before he became a professional politician, by the late 1850s Johnson had risen to the U.S. Senate, where he defended slavery, states' rights, and Jacksonian Democracy, southern style. True to the heritage of Old Hickory, in 1861 Johnson denounced secession as treason and refused to follow Tennessee out of the Union. When Tennessee fell to Union occupation, Lincoln appointed Johnson military governor. Running for reelection in 1864, Lincoln wanted his campaign to represent national unity. As a southerner and a Democrat loyal to the Union, Johnson made an attractive running mate. He also appealed to radical Republicans, who liked his disdain for the planter aristocracy and his repeated statement, "treason must be made odious and traitors punished." Radicals overlooked another facet of Johnson's politics. Like many southern Unionists, Johnson hated the region's slaveholding elite, but he also hated the slaves. Firmly committed to white supremacy, Johnson was determined to keep the South a white man's country.

Johnson became president in April 1865, upon Lincoln's assassination. Congress was then out of session and would not reconvene until December, leaving Johnson in sole control of Reconstruction policy. Following Lincoln's plan, Johnson promised amnesty to southerners who would take loyalty oaths. (He exempted high Confederate officials and persons owning property worth more than $20,000. These members of the Confederate elite would have to apply directly to the president for a pardon. As it turned out, Johnson handed out pardons like candy to almost anyone who asked.) Johnson urged the former Confederate states to hold conventions to draw up new state constitutions, which he insisted must include provisions to abolish slavery, nullify secession, and repudiate the Confederate debt. Like Lincoln, Johnson suggested that the new state constitutions might include provisions allowing black male property owners to vote.

The Republicans and Black Suffrage

Republican Party leaders realized that their victory in the war had actually injured the party itself. Under the Constitution, each southern slave had been counted as three-fifths of a person for representation in the House. With the end of slavery, former slaves would be counted the same as whites, and the South would gain a dozen new congressional seats. Republican leaders expected that most of those seats would be filled by Democrats, since few white southerners would vote for members of the party of Lincoln. However, Republicans had reason to believe that former slaves would.

Giving black men the right to vote was a radical move in 1865. Only a few years previously the Supreme Court, in the *Dred Scott* decision, had ruled that blacks were not citizens. Moreover, most northern states did not allow blacks the right to vote. To give African-Americans suffrage in Mississippi without doing so in Minnesota would be a difficult trick to pull off. In the fall of 1865 Republicans took the issue of black suffrage to three northern states, Connecticut, Minnesota, and Wisconsin. In all three cases, voters rejected proposals to let black men vote. Republican leaders realized that they lacked support for African-American suffrage and put aside the issue for the time being.

Good Old Rebels

During the summer and fall of 1865 former Confederates took oaths of new loyalty, created new state constitutions and state governments, and elected representatives to send to the U.S. Congress in December. In doing so, southerners signaled that their version of the meaning of the Civil War differed in significant ways from that of the Republican Party and of many northerners. Defeated but not humbled, southerners did not consider their losses a negative verdict against their entire society. Instead, they clung to their traditional beliefs in white supremacy, states' rights, and the personal liberty of white men. They expected the Reconstructed South to be very much like the Old South, but without slavery.

Southerners accepted the demise of slavery. Indeed, anyone who reads southern letters and diaries from the period will be struck by how often people—particularly women—express relief at being delivered from the burden of slavery and the care and maintenance of slaves. However, planters still needed to control black labor, and southerners of all classes continued to support white supremacy. In 1865, many southern states enacted Black Codes designed to codify the status of all blacks as less than full citizens. In some states, blacks were forbidden to buy property in towns; in others, forbidden to work at anything but agricultural labor. Most of the states' Black Codes restricted gun ownership for blacks. Even more ominously, some states provided that blacks without jobs would be arrested as vagrants. Their labor would then be sold at auction. Black children could be taken from their parents and "apprenticed" to whites, who would keep them as workers until adulthood. The Black Codes indicated that white southerners still thought they had a right to control black lives and labor; as one Freedmen's Bureau official commented, white southerners had a hard time understanding that abolition meant blacks were free just like they were.

None of the southern states took Johnson up on his suggestion to give the vote to blacks with property. Instead, through the Black Codes, the states reduced antebellum free blacks, often educated property owners, to the same status as illiterate former slaves. Moreover, southern whites enforced white supremacy with violence, attacking blacks who acted "uppity"—that is, like free men and women.

When they formed new governments, southerners indicated that military defeat had destroyed neither their belief in the right to secession nor their loyalty to the men who had led the secession movement. Some southern constitutional conventions refused to nullify secession, an action acknowledging its illegality. Instead, these states repealed secession. Other states refused to repudiate the Confederate debt, again signifying a belief that the Confederacy had been a legitimate government. Mississippi and Texas did not ratify the Thirteenth Amendment, which abolished slavery forever in the United States. When new governments were formed in the summer of 1865, they looked very much like the old Confederate state governments, with a lot of ex-Confederate soldiers added. Southern Unionists complained to their Republican supporters in the North that the rebels were back in power and were taking revenge on men who had been loyal to the Union.

When Congress reconvened in December 1865, the composition of the southern delegations enraged northern politicians. The southern states sent to Congress nine Confederate congressmen, seven Confederate state officials, four Confederate generals, four Confederate colonels, and the former vice president of the Confederacy. To expect northern politicians to accept as colleagues men who had only a few months previously been shooting at their sons and brothers was politically naive at best. Congress exercised its right to rule on the qualifications of its own members and refused to seat the southern delegations.

Johnson vs. Congress

The new Congress immediately formed a Joint Committee on Reconstruction. Led by moderate Republicans, the joint committee at first had no plans for radical Reconstruction of the South. Instead, Republican moderates wanted to protect the freedmen. The chair of the committee proposed to Congress an extension of the Freedmen's Bureau and a civil rights bill that would have protected blacks from infringements on their liberties such as those enacted in the Black Codes. At this point, moderate Republicans seem to have envisioned a status for blacks, male and female, equivalent to that of white women. In most northern states, laws protected white women's rights to own property and to be secure from attack, but women were not allowed to vote and could be denied access to educational facilities and to employment on the basis of sex. Moderate Republicans wanted to stop southerners from reenslaving blacks but did not yet support full equality for former slaves. They had every reason to think that President Johnson agreed with their position.

Instead, Johnson vetoed the Freedmen's Bureau extension and the civil rights bill. The president said that the bureau was providing blacks with economic support that had never been given to whites. Johnson suggested that welfare would destroy the characters of the former slaves and make them dependent on the federal government. In addition, Johnson charged that the bureau was too expensive and too intrusive into the affairs of the southern states. As for the civil rights bill, Johnson said that it was a "stride toward centralization, and the concentration of all legislative powers in the national Government." Besides, Johnson said, by protecting black rights the bill discriminated against whites.

With these two vetoes, Johnson lost the support of moderate Republicans and pushed the entire Republican Party closer to radicalism. Congress passed both bills over the president's veto and set out to remove Reconstruction policy from the hands of the man one historian referred to as the "last Jacksonian Democrat."

The Fourteenth Amendment

In June 1866, Congress passed the Fourteenth Amendment, the keystone of the joint committee's Reconstruction policy. By defining as citizens all those born in the United States, the amendment overturned the *Dred Scott* decision and gave citizenship to the former slaves. It also required that states respect the rights of all U.S. citizens, thus making racially specific legislation like the Black Codes illegal. The amendment dealt with the issue of black suffrage by saying that states that refused to let citizens vote could not count those citizens for apportionment purposes. This would mean that southern states who restricted suffrage would lose representations, while northern states would not, since the black population in most northern states was minuscule. The Fourteenth Amendment disqualified from voting men who, as members of prewar state or federal governments, had violated their oaths to support the Constitution by joining the Confederacy. However, this disfranchisement could be removed by action of Congress. Finally, the amendment guaranteed the national debt and repudiated the Confederate debt. Of the Confederate states, only Tennessee ratified this amendment, and it was readmitted to the Union in 1866.

The congressional elections in the fall of 1866 became a northern referendum on Reconstruction. The Republicans presented the Fourteenth Amendment as necessary to save the peace for which so many northern soldiers had given their lives. Without it, the former Confederates would regain control of the South and the lives of the freedmen would be endangered. The latter argument was strengthened in May 1866, when a white mob in Memphis, including many members of the city police force, attacked a black neighborhood and killed forty-six people. In July a white mob assault on an African-American political meeting in New Orleans re-

HARPER'S WEEKLY

JOURNAL OF CIVILIZATION

VOL. X.—No. 491.]   NEW YORK, SATURDAY, MAY 26, 1866.   [SINGLE COPIES TEN CENTS.
[$4.00 PER YEAR IN ADVANCE.

Entered according to Act of Congress, in the Year 1866, by Harper & Brothers, in the Clerk's Office of the District Court for the Southern District of New York.

THE MEMPHIS RIOTS.

THERE was in Memphis, on the first two days of May, an excitement unequaled since the close of the war. The origin of the disturbance between the whites and negroes of that city was highly discreditable to the colored soldiers, and the riotous proceedings which followed were a disgrace to civilization. For the riot the lower class of white citizens were as responsible as were the soldiers of the Third United States Colored Infantry for the original difficulty. This regiment, whose reputation has been a bad one, had been mustered out, since which they had frequented whisky-shops in the southern part of the city, and had been guilty of excesses and disorderly conduct. On the evening of May 1 some drunken members of the regiment were on South Street, talking noisily, when in an insolent manner they were ordered by two policemen to cease their noise and disperse. Words ensued, followed by blows, throwing of missiles, and firing of revolvers.

To understand what followed it must be remembered that the police force of Memphis is composed mostly of Irishmen, whose violent prejudice against negroes was so shamefully displayed in the New York riots of 1863. The *Times* correspondent thus described the riot:

Word was sent to police head-quarters, and the whole force at once proceeded to the scene of the fray, being joined on this way thither by armed and excited citizens. Meanwhile the firing had brought other negroes to the spot, some armed with clubs and some with revolvers, so that by the time the police force came up the two parties were about equal in number. The negroes held the original

position, and, upon the approach of the police, showing no determination to abandon it, were fired upon by the police and citizens who accompanied them. This fire was returned, and for a while both parties busied themselves in discharging their revolvers as rapidly as possible. Meanwhile word was sent to General STONEMAN, who promptly dispatched to the scene of action a company of Regulars (white), when the negroes were quickly dispersed and driven in every direction.

During the evening the wildest and most exaggerated reports soon spread throughout the city. Every communicator of the intelligence of the fight told a different story, and the highest excitement prevailed. Each rumor placed a worse aspect upon the affair than the preceding one, and only served to develop the pent-up prejudice against the negro. Soon after dark this excitement and prejudice found vent. Large numbers of armed citizens repaired to the scene of the fight and commenced firing upon every negro who made himself visible. One negro upon South Street, a quiet, inoffensive laborer, was shot down almost in front of his own cabin, and after life was extinct his body was fired into, cut and beat in a most horrible manner. In all parts of the city, wherever they could be seen, negroes were fired upon by policemen as well as citizens. They were shot while driving hacks, and quietly walking in the streets about their business. The police seemed to make it their special business to shoot every negro they could see, no matter where he was or what he was doing. The result was that by 9 o'clock the colored population were in-doors trembling with alarm. How many negroes were killed during the night it is impossible to ascertain, as firing was constantly heard during the earlier hours in all parts of the city. It is estimated that from 15 to 20 were killed. So far as I have been able to learn, not a white man was fired upon by a negro during the whole night.

After the fight of Tuesday evening the negro soldiers and most of the colored population residing in the vicinity of the fight fled to the fort for security. They were perfectly quiet—in fact, were terribly frightened for their own safety. At an early hour yesterday morning every thing

SCENES IN MEMPHIS, TENNESSEE, DURING THE RIOT—BURNING A FREEDMEN'S SCHOOL-HOUSE.

[SKETCHED BY A. R. W.]

Republicans in Congress were stirred to action in May 1866 by news of white attacks on blacks in Memphis. Shown above is the front page of *Harper's Weekly,* giving details of the Memphis riots. Library of Congress.

sulted in the death of thirty-seven blacks and three white Unionists. Faced with southern defiance and violence, northern voters agreed with the Republicans. Although Johnson campaigned vigorously against Republican candidates for Congress, the party of Lincoln won a two-thirds majority in both houses of Congress.

This was the majority necessary to pass legislation over a presidential veto, or to impeach a president, as Johnson found out when he impeded Republican Reconstruction plans. Impeached by the House of Representatives, he was acquitted after a Senate trial in 1868, and he retired at the end of his term to Tennessee, where he went back into politics and was reelected to the Senate.

In 1868 Ulysses S. Grant won the presidency for the Republicans; he was reelected in 1872. A soldier without much talent for politics, Grant followed the congressional Republicans' lead on Reconstruction policy.

Congressional Reconstruction

Now firmly in control, Republicans in Congress passed the Reconstruction Act of 1867, putting the South back under military occupation. In each of five military districts, officers were charged with supervising the Reconstruction process. The Reconstruction Act required that each of the Confederate states allow all adult males to vote for delegates to constitutional conventions, which were then required to draw up new constitutions giving adult males, regardless of race, the right to vote. The states also had to ratify the Fourteenth Amendment. Men disqualified from voting by the Fourteenth Amendment could not participate in these elections. Having complied with these requirements, southern states' representatives would be admitted to Congress. To supplement this plan, the Second Reconstruction Act, passed a few weeks later, required that the generals in command in the South register eligible voters and get the Reconstruction process under way.

By 1869 Republicans realized that even military occupation was not enough to ensure black suffrage. Therefore, Congress passed the Fifteenth Amendment, giving black men the right to vote, and added this new amendment to the list of items southern states would have to sign off on before readmission to the Union.

Reconstruction in the South

Congressional Reconstruction lingered long in southern memories, where it was generally termed "Radical Reconstruction." A popular historian, writing in the early twentieth century, insisted that between 1867 and 1877 southern whites had been "literally put to the torture" by white Yankees who incited normally docile blacks to rebellion and to lust after white women. Modern historians have been unable to find any evidence of torture, or indeed of any atrocities enacted upon white southerners at the orders of the federal government. By the standards of the twentieth century, the postwar punishment meted out to the South was mild indeed. Rebel leaders were allowed to go home. Their lands were not confiscated. By 1867 many high-ranking Confederate officers had become successful businessmen. Lee himself took a position as president of Washington College.

The federal government did single out Jefferson Davis for punishment, keeping him confined in prison for two years. In addition, the commandant of the horrific Confederate prisoner-of-war camp at Andersonville, Georgia, was hanged for war crimes, the sole such execution in the Civil War-Reconstruction period. Compared wth what victorious nations usually do to defiant rebels, the South got off easy.

Why, then, the long memory of Reconstruction as a period of degradation, humiliation, and "torture"? Recent historians have suggested that the real issue of Reconstruction was race. With the support of the federal government, blacks who had been slaves two years previously registered, voted, and held public office. Conversely, whites who had been the region's traditional leaders were disfranchised. To the restrictions on voting contained in the Fourteenth Amendment and the Reconstruction Acts, Congress later added more legislation allowing local voting registers to determine whether a person's participation in the rebellion disqualified him from voting. As a result, about 10 to 15 percent of the white electorate lost the right to vote. These restrictions did not last long; all had been removed before 1877. Yet in five Deep South states, white disfranchisement created black voting majorities. When white southerners boycotted elections, as they did periodically throughout the Reconstruction period, blacks also gained political power. With as much as 30 percent of the white electorate staying home, black votes could swing elections.

For southerners committed to white supremacy, a system allowing freedmen to vote while disqualifying whites was unnatural; blacks holding political power instead of whites, unthinkable. In a culture where voting was an attribute of manhood, Reconstruction voting restrictions stripped masculinity from whites and bestowed it on blacks: for a brief time, the freedman was "the man."

Southern whites' legends describe the freedman politician of Reconstruction as an illiterate former slave right out of the cotton fields. Although some leaders did emerge from the agricultural labor force, most prominent black politicians during Reconstruction were literate, educated men. Many had been free before the war and owned businesses or plantations. Some had been runaway slaves. Many were the mulatto sons of plantation owners. Still others were natives of the North, come south to pick up on opportunities for black men not available in the northern states.

Former slaves learned about politics through "Union Leagues," political clubs formed to promote Republicanism in the South. There, teachers, preachers, and skilled craftsmen often took the lead in educating freedmen. Although southern whites scornfully asked how illiterate former slaves could possibly understand politics, observers noted that the freedmen clearly grasped their own political situation: they were poor and powerless and needed economic opportunity and political rights. For that matter, southern politicians had long expected illiterate whites to participate in politics, and no restrictions had ever prohibited them from voting.

Former Confederates also detested Reconstruction because it brought to power poor whites and men from the North. Many of the southern common folk had exhibited limited support for the Confederacy, and as noted earlier, the mountain districts of the South had been bastions of Unionism. At the end of the war, with their old political adversaries from the plantation districts disfranchised, men from the hill-country districts emerged as political leaders, joining the newly organized southern branch of the Republican Party. So did former southern Whigs. Unreconstructed Confederates called southern-born Republicans "scalawags," a term usually denoting poorly bred, runty cattle. For many members of the traditional southern elites, common folk, like blacks, were inferior beings incapable of political leadership.

Yet old rebels saved their most biting contempt for those northern-born newcomers to the South who went into politics: the carpetbag-gers. In the 1860s, a carpetbag was the cheapest form of luggage. The term "carpetbagger" implied that the northern-born politician was a poor man who had come south to get rich, like a vulture battening upon the fallen South. In fact, many northerners had come to the South after the war to start businesses or to plant cotton; some worked as Freedmen's Bureau of-ficials, while others were Union army veterans who simply liked the climate and the people of the South.

With the support of the federal government and the backing of federal troops, coalitions of blacks, southern whites, and northern new-comers formed local and state Republican Party units in 1867 and pro-ceeded to follow Congress's plan for Reconstruction. By the winter of 1867–68, Republican-dominated state conventions began to draw up new state constitutions. These constitutions were more liberal than many in the North. Most mandated universal manhood suffrage, while many northern states still did not allow blacks to vote. In addition, the new southern state constitutions created the region's first real public school systems and other institutions of public welfare ranging from asylums for the orphaned, blind, and mentally handicapped to systems of poor relief. After fierce debates, some of the conventions wrote into their constitutions provisions disfran-chising ex-Confederates, but when these voting restrictions proved un-popular, they were removed from the constitutions or quickly repealed. (Many black political leaders, committed to universal manhood suffrage, were less supportive of voting restrictions than white Unionists.) Ultimately, only Arkansas disfranchised large numbers of former Confederates, and even there voting restrictions were removed by 1872.

Almost overlooked in the controversies over schools, segrega-tion, and voting restrictions was an issue that proved of great long-term sig-nificance: taxation. White southerners had a long tradition of opposing anything but the most minimal taxation to support the most minimal state governments. The new state constitutions proposed much more active state governments than had ever existed in the region before. This would re-quire tax increases. One major source of prewar tax revenues, the tax on slaves, had disappeared with the institution. Therefore, the new state con-stitutions included new state taxes on land. Many delegates to the conven-tions approved of higher land taxes for social and economic reasons as well: by hiking the land tax above the ability of planters to pay, they could force the sale of lands to freedmen.

Once written, the new state constitutions were then submitted to the voters for approval, with a majority of registered voters necessary for ratification. Southern Democrats, seeing an opportunity to thwart Reconstruction, urged white voters to boycott the elections, but Congress passed in March 1868 yet another Reconstruction act saying that constitutions could be ratified by a majority of those voting. With as many as half of the South's eligible white voters staying home, Republicans carried the ratification votes throughout the region and then formed new state governments, which then ratified the Fourteenth Amendment. In June, the U.S. Congress voted to readmit seven former Confederate states to the Union; the remaining three, Texas, Virginia, and Mississippi, were readmitted in 1869.

Southern Democrats believed that their last hope of staving off "black rule" lay in the 1868 presidential election. They still found it hard to believe that white Yankees would vote for policies designed to enfranchise and empower blacks. The national Democratic Party leadership apparently agreed. The party platform denounced the Reconstruction acts as unconstitutional, and the party's vice presidential candidate accused the Republicans of having placed the South under the rule of "a semi-barbarous race" awaiting opportunities to "subject the white women to their unbridled lust." Calling for an immediate end to Reconstruction and the return of "white rule" to the South, Democrats throughout the nation joined to campaign for white supremacy.

In the South, whites formed terrorist groups and attacked Republican voters of both races. The most famous of these groups, the Ku Klux Klan, originated as a Confederate veterans' fraternal organization at the end of the war but was quickly transformed into a political terror group in 1868. The Klan and similar organizations throughout the South drew membership from all classes of southern society for their terrorist campaigns. During the months before the election of 1868, historians estimate that thousands of potential Republican voters, most of them black, died at the hands of terrorists throughout the region.

Reports of widespread disorder and violence in the South helped the Republicans carry the election of 1868. Ulysses S. Grant won the presidency, and the Republican Party kept its two-thirds majority in both the House and the Senate, thus ensuring that Reconstruction would continue.

Reconstruction State Governments

Between 1868 and 1870 Republican governments came to power in all the southern states. Long stigmatized as "carpetbagger governments" and lumped together in the public memory as uniformly corrupt and inefficient, the Republican governments actually varied widely from state to state. In Tennessee, which rejoined the Union early, in 1866, white Unionists dominated Reconstruction, while in Mississippi the Reconstruction governor was an idealistic northerner chiefly concerned about the rights of the freedpeople. In South Carolina, blacks formed the majority of the lower house of the legislature, while in other states whites, either northern newcomers or southerners, predominated. Some Reconstruction-era politicians used their power to enrich themselves with bribes, kickbacks, and insider information, while others, including prominent black leaders, were models of enlightened and honest public service. With so much diversity from state to state, it is hard to generalize about the famed "carpetbagger" governments. However, the governments did have certain things in common.

First, and most infuriating to the southern white elite, was the personnel of Reconstruction governments. Staffed by mountain people, poor whites, former Whigs, Union veterans, and blacks, the Reconstruction governments could never satisfy people who believed they had a hereditary right to regional leadership.

Second, Reconstruction governments greatly extended state services and required southerners to pay higher taxes, to the great disapproval of the farmers who made up most of the southern population. Small farmers, accustomed to paying little to no land tax, winced at the prospect of tax increases to pay for services they did not want, such as public schools and poor relief, and grumbled that the freedmen, who did want and need the services, paid no taxes because they owned no lands.

Third, Reconstruction governments attempted to bring the blessings of industrial capitalism to the South and failed disastrously. Convinced that railroads would open up the South for industrial development, most of the state governments encouraged railway construction by guaranteeing railroad bonds. When the railroads failed, as they often did, state governments were left with massive debts, the payment of which required still higher taxes.

Fourth, Reconstruction governments were corrupt, with personnel on the take at every level up to the top. Many Reconstruction political leaders had come into politics to make money; few had jobs or careers to fall back on if they lost elections. In the fast and loose atmosphere of post-Civil War politics, southern politicians who came into office with assets of a few thousand could leave with hundreds of thousands stashed away in banks. Although southern corruption paled before the mountains of boodle raked in by politicians in New York City, or in the national government itself, the fact of corruption played into the hands of people who did not believe that blacks or poor whites were fit to govern.

Fifth, and finally, all the Reconstruction governments faced continual and violent opposition from unreconstructed rebels, determined to keep the South a white man's country. During the early 1870s white terrorist groups including the KKK attacked institutions of black advancement like schools and churches and terrorized black voters. Meanwhile, whites who supported the Republican Party found themselves ostracized by white society, while whites throughout the South complained of a rising crime rate.

The inability of Republican governments to keep the peace and protect property graphically illustrated how tenuous Republican control over the South really was. Reconstruction governments could not exist without the support of Union troops, still stationed in the South five years after Appomattox. Northern politicians, increasingly tired of Reconstruction, asked why the legitimate governments of the South could not defend themselves? In some cases, they could. In Arkansas and Tennessee, the governors sent in state militia units to put down the Klan in selected counties. However, in most of the South Republicans did not even organize resistance against the Klan, preferring to rely on the law and the protection of the federal government. Unlike the Klansmen, most of them Confederate veterans, blacks generally lacked military skills. Besides, black leaders believed that any attempt to organize militarily and fight white terrorism would create a white backlash. Taking the high ground, black leaders condemned white terrorists as the real "barbarians," and fought for their rights under the law.

In 1870 and 1871, the federal government passed a series of acts designed to attack the Ku Klux Klan by making interference with voting a felony. Empowered by Congress to use the U.S. Army to enforce the new "Ku Klux Klan Act," as it was popularly called, President Grant sent troops into counties known to be KKK strongholds and arrested thousands of sus-

pected Klansmen. The resulting federal prosecutions helped drive the Klan underground but did not stop white southerners from resorting to terrorism in defense of white rule. Wearily, northern politicians, and President Grant himself, wondered how long the federal government would have to police southern elections.

Reconstructing Southern Society

White southerners who thought that the postwar South would be like the antebellum South, minus slavery, did not realize how impossible that dream was. The Civil War, emancipation, and Reconstruction brought rapid social changes for which most southern whites were unprepared. Accepting slavery as an organic part of their lives, white southerners did not know how deeply the institution was embedded in all southern institutions until, suddenly, it was gone. Filling in the vacuum required adjustments in every facet of southern life.

Land and Labor   When the war ended, freedmen throughout the South waited impatiently for the federal government to reward their loyalty by confiscating the rebels' land and giving to them each "forty acres and a mule." These hopes were most cruelly dashed. With rare exceptions, neither the federal government nor the Republican Reconstruction governments made any serious efforts to redistribute land. In fact, the federal government even evicted blacks from lands upon which they had been settled by the army during the war. As the head of the Freedmen's Bureau told black leaders, they had been given nothing but freedom. Freedmen wanted to be independent farmers like the white common folk around them, but without land that dream would remain unfulfilled.

The Freedmen's Bureau had its own plans for the former slaves: they were to become wage workers like the whites employed in northern factories. Imbued with the free-labor ideology, bureau officials expected former slaves to save their wages and, through thrift and industry, rise in the world to become landowners and businessmen. Many of the bureau's policies, such as its sponsorship of schools, were calculated to speed the formation of a self-supporting black middle class. However, the bureau's plans ran aground against a basic fact of the postwar southern economy: southern planters had no cash with which to pay wages.

Planters wanted a labor system as close to slavery as possible. Insisting that blacks would not work without coercion, planters wanted to continue the system of gang labor typical of plantation agriculture before the war. Under that system, men and women worked in groups under an overseer's direction. Planters laughed at the idea of paying weekly wages, telling bureau officials that hands would immediately take their pay and leave, not to return until all the money was spent. Most of all, planters needed to be sure that their hands would not leave at critical moments in the agricultural year, such as planting and harvest. Moreover, planters wanted control over the freedmen's home life, preferring that their workers live in the old slave quarters under close white supervision.

In this conflict of goals and dreams, none of the parties could win. What eventually emerged out of the shambles of the postwar agricultural economy was a system no one really wanted: sharecropping. With bureau support, planters contracted to rent lands to tenants in exchange for a portion of the harvest. (The portion varied depending on whether the planter provided tools, draft horses or mules, seeds, and so on.) Because the worker would not be paid until after the harvest, the planter could be sure that he would stick around. On the other hand, freedmen extracted from planters an end to the gang labor system and a certain amount of privacy for their families. Freedmen demanded that planters give them a set acreage to farm on their own, without constant white supervision, and a cabin in which their families could live. Unable to get the land that made economic independence possible for white common folk, blacks approximated small farming as closely as possible through sharecropping. This system was not completely satisfactory to freedmen, planters, or the bureau, but seemed acceptable as a temporary expedient at a time of crisis. No one foresaw what would happen: the sharecropping system lasted until the middle of the twentieth century, to the great detriment of southern agriculture.

Domestic Relations: Work and Law   Southern jurists classified laws governing slavery under "domestic relations." With the removal of slavery, domestic relations for all southern families, black and white, went through a period of change, both legally and socially. For the first time, whites and blacks encountered each other as legal equals within the judicial system. Reconstruction governments wrote into their constitutions and their new legislation provisions significantly liberalizing family law.

Meanwhile, black families adjusted to gender role changes following upon emancipation.

Prior to the Civil War, southern family law followed the ancient English common law, by which women ceased to be individuals under law when married. As English legal scholars explained, by marriage man and wife became one person—and that person was the husband. Wives could not buy, sell, or make contracts without their husbands' consent. Through marriage, husbands acquired ownership of any property that wives brought to the marriage or earned by their own work. Although the northern states' original family law codes were similar, those laws had been modified to reflect the changing realities of middle-class family life in an industrial society. During Reconstruction, Republican legislatures reformed southern law to reflect the growing individualism of American society. In several states, married women were given the right to control their own property, a development conservatives denounced as part of "the mighty tide of progress which has already swept away the Constitution, and slavery, and State's rights." Conservatives protested that such laws destroyed the old domestic order under which only male heads of families had an individual relationship with the state. In addition, divorce laws were liberalized throughout the South, and judges became less likely to automatically award children, as a kind of property, to fathers.

The antebellum tendency toward patriarchy inherited from English law had been strengthened by slavery. Southern law codes and courts had argued that white male family heads needed to have almost all of the power within families, since they, as masters, were responsible for dependents, including their own wives, children, and slaves. Southern conservatives noted that antebellum southern society had hardly needed jails or prisons, since most "crimes" were domestic, occurring on plantations and dealt with informally by masters.

The Civil War destroyed this informal judicial system, and the more formal one as well. The result was a period of great confusion. Anecdotal evidence indicates that postwar economic and social conditions led to an increase in theft. With white refugees, freedpeople, and starving Confederate veterans floating through rural districts and crowding into towns, property owners guarded their food and money with guns. In the immediate postwar period, Union officers administered martial law in occupied territories, much to the relief of property owners, who found to their chagrin that they needed the Yankees' protection. After the war, the Freedmen's Bureau acted as a small-claims court to rule on conflicts between planters and workers, while the southern judicial system underwent its own reconstruction, with Republican judges replacing former Confederates on the bench, and blacks in the jury box, much to the disgust of many southern whites. Southern whites charged that the Reconstruction governments failed to protect their property, and both blacks and whites complained about racially biased courts, each charging the other side with failing to provide color-blind justice.

Antebellum southern laws had no provisions dealing with slave families, since under the law no such entities existed. For freedpeople, the right to form families and have the legitimacy of those families recognized by the state was one of the most cherished fruits of freedom. In 1866, a Freedmen's Bureau official gave a sermon on marriage to black Union troops stationed in Virginia and recorded the testimony offered by one of the soldiers, Corporal Murray: "*I praise God for this day!* . . . The Marriage Covenant is at the foundation of all our rights. In slavery we could not have *legalized* marriage: *now* we have it. Let us conduct ourselves worthy of such a blessing—and all the people will respect us—God will bless us, and we shall be established as a people." After emancipation, freed men and women hurried to legitimate long-standing relationships, often standing up before their children and grandchildren to say their marriage vows.

In freedom, black men insisted to their landlords that their wives and daughters would no longer take orders from white bosses as they had under slavery, and many withdrew their wives from field labor altogether. Whites disapproved when freedmen appropriated to themselves concepts typical of white society, such as the obligation of men to support women. Whites thought that a black woman carrying no more than the normal load of work for farm wives was not really working, and they mocked the pretensions of black "ladies." For their part, many freedpeople found middle-class gender roles impossible to sustain: survival required the work of the entire family, parents and children alike.

In a less striking fashion, Reconstruction saw the beginning of changes in gender roles for white southern families as well. The war had taken the lives of approximately one-quarter of the white men of military age in the South and had left many others physically disabled and mentally shattered. After the war, white women found themselves managing plantations and running businesses, jobs for which many of them had not been prepared, either educationally or emotionally. Their daughters and sons would grow up aware that patriarchy had its limitations. Contrary to myth, men did not always protect women from the harder side of life.

White women also became the chief mourners of the Confederacy. Unwilling or unable to let the memory of the men of the Lost Cause fade away, women throughout the South formed Ladies' Memorial Associations in 1866 and created a new holiday: Confederate Memorial Day. Over the years, the Ladies' Memorial Associations moved from decorating graveyards and putting up statues of Confederate soldiers to founding homes for the widows and orphans of fallen soldiers. Although memorializing the Lost Cause led white women into public activism, the ladies never ceased to uphold conservative concepts of white supremacy and the duty of white men to protect southern white womanhood.

The End of Reconstruction

The Rise of the Redeemers

Southern whites might have lost the Civil War, but they were determined not to lose the battle for home rule. Although Grant's reelection in 1872 seemed to signal that northern voters still supported Reconstruction, southern Democrats soon began a resurgence that toppled Republican governments throughout the South. When Democrats took power back from Republicans, they called it "Redemption," a word freighted with deep meaning drawn from law and religion: to pay all debts on a property is to "redeem" it; Christ's death "redeemed" the sins of the world. The southern Democrats called themselves Redeemers. By 1874 they had taken power in Virginia, Tennessee, North Carolina, Alabama, Georgia, Texas, and Arkansas.

The Redeemers began their return to power by winning the support of most white voters throughout the South. Never really reconciled to sharing power with blacks, white common folk also had reason to resent Republican governments' tax policies, which fell most heavily upon them. No one who valued good government could have approved of the level of corruption prevalent in many Republican-controlled legislatures and governor's mansions. Finally, the Redeemers made cooperation with Republi-

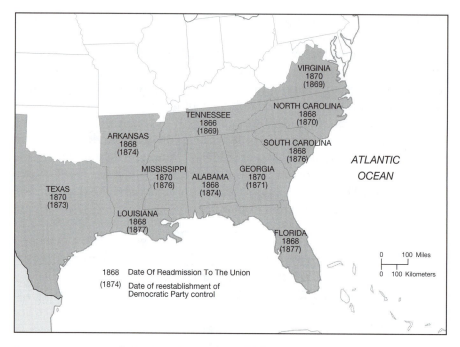

Reconstruction of the South, 1866–1877.

cans a distinct social liability. According to one well-known story, one southern man justified his decision to vote Democratic in the next election by explaining that he had five daughters, all single and all likely to remain that way as long as he supported the Republicans.

Republican disarray and factionalism also helped fuel Democratic resurgence. In several states, black Republicans charged that whites hogged all the patronage and offices, while in other states the party split, with some Republicans appealing for conservative Democratic votes and others drawing support mainly from blacks. In South Carolina, the only state where blacks held significant power during Reconstruction, black factionalism contributed to the Republican Party's difficulties. As educated black leaders became more prosperous, their interests more often coincided with those of conservative whites than with workers on the rice plantations.

Ultimately, however, the Redeemers took back power in the same way the Confederates had lost it: with guns. While encouraging white voters to support them, Democrats also discouraged blacks from voting, using the most forceful measures possible. Whites organized "rifle clubs" and other quasi-military groups to terrorize black voters. In Louisiana in 1874, "White Leagues" battled black militiamen in the very streets of New Orleans, took control of the city hall and arsenal, and were only put down by federal troops. In Mississippi in 1875, whites attacked black political meetings and rode through the countryside assassinating black political leaders, teachers, and ministers.

In previous years, such actions by unreconstructed southerners led to repeated federal intervention. However, by 1874 northern support for Reconstruction had waned. The entire nation slid into a major depression in 1873, and many voters worried more about their own economic prospects than about what many called the "Negro question." In the North, the children of the reform-minded people who had worked for abolition in the 1850s turned their attention to the problem of political corruption. Grant's own ability to govern, and his personal reputation, suffered when investigations revealed that several of his cabinet officers and his personal secretary were involved in schemes to defraud the taxpayers. Republican reformers found it difficult to defend Reconstruction governments noted for corruption.

Yet the North's retreat from Reconstruction represented more than just fatigue, distraction, or disapproval of corruption. Many northern politicians had supported abolition, citizenship for blacks, and suffrage for black men as ways of getting at the rebellious South. With the exception of true believers like Charles Sumner, who in 1875 pushed through Congress the last Reconstruction-Era civil rights bill, few northern politicians cared much about what happened to blacks in the South. Many northerners, as much convinced of white superiority as any southern Democrat, doubted whether blacks were, or ever could be, capable of governing themselves. The new popularity of Social Darwinism, which applied Charles Darwin's theory of evolution to economics and society, reinforced such prejudices.

To Social Darwinists, blacks were lower on the evolutionary scale than whites of British descent—but so were many other ethnic groups, such as the Irish immigrants who formed the majority of the working class in many northern cities. As labor strife rocked northern cities in the 1870s, upper-class Republicans found themselves thinking that perhaps the southern white elites were right: the working classes, whether white Irish immigrants in the North or blacks in the South, could not be trusted and needed supervision from their natural superiors. In addition, Social Darwinists, believing in the survival of the fittest in the socioeconomic world as in the jungle, thought that all people should be left alone to sink or swim on their own. Such attitudes reduced public support for continual federal intervention in the South to protect the freedpeople.

Reconstruction had failed, many northern leaders believed, and it was past time to withdraw support from a policy that simply did not work. Businessmen complained that investment in the South could never proceed until good governments and law and order replaced corruption, violence, and chaos. After almost a generation of political upheaval and war followed by more political upheaval, northerners wanted to forget the "southern question" and the "Negro question" and get on with their lives. As the *New York Herald* noted, "The plain truth is, the North has got tired of the Negro."

Therefore, when the governor of Mississippi, the carpetbagger Adelbert Ames, asked for troops to protect blacks and put down white violence, President Grant refused, saying "The whole public are tired out with these annual autumnal outbreaks in the South . . . [and] are ready to condemn any interference on the part of the Government." Grant's attorney general wrote to the governor instructing him to "Preserve the peace" in Mississippi with his own forces: "[L]et the country see that the citizens of Mississippi . . . have the courage to *fight* for their rights." Unwilling to send black militiamen into battle with whites for fear of provoking even more white violence, Ames negotiated a deal with Democrats that included disbanding the black militia. Without federal troops to back them up, the Republicans lost the 1875 elections in Mississippi.

The Compromise of 1877

In 1874 the Democratic Party made a surprising recovery from its years of unpopularity among northern voters, while the Republicans suffered public blame as the party that had presided over the Depression of 1873. Democrats won a majority of seats in the House of Representatives and made similar gains in many northern states. Hopeful of winning the presidency in 1876, the Democrats nominated Samuel Tilden of New York and issued a platform statement condemning "a corrupt centralism which, after inflicting upon ten States the rapacities of carpet-bag tyrannies, has honeycombed the offices of the Federal Government itself with incapacity, waste and fraud."

The Republicans nominated their own reform candidate, Rutherford B. Hayes of Ohio. Evoking the Civil War and capitalizing on white southern atrocities against blacks in Hamburg, South Carolina, the Republicans asked the northern public to rally once again, as Hayes wrote, against "the dread of a solid South, rebel rule, etc., etc." Though the Republicans expected their opponents to win most of the South, they had hopes of carrying the three remaining southern states under Republican governments—Louisiana, South Carolina, and Florida.

The election of 1876 produced one of the strangest outcomes in all of American political history: a kind of tie. With electoral and popular votes almost even, the winner of the election would be the man who was awarded the electoral votes of Louisiana, South Carolina, and Florida, all of which had sent in two sets of returns, one certified by the Democrats and one by the Republicans. Which set one believed the "true" vote depended on one's politics, and in fact both sides cheated. Congress set up a commission to resolve the question, but the commission divided on party lines.

What followed has been the subject of considerable debate and conjecture among historians. We know that leading southern Democrats met in February 1877 with prominent Republicans from Ohio, Hayes's home state. We also know that after that meeting southern politicians in Congress withdrew their opposition to Hayes's election, and he was inaugurated in March. Apparently the southern leadership and Hayes's people cut a deal: the Republicans could have the presidency if Hayes would end Reconstruction. Although no documentation of such a bargain exists, historians have dubbed it the Compromise of 1877. Hayes removed all federal troops from the South, allowing Redeemers to take power in South Carolina and Louisiana; he made an ex-Confederate from Tennessee postmaster general, thus giving him control over highly coveted federal patronage jobs in the postal service; and he urged Congress to appropriate moneys for internal improvements in the South.

In 1877 the Republican Party gave up on Reconstruction, and with it, the party's long-term commitment to securing for blacks equal rights as American citizens. It would be eighty years before the federal government again dispatched troops to protect black rights in the South. The northern public acquiesced in this betrayal of black hopes. The leading journal of middle-class northern opinion, *The Nation,* welcomed the end of Reconstruction: "The negro will disappear from the field of national politics. Henceforth, the nation, as a nation, will have nothing more to do with him." Southern blacks understood their situation. As one Louisiana black leader said, "The whole South . . . had got into the hands of the very men that held us as slaves." Although Democratic leaders had promised to respect black rights, they clearly expected the freedmen to accept subordinate positions in southern society.

In 1861 southerners went to war to defend their way of life, and by doing so destroyed it. Unable to salvage slavery out of the wreckage of the Civil War, white southerners mounted a successful resistance movement in defense of the other cornerstones of southern ideology, white supremacy and states' rights. Twelve years after Appomatox, the white South won the battle of Reconstruction. With the Old South dead, and Reconstruction over, southerners focused on a different kind of rebuilding: the economic transformation of the New South.

Suggestions for Further Reading

PETER BARDAGLIO, *Reconstructing the Household: Families, Sex and the Law in the Nineteenth Century South* (1995)

W. E. B. DuBOIS, *Black Reconstruction* (1935)

ERIC FONER, *A Short History of Reconstruction, 1863–1877* (1988)

JOHN HOPE FRANKLIN, *Reconstruction: After the Civil War* (1961)

THOMAS HOLT, *Black over White: Negro Political Leadership in South Carolina During Reconstruction* (1977)

J. MORGAN KOUSSER AND JAMES M. McPHERSON, EDS., *Region, Race and Reconstruction* (1982)

LEON F. LITWACK, *Been in the Storm So Long: The Aftermath of Slavery* (1979)

ROBERT C. MORRIS, *Reading, 'Riting and Reconstruction* (1981)

MICHAEL PERMAN, *The Road to Redemption: Southern Politics, 1869–1879* (1984)

LESLIE A. SCHWALM, *A Hard Fight for We: Women's Transition from Slavery to Freedom in South Carolina* (1997)

KENNETH STAMPP, *The Era of Reconstruction, 1865–1877* (1965)

ALLEN W. TRELEASE, *White Terror: The Ku Klux Klan Conspiracy and Southern Reconstruction* (1979)

Index